CHINESE IMMIGRATION.

The Social, Moral, and Political Effect

OF CHINESE IMMIGRATION.

TESTIMONY

TAKEN BEFORE A COMMITTEE OF THE SENATE OF THE STATE OF CALIFORNIA,

APPOINTED APRIL 3D, 1876.

REPORTED BY FRANK SHAY, OFFICIAL REPORTER OF SAID COMMITTEE, AND PUBLISHED UNDER AN ORDER OF THE SENATE BY F. P. THOMPSON, STATE SUPERINTENDENT OF PUBLIC PRINTING.

SACRAMENTO:
STATE PRINTING OFFICE.
1876.

INDEX.

ERRATA.

Page four, line three from top—For "April 14th," read "April 4th."
Page fourteen, line two from bottom—For "thirteen" read "three."
Page fourteen, line three from bottom—For "the same" read "similar to that."
Page fifteen, line seven from bottom—After the word "else" read "in the Old World."
Page sixteen, line four from bottom—For "pretense" read "accusation."
Page seventeen, line six from top—Before "children" read "female."
Page seventeen, fourth answer—After words "Yes, sir," read "somewhat so."
Page seventeen, line eight from bottom—For the word "individuals" read "communities."
Page eighteen, line twelve from top—After "into" read "the interior of." And add at the close of that paragraph: "and they are now, or were, when I was there, only allowed to trade in the interior when given a special government permit so to do."
Page nineteen, line two from top—In place of "where" read "upon the top of which."
Page twenty, line five from top—For "the church" read "their church."
Page twenty, line nine from top—Before "high" insert "so."
Page twenty, line fourteen from top—After "brick" read "and wood."
Page twenty, line fifteen from top—Before "the Temple of Heaven" insert "in." Strike out "It is" and insert "There is a high altar there."
Page twenty, line seventeen from top—After "The place" insert "called the Temple of Heaven;" and after "very pretty," in next line, insert a period, and read: "The roofs are tiled, and as regards architectural beauty those temples," etc. And in last line of same answer, after "dwellings" read "in the city.
Page twenty, line twenty-two from bottom—Strike out "of wit and." After "harmony" read "Their writings are devoid of wit."
Page twenty-one, line three from top—Strike out "as."
Page twenty-one, line twenty-eight from top—After "hold office" read "and that diploma places them in the ranks of a sort of nobility, none below them being permitted to hold any civil office." And after the word "caste," at end of that answer, read: "But it bears no resemblance to caste in India."
Page twenty-one, line eleven from bottom—After "Yes, sir," read "the number is not limited."
Page twenty-two, line seven from top—Before "labor" read "white."
Page twenty-three, line three from bottom—After "Burlingame," add: "and, indeed, I had the highest official authority for knowing that the Chinese Government had invested Mr. Burlingame with no such authority, and had not requested the United States to make any such treaty. The knowledge of it was a surprise to the Chinese Government, and all foreign ministers at that court, including our own."
Page twenty-four, line twenty-three from bottom—After "language," read "and engaging in trade."
Page twenty-four, line fourteen from bottom—Strike out "can."

CHINESE IMMIGRATION.

THE SOCIAL, MORAL, AND POLITICAL EFFECT OF CHINESE IMMIGRATION.

TESTIMONY

TAKEN BEFORE A

Committee of the Senate of the State of California,

APPOINTED APRIL 3, 1876.

CHINESE IMMIGRATION.

On the third day of April, eighteen hundred and seventy-six, in the Senate of the State of California, the Hon. Creed Haymond, Senator from the Eighteenth Senatorial District, offered the following resolutions, which were unanimously adopted:

Be it resolved by the Senate of the State of California, That a committee of five Senators be appointed, with power to sit at any time or place within the State, and the said committee shall make inquiry:

1. As to the number of Chinese in this State and the effect their presence has upon the social and political condition of the State.
2. As to the probable result of Chinese immigration upon the country, if such immigration be not discouraged.
3. As to the means of exclusion, if such committee should be of the opinion that the presence of the Chinese element in our midst is detrimental to the interests of the country.
4. As to such other matters as, in the judgment of the committee, have a bearing upon the question of Chinese immigration. And be it further

Resolved, That said committee, on or before the first day of December, eighteen hundred and seventy-six, shall prepare a memorial to the Congress of the United States, which memorial must set out at length the facts in relation to the subject of this inquiry, and such conclusions as the committee may have arrived at as to the policy and means of excluding Chinese from the country. And be it further

Resolved, That said committee is authorized and directed to have printed, at the State Printing Office, a sufficient number of copies of such memorial, and of the testimony taken by said committee, to furnish copies thereof to the leading newspapers of the United States, five copies to each member of Congress, ten copies to the Governor of each State, and to deposit two thousand copies with the Secretary of State of California for general distribution. And be it further

Resolved, That such committee shall, on or before the first Monday in December, eighteen hundred and seventy-six, furnish to the Governor of the State of California two copies of said memorial, properly engrossed, and the Governor, upon receipt thereof, be requested to transmit, through the proper channels, one of said copies to the Senate and the other to the House of Representatives of the United States. And be it further

Resolved, That said committee have full power to send for persons and papers, and to administer oaths and examine witnesses under oath, and that a majority of said committee shall constitute a quorum. And be it further

Resolved, That said committee shall have power to employ a Sergeant-at-Arms, at a compensation not to exceed two hundred and fifty dollars, and a phonographic reporter at a compensation not to exceed one thousand dollars, and that two thousand dollars of the Contingent Fund of the Senate be set aside, out of which such compensation and the contingent and traveling expenses of the committee shall be paid upon the order of the Chairman thereof. And be it further

Resolved, That said committee report to the Senate, at its next session, the proceedings had hereunder.

Subsequently, on motion, the Senate increased the number of the committee to seven, and the following Senators were appointed on said committee: Senators Haymond, McCoppin, Pierson, Donovan, Rogers, Lewis, and Evans.

PROCEEDINGS OF THE COMMISSION.

State Capitol,
Sacramento, April 14th, 1876.

The committee appointed by the Senate of the State of California to investigate the subject of Chinese immigration met at two o'clock P. M.

Present—Senator Haymond, Chairman; Senators Evans, Lewis, Donovan, McCoppin, Rogers, and Pierson.

Frank Shay was elected official reporter, and —— Cronk, Sergeant-at-Arms.

* * * * * * * *

The committee adjourned to meet at the City of San Francisco on the eleventh day of April, eighteen hundred and seventy-six.

San Francisco, April 11th, 1876.

The committee met pursuant to adjournment—present, all the members—and proceeded to take testimony, as follows:

F. F. Low sworn.

Mr. Pierson—How long did you reside in China?

A.—I resided there about three years and a half.

Q.—In what parts of China?

A.—Chiefly in Pekin; that was my residence.

Q.—Are you familiar with the immigration of Chinese to this State?

A.—Not from personal observation, because I was in a different part of the empire than from whence this immigration comes.

Q.—From where does it come?

A.—Principally from Hong-kong.

Q.—What position did you occupy in China?

A.—Minister Plenipotentiary from the United States to the Emperor of China.

Q.—During what years?

A.—Eighteen hundred and seventy, eighteen hundred and seventy-one, eighteen hundred and seventy-two, and a portion of eighteen hundred and seventy-three.

Q.—Have you any knowledge of the terms upon which the Chinese emigrate from China to this country, either officially or personally?

A.—I have no knowledge.

Q.—Is it voluntary or involuntary? Do they come voluntarily, or are they sent here?

A.—Before I can answer that question perhaps it will be well for me to state that the emigration from Hong-kong is not from China, a fact which seems to have been lost sight of by almost everybody that discusses this question. The Island of Hong-kong is a British possession, ceded to the British Crown by the Government of China, and is organized, I think, the same as Australia. It is a British colony, governed the same as any other British possession.

Q.—Under no jurisdiction of the Chinese Empire at all?

A.—No more than Canada. How these people get to Hong-kong I do not know. I suppose they go in sam-pans, in boats, steamers, and all sorts of ways, and then emigrate from Hong-kong to San Francisco.

Mr. McCoppin—Don't the Chinese come from different parts of China to Hong-kong to take ships there, just as emigrants from England, Ireland, and Scotland used to go to Liverpool?

A.—Yes, sir. But take the Chinese here and you would not find one in a thousand—probably one in five thousand—but that came from Kwang-tung, the province of which Canton is Capital. There are their homes; they are all from one section of the country. We have anglicized "Canton;" made that name out of the original Chinese words "Kwang-tung." So far as it appears from all evidences, all the emigrants from Kong-kong are freemen; indeed, I understand that the British emigration law forbids anybody but voluntary emigrants embarking; forbids a vessel clearing unless all the emigrants on board are voluntary emigrants, and that is to be certified to before the vessel can have a clearing.

Mr. Pierson—Who is the American Consul at Hong-kong, now?

A.—It is not easy to tell you that, the mutations of office are so frequent. David G. Bailey was the last one that I heard of.

Mr. Evans—You are then of the impression that the people do not come here as peons, under contract—that that theory is not correct?

A.—No, sir.

Q.—You think that they come here as free people?

A.—On the face of it, yes; that is the only impression that I have.

Mr. Pierson—Do you know of the existence in Hong-kong, or any part of China, of companies such as they have here?

A.—These companies all have agents in Hong-kong.

Mr. McCoppin—Each company here has an agency there?

A.—I do not speak from absolute knowledge, but that is my understanding. The Chinese people are made up of guilds, of all sorts and kinds, and rule, in this manner, everything sold—as tea, silks, etc., even to the transportation on wheelbarrows. It is all governed by guilds or associations, and these, probably, have some general headquarters in China; probably at the hospital to which the companies here telegraphed a short time since.

Q.—I suppose that is the place where all the people are received or taken prior to being shipped?

A.—That is my belief; I do not know. These people deny that such are the facts; practically, all Chinese come here through means advanced by these companies or individuals, or by people here, through these companies. I think it is by no means sure that the Southern Pacific Railroad Company is not importing Chinese to-day through these companies. I know the Central Pacific Railroad Company did it.

Mr. Evans—Oftentimes friends and relatives here send for their friends and relatives there, don't they?

A.—There may be individual cases, but not many. I know the Central Pacific Railroad Company imported thousands and thousands of coolies through Chinese agents, and that they advanced money for passage, and took it out in work, with a bonus.

Mr. Pierson—Do you understand that these Chinamen here come under contracts, and that they must work themselves free from them?

A.—Their contract is simply to repay the amount advanced for their passage, with a sufficient bonus to recompense them for the risk, interest, etc. In other words, if they advanced forty dollars for passage they exacted that they should pay one hundred dollars, perhaps, in return, to be deducted from wages—five dollars a month or ten dollars a month, after they arrive; after they work that out they are free.

Q.—In an interview between you and a *Chronicle* reporter——

A.—That was a very imperfect report.

Q.—I did not gather what your ideas were about the Burlingame treaty. From your answers, I infer that no modification of the treaty can help us?

A.—You can see that yourself. Suppose the Chinese come from Australia, any inhibition in the Burlingame treaty could not have anything to do with them. Divest yourself of the idea that Hongkong is not China, and you have the question in a nutshell.

Mr. McCoppin—So that any modification of the Chinese treaty——

A.—If the British Government and the United States Government should agree to any inhibition regarding the emigration of Chinese from a British port, then the Chinese Government might have cause for a grievance, for they had a treaty with this country, but a modification of the Burlingame treaty could have no effect one way or the other.

Q.—Is not the whole remedy of this evil with Congress? Has it not the power to pass laws restricting this class of immigration?

A.—It is not easy to map out.

Q.—Is not the power there?

A.—Yes, sir; the same as—it all lies there, if anywhere. It is not an easy problem to solve by any means, because of our treaties with China. We derive a large portion of our rights and privileges in China from the fact of the "favored nation" clause in those treaties; that is, when China makes a treaty with the United States, France, Great Britain, and all other countries, it is usual, and I think it is universal, to insert this "favored nation" clause, which reads substantially as follows: "That any rights other than those granted in this treaty, that have or may be granted to any other nation, shall inure to the nation that makes this treaty;" so that all our treaties with China contain that clause, and a very large proportion of our rights that we have there comes through the operation of the "favored nation" clause in our treaties, that we have gathered from other treaties.

Mr. Pierson—The great mass of the immigrants here, of the Chinese, is of the very lowest order of Chinese, is it not?

A.—They are the laboring classes, and, usually coming from sea-port towns, might be considered the lowest class of laborers; the agricultural laborers ranking next to the officials.

Q.—Then we get most of our Chinese immigration from sea-port towns?

A.—I am assuming that they come from the neighborhood of Canton—boatmen and men who work for hire, or the common class of laborers. Agricultural laborers are regarded with great consideration in the social ethics of China; indeed, agriculture has been ennobled by the action of the government. In the gradation of Chinese society the officials hold the highest rank; next come the agricultural laborers; then the manufacturers who increase values by working raw materials into articles of use; then the trader, let him trade in anything—peanuts, or dry goods at wholesale. They are dealers all the same; they exchange commodities, producing nothing.

Q.—His caste is lower than the laborer?

A.—Yes, sir. Then we have the professional man—he is lower still. A lawyer in China is pretty nearly as bad as actors and barbers, who are without the pale of social life.

Mr. Donovan—Then the lawyers are a stage above actors and barbers?

A.—Yes, sir. When I say lawyers, there is practically no such thing; there are men who hang about the Courts, but they answer more to the description of French notaries or conveyancers—men who draw papers. There are no differences in their grades.

Mr. Pierson—Where do we get the bulk of our immigration?

A.—From the laboring classes.

Q.—What are the customary wages of laborers in China?

A.—From ten to twenty cents a day. Perhaps ten cents will be nearer the average for common laborers.

Q.—They support themselves out of that?

A.—Yes, sir.

Q.—How do those people live? What is their social position there? Do they live on the water or on the land?

A.—They live on the land, with the exception of around about the City of Canton, where a great many people live in boats, knowing no law. They make their homes in boats, but that is a very small portion of the population. China is an immense empire, and we are only dealing with the little fringe around the edges. We know comparatively little of the interior.

Q.—I was asking to see if we drew the mass of our immigration from sea-port towns?

A.—I assume we do, for the laborers; the men who own a little piece of land and cultivate it will not come here, because they are independent. Those only who are obliged to work for wages will come. I speak now of the mass. Of course some merchants come here, because they will go anywhere where there is profit to be made in trade and traffic.

Q.—Now as to their education—can the lower classes of people read and write?

A.—Most of them can, to a certain extent.

Q.—What is their system of education; is it a governmental system?

A.—No, sir. It is all private education. They have neighborhood schools that are supported by the voluntary contributions of the neighborhood; sometimes by assessments levied, but that is all voluntary. There is nothing compulsory in it.

Q.—What about their domestic relations in regard to marriage?

A.—It is incumbent upon every man to marry. This is the custom of the country. The public opinion of the people makes it absolutely compulsory, and everybody does marry. Even at a young age, marriage contracts are made by the parents of either side, and they are betrothed from infancy, frequently. As soon as they are old enough to marry, they marry.

Q.—Do we get any considerable proportion of married Chinamen here?

A.—Very likely.

Q.—Do they leave their wives in China?

A.—They leave their wives at home.

Q.—Is it not a fact that the great bulk of the Chinese women that come here are prostitutes?

A.—That is to be presumed. I assume that as the fact.

Mr. Evans—How are the people there—in China—as regards chastity?

A.—The bulk of the people are chaste. It is only around large cities where we have immorality and vice. On this point I have the testimony of those who have traveled a great deal in the interior, where immorality on the part of married women is punished with terrible severity—where they are tabooed from society.

Mr. Pierson—Are men restricted, by the laws of China, to one wife?

A.—No, sir. The others, after the first, are called wives, and the children are legitimate, too. A Chinaman who has wealth can take as many wives as he chooses—as many as he can support. It is a mere matter of bargain and sale with the parents. If a family have a surplus of girls that cannot be betrothed in the regular way, they dispose of them as second and third wives.

Mr. Donovan—They can have as many wives as they can buy?

A.—Yes, sir. But the second, third, fourth, and fifth wives are all subordinate to the first; she is mistress of the household.

Q.—Can the women have as many husbands as they like?

A.—No; they are restricted.

Mr. Pierson—What do you understand to be the population of China?

A.—It is popularly thought to be four hundred millions, but my opinion is that it is overestimated. Three hundred millions would be a fair estimate, although we have so little data that it is impossible to tell with anything approaching accuracy. The population of China has decreased in the last century very largely. That don't admit of doubt.

Q.—From what causes?

A.—From rebellion, insurrection, famine in certain districts, and more than all, the consumption of opium; for it is an established fact, I think, by the medical fraternity, that the confirmed opium-eater is incapable of procreation.

Q.—Do you understand, Governor, that there is any particular prevalence in China of syphilitic diseases?

A.—No more than here.

Q.—Or elephantiasis?

A.—In the southern provinces. Elephantiasis is in Hong-kong, as in all tropical countries.

Q.—It is common, then, to India and southern China?

A.—To all tropical countries—Central America, for instance.

Q.—Any prevalence of leprosy?

A.—Leprosy is not uncommon in China, although it is not prevalent in the north of China. Goitre, a swelling of the glands of the throat, is frequent, and is supposed to come from the water. The whole valley on the northern part of the Yang-tse-kiang is impregnated with muriate of lime, and this disease was attributed to the lime water. Whether this was the cause, or not, I do not know.

Mr. McCoppin—The introduction of opium, was that in this century?

A.—In the year eighteen hundred, according to the best statistics I could obtain, the importation of India opium into China was about four thousand chests, one hundred and thirty-three pounds each, according to the best data I could obtain. In the year eighteen hundred and seventy-three, or we will take the year eighteen hundred and seventy-one, the importation of opium into China was ten thousand five hundred tons. In addition to that, the native production amounts to fully the foreign importation.

Q.—The English first introduced opium there?

A.—Yes, sir; it came from India—the East India Company.

Mr. Pierson—How far is the island upon which Hong-kong is situated from the mainland?

A.—Oh, it is just a passage for the ships of the Chinamen; not farther than from here (City Hall) to Goat Island.

Mr. Evans—Do you know the area of that island?

A.—I do not know. It is just a rocky sort of island, a forbidding sort of place, although they have spent a great deal of money improving it.

Q.—What is the population?

A.—I won't pretend to say. It is very largely Chinese. Most of the population is Chinese. There must be half a million, I suppose.

Mr. McCoppin—What benefit, if any, does America, as a nation, derive from this immigration from China, outside of its trade? Does the immigration give the right to Americans to go into China, and trade to any extent, and have they availed themselves of it?

A.—Very largely.

Q.—I mean outside of Hong-kong—China proper?

A.—There is a good trade with Shanghai. On the Yang-tse-kiang River there is a line of steamers owned by Americans, where they must have, I should think, fifteen, perhaps not as large as the largest river steamers in America, but larger than any we have here; larger than the steamer Capital. The freight-carrying capacity of those steamers is between two thousand five hundred and three thousand tons, besides a large passenger capacity.

Q.—Owned and operated by Americans?

A.—Yes, sir.

Q.—Where do they run?

A.—Run from Shanghai to Hang-kow; that is the head of navigation.

Mr. Pierson—Have you any idea how large an American population there is in China to-day?

A.—I cannot tell from memory. I have some books that I can consult, and give a pretty accurate estimate. We have a very large trade in cotton goods in China, also in heavy cottons and drills and twilled goods. During the war, when cotton was high, the English dug into the trade, and counterfeited our trademarks, thus securing the bulk of the trade, which they have kept ever since, by making lighter goods, and sizing them differently. I have seen bales of drills at Hang-kow marked "Lawrence Mills, Mass.," that never saw the United States.

Mr. Donovan—Do you think there are five thousand Americans in China?

A.—I should say yes, for a guess. I do not speak from knowledge.

Q.—Do you think that would be a fair estimate?

A.—I would not like to make an estimate without consulting some statistics, since it would be a wild sort of a guess.

Mr. Pierson—From what source do you think we would be able to get any accurate information as to the terms upon which the Chinese come to this country?

A.—You can get it only by digging down into those affairs here.

Q.—Would the Minister to China be able to give any information?

A.—Oh, no!

Q.—There are Consuls——

A.—There are Consuls; but the government does not provide them with any machinery. They give them secretaries; but they are posted two hundred miles from where the emigrants come.

Q.—Then what we do get will have to be obtained here?

A.—This seems to be the place.

Q.—Practically, I understand you, if any such system exists as involuntary emigration——

A.—You can hardly call it involuntary emigration.

Q.—If that system does exist, it is in violation of our treaty, is it not?

A.—It is in violation of our treaty, and in violation of the Chinese law. The Chinese themselves are opposed to the exportation of coolie labor, more than we are to the immigration. They have three great griefs against foreign nations. One is opium; the second is coolie emigration. When I speak of coolie emigration, I mean as it has gone on in years past, as the exportation of coolies from Macao to Peru and Havana. Those coolies thus taken away under contract, we know, were ill-treated, and the contracts violated. The Chinese felt very sore about this, and appointed a commission a year ago; and I think they abrogated their treaty with Spain on account of it. Spain had a sort of treaty that permitted the taking away of contract labor, and they shut down on it. I sustained them in it, too.

Mr. Donovan—The proposition, as I understand it, is that as long as they keep the contract the Chinese take no exceptions; but when they break the contract they do take exceptions.

A.—It takes a long story to explain that. When the English and French captured Pekin, in eighteen hundred and sixty, they made a supplemental treaty, which provided, among other things, that the Chinese might be taken under contract to go abroad, under such rules and regulations as might be prescribed by government. The view of the English was to get laborers to take to the West India possessions, where they wanted labor, and subsequently Alcock, the British Minister, together with the French Government, concluded some articles of agreement by which contracts might be made. These contracts required five years' service and the return of the men by the contractors, etc. So many conditions were required that the British Government rejected the articles, and since that there has been nothing. Involuntary emigration, or immigration under contract, has been and is discouraged by the Chinese Government. You must understand that this treaty was made under duress. It was dictated to China, with cannon planted around her capital—Pekin. That treaty was written for them. They did not write it themselves, and they have obstructed, in every way possible, emigration other than free emigration.

Mr. McCoppin—What is the name of the gentleman, in China, connected with the American Embassy?

A.—Mr. Williams.

Q.—Where is he?

A.—He sailed on the last steamer for China. He has been Secretary of the legation, speaks the Canton dialect as well as English, and if you had some man like that here your committee could gain much information of value. He goes among the Chinese and talks with them in their own language. His residence is Pekin.

Mr. Pierson—Will you explain the *modus operandi* of shipping men—the forms that they have to go through with in order to ship them at all?

A.—I don't know. That is what I want to find out. What I know is, that a manifest—a list of passengers, with their various occupations. All appear to be free, voluntary emigrants, and the Consul certifies to that fact, nothing to the contrary being asserted.

Mr. Donovan—It seems that the Chinamen who come here have some sort of a contract with some one, by which their bones are to be returned to China in case of death?

A.—That seems to be the fact.

Q.—And they won't come here except under contract to take their bones back?

A.—I assume that to be the case.

Mr. Pierson—You assume they all do come under contract?

A.—So I assume. Forty or fifty dollars is the passage money by steamer. You take a common laborer, one who has not that amount of money, and advance it; he agrees to work it out. Those who have that much money will not come, because they are independent.

Mr. McCoppin—I suppose that to be buried in China is a part of the religion of that country.

A.—It comes from Confucius' doctrine of the worship of ancestors; but then a great many Chinese go to the East Indias, die there, and their bones are never brought back to China. It is a short distance, and I presume those who go there do so on their own hook, there being no contract by which some one must see to the sending back of the bones. At the same time there is that feeling among the Chinese, inculcated by their religion—if religion it may be called—that they sleep better if they can have their descendants make offerings at their graves when they are buried. They think they will be happier in the other world, and all of them, therefore, desire it.

Mr. Pierson—If they ship here under contract, it is in direct violation of the British colonial laws, as well as our treaty?

A.—Yes, sir.

Q.—So that the British Government must wink at their deception?

A.—Yes; it seems as if they must. The English Government has a law for ferreting out the fact whether they are free emigrants or not. If they are free, they are permitted to go on board the English ships. At the present time there are very severe pains and penalties provided for the importation of coolies in American vessels; but these do not apply to foreign governments. Where emigrants embark in English vessels they are beyond the reach of our laws.

Q.—Have you any means of knowing, approximately, the number of Chinese in California, or in San Francisco?

A.—No, sir; I have a sort of general impression that the number is overestimated. Of course the statistics of those who have arrived, and the departures by steamers for China, and the number of deaths, might be ascertained. A great many go back to China. They come here because they have good wages, and after serving two or three years they have a competence, and away they go. In the autumn a great many go home, so as to be there during the Chinese new year, and have a grand blow-out.

Mr. Haymond—Is it not your impression that the immigration here is an off-shoot of the coolie trade, the only difference being that that trade is under the auspices of the government, while this is a private enterprise?

A.—No; I think this emigration sprung up originally from the building of these great railroads. They brought us a large Chinese immigration to this coast.

Q.—You have spoken of free emigration and enforced emigration, how would you class this?

A.—I class this as enforced emigration; but that is hardly the proper name for it, because they are not bound to any certain term of service, as I understand it. The contract is simply to repay advancements made for passages, with a certain bonus to pay for interest and risk.

Mr. McCoppin—I suppose that Chinamen wishing to come to this country, in the hope of bettering their condition, and not having money to pay the passage, make contracts with these companies to pay them back for advances made, with interest, etc.?

A.—Yes, sir.

Mr. Evans—Don't you know white immigrants that came to California that way?

A.—Yes, sir; and they never kept their contracts as the Chinese do. There was a very large sprinkling of immigration that came to California that way in forty-nine.

Mr. Donovan—Do the Chinese keep their contracts better than the Americans?

A.—They don't know our laws here, and the companies have such absolute power over them that they keep their contracts. The guilds have absolute power over them here and in their own country.

Mr. Pierson—Have the Chinese Government any tribunals in Hongkong?

A.—It is an entirely British colonial government. The Chinese have no government there.

Q.—Are Chinamen tried in British tribunals?

A.—Certainly.

Mr. Haymond—You say the guilds in China have absolute control over them. To what extent—to the extent of life and liberty?

A.—They cannot take a man's life by law, but they can persecute and depress him.

Q.—He then is absolutely at their mercy?

A.—You take the merchants' guild—the tea merchants' guild for instance; it decides that the members shall not sell tea below a certain price. Suppose a member breaks that agreement; he will be ruled out, and his credit will be destroyed; he will be bankrupted. There are various ways in which they can enforce their decrees. The great power of these Chinese companies over the people here is due, in a measure, to the fact that the Pacific Mail Steamship Company will not sell them tickets for China until they get certificates from their companies, and the companies will not give the certificates until the people shall have paid their debts.

Mr. Donovan—I have been told that the Pacific Mail Steamship Company have a contract with the Chinese companies, that it will not sell Chinamen tickets unless they get certificates from the companies that they are free; that they have served their term of servitude?

A.—Substantially that is a fact. I recollect having a conversation with Mayor Otis about it, and he said that company had to conform to the wishes of the companies, because the trade was worth too much. I know, from my knowledge of the Chinese people, that very few can raise money enough to pay for a passage here. Somebody has to pay it. A common laborer, who has fifty dollars, will not come here; he is independent.

Mr. Haymond—And this money is advanced by the companies, and they enforce payment by having a contract with the Pacific Mail Steamship Company by which they can keep these Chinamen here until they shall have paid everything?

A.—That is their safety in making advances; but that is only a supposition on my part—an opinion I have formed from facts that have come under my own observation.

Q.—Is it not the prevailing opinion in the neighborhood of the ports from which these people are shipped, that a great many are shipped against their will—for instance, the women?

A.—No.

Q.—It is with their consent?

A.—Yes, sir. Where a woman is under age she has very little to say. The parents make contracts to sell them in marriage, or anything else they please.

Mr. Donovan—As I understand it, the parents have a right to make marriage contracts, and the woman really has no control of herself in China?

A.—Nor the boy either.

Q.—I mean the woman; if she is of age and unmarried?

A.—No, sir.

Q.—And consequently the women that come here must be sold or given away?

A.—That would be a fair assumption.

Q.—And brought to this country for ——— Of course we know the purposes for which they are brought here?

A.—There may be some exceptions; but that is the general assumption.

Mr. Haymond—How long have you been a resident of California?

A.—I have been a resident here since the fourth of June, eighteen hundred and forty-nine.

Q.—What business have you been engaged in?

A.—Merchant and banker. I have been Governor of the State, member of Congress, Collector of the Port of San Francisco, and Minister to China.

Q.—What commodities or products of the United States are now sold in China—exported in any quantities?

A.—Most every product of the country. Quite a large trade has sprung up between here and there in domestic produce, breadstuffs, etc.

Q.—Are these consumed by China proper or by the foreign population?

A.—They do not go into the interior, and are consumed principally by the foreigners. The Chinese themselves could not afford to live on flour. As the Chinese become more anglicized they may change in this respect. Flour is a sort of luxury there just now, and cannot be used extensively.

Q.—What is the general condition of the working classes, as compared with that of the working classes of this country?

A.—More average comfort, according to their ideas of comfort. According to our ideas, it would be misery. There are fewer abject poor. That comes partly from the fact that labor is honorable, and everybody works; everybody is expected to work, and a drone has no sympathy.

Q.—Do you know the average amount required to support a laborer per day?

A.—I can judge from the fact that the wages are small and that the families are supported on them.

Q.—Ten cents a day?

A.—Yes; and in foreign settlements a common laboring coolie, employed by a foreigner, would get five or six dollars a month. Out of that they support considerable families, but they make the families work also. Every individual works—the wife works and all work.

Mr. Donovan—Could the Collector of the Port do anything to prevent these people coming here as they do?

A.—No. When the manifest comes to him properly certified, I don't think the Consul would have the power to go behind it.

Q.—How many children, as a rule, do families average, that are supported on ten cents a day?

A.—About the same as it is here.

W. J. SHAW sworn.

Mr. Haymond—State generally what you know of the social and political condition of the Chinese in their own country, their habits, mode of life, manner in which they work, wages, and customs generally.

A.—I went to China when I was abroad. I went to Shanghai, to Tien-tsin, to Pekin, the Great Wall and back, up the Yang-tse-kiang, and into the interior about five hundred and fifty miles. I visited several of the chief towns, and studied the country and the people as well as I could; but I don't know that I have anything new to communicate. I found the Chinese a peculiar people. Their government is one of the most remarkable that I have ever studied. While it is hardly any government at all, yet it maintains a kind of control over the largest population of any one government in the world. I attribute this to what we may call their religion. They are educated in a manner ever the same—the same which prevailed in Christendom thirteen hundred years ago. They are taught that all the knowledge that is of real value is found in the works of Confucius.

In their schools they are educated in his works; and the learning to be found in them, and in the works of his contemporaries, constitute the whole of their system of education. Among the most striking features of that education is their devotion to parents; and that parental relation seems to me to afford some clue to their extraordinary condition governmentally. They live in families, and sometimes these families are very large. I have been assured that sometimes twenty to forty married people constitute one family, and they bring up their children all together. It is a family relation emphatically; and in such a country, under such a condition of things, there is very little necessity for governmental interference. The families are held responsible for the conduct of their children. When a child of bad habits, disregarding the example and teachings of his parents, becomes uncontrollable, and the parents don't know what to do with him, they have the right, as I am assured—a right that is very often practiced—to rid the world of that child. They say: "We can do nothing with this child. It will only disgrace us; and it is better for us to drown him in the river than to bring him up in this way." Their teachings lead them to literally worship their parents. I have seen them bow reverentially to their parents as a pagan would to his god. The idea of resisting parental authority is regarded with horror; and it does not enter their minds, except under extraordinary circumstances. The consequence is, that the parental rule of the family provides a rule for the whole country, without the interference of government, as we understand it. In some districts, however, particularly in the interior, up the Yang-tse-kiang River, it is customary for the natives to form expeditions to rob from village to village; and as they increase the number of villages captured, the horde becomes more extensive, and they continue on robbing and pillaging until their numbers amount to almost an army. I was shown on the Yang-tse-kiang River an extensive territory recently pillaged. The whole place was devastated. The central government has no particular power over them. I was told that when such occurrences happened, the government would send its mandate to the Governor of the province, insisting that order should be preserved. Sometimes they succeeded in quelling the disturbances, and sometimes they were quelled by the voluntary dispersion of the members of the gangs. I was assured that in that country these things are not of rare occurrence. I was also assured that a very large portion of the population, particularly the working population, were simply slaves—some of them slaves from birth; but as a rule, or at least in very frequent instances, they were enslaved in a manner not unknown to foreign nations, being sold to pay debts. A very large proportion of the laboring classes composes this latter class. The labor of agriculture is encouraged by the example of the Emperor himself. At certain times in Pekin he holds the plow himself. It is undoubtedly to show that the government has a high respect for agriculture. But although this high example is set, and agriculture is so ennobled, yet it is in China, like everywhere else—the real work is done by the lower classes. The highest members are those who are considered to be nearest the courts. The army proper consists of agriculturists; that is to say, the members are given ground to cultivate, and they cultivate the land, thus maintaining themselves and their families by their own labor. They are not paid salaries as in other countries, but are made to earn their own living in that way. The regular army in China is considered, in villages where it is sent to quell disturbances, as the most dangerous element that could visit them, because they are usually hungry, and consider themselves at liberty to help themselves to any provisions or property that are loose. Shortly after the Tae-ping rebellion, I was told that the towns preferred the visits of the rebels to the visits of the regular army.

Mr. Pierson—What do you understand by coolie labor?

A.—Slave labor, I should understand; what we call slave labor; perhaps more closely resembling peonage than strictly slave labor.

Mr. Haymond—There is no obligation on the part of the person holding them to take care of them?

A.—What the law may be on that point I cannot say.

Mr. Pierson—How long were you in China, Mr. Shaw?

A.—I do not remember. I think about three or four months.

Q.—During what year?

A.—In eighteen hundred and sixty-eight.

Q.—Were you in Hong-kong?

A.—Yes; I remained at Hong-kong some little time, two or three weeks, I think, visiting in that vicinity.

Q.—Do you know anything about the mode of the shipping of Chinese to this port?

A.—I do not know anything about it.

Mr. Rogers—How do these Chinamen you see here compare with the generality of the Chinese?

A.—The masses are about the same as we see here. In cases where they are better here, the change is caused by the better country.

Q.—Are the women there very little lower than these we see here?

A.—The women there are, of course, in a very peculiar condition. Prostitution, for instance, in China, is not regarded as a disgrace, but is regarded as a profession, a calling, like that of beggary, or any of the low professions—a condition in which they must remain, because they have been occupying it. It is supposed that they are not responsible for it. The condition of the lower classes is as near, as I should think, that of the brutes as any human exhibition can be found any where in human society. In Pekin, I visited the Sisters of Mercy, who have a society there, and I saw in that house children, girls from infancy, still unweaned, up to fourteen and fifteen years of age. I was assured by the Sisters—and have no question of its truth—that those children were picked up, for the most part, by them out of the streets. Frequently mothers have brought their girl children to the Sisters, and voluntarily delivered them, to be raised by them; and it was no rare occurrence when a girl was born to place it on the street, abandon it to its fate, because the parents had no means to bring it up. I cannot give any accurate idea as to the number I saw in that institution. At that time I gained the impression that infanticide and the abandonment of female infants were things much practiced there—to an extent unheard of amongst us or any other nation. At Tien-tsin more Sisters have a convent, and most of the inmates were children picked out of the gutters, where they were left by their parents. The inmates of this convent, as you are aware, were massacred by the Chinese population on one occasion, under the pretense that they were bringing up these children as Christians. That organization is sustained by the Catholic Church; they are Catholic institutions, sustained as they are in other countries. Most of th

Sisters in the convent at Pekin were French, two of them, I think, being Irish by birth. They were sent there and maintained as those organizations are in other countries. I found the numbers in these institutions to be governed by the room in their buildings more than the supply. They were all filled, and there were subjects for many more besides—children abandoned by their parents.

Q.—How does living in Chinese cities compare with living here?

A.—Their living here must be very far superior to their living there. I mean the laboring classes, what would be called there the coolie class. So far as I observed, they seemed well satisfied if they got plenty of rice.

Q.—What wages did they get?

A.—That I never went into sufficiently to give me any proper ideas as to the rule of wages. With regard to the coolies, their wages would, of course, simply be their rice.

Mr. Donovan—Do they have more wives than one?

A.—Yes, sir. They are allowed to have as many as they want. Strictly speaking they have but one wife. That wife is permitted, and it is considered no disgrace to encourage the husband to have as many more women in the same house as he can support. They are his concubines. They would more nearly correspond, according to our ideas, to concubines than to wives. They have a claim for support, and the children are the children of the wife. In law they are held to be the legitimate children of the father. They are credited to the first or legal wife. The wife, when she loves her husband, considers that she does him a kindness in inviting in others to assist in the domestic relations.

Q.—I understood you to say that in these little villages and places in China, where one makes war upon another, they feel that they have a right to decide that quarrel without respect to the central government, and punish criminals as they see fit. The central government is of secondary consideration?

A.—Yes, sir.

Q.—And regarding these guilds or companies, is their authority regarded as paramount to that of government?

A.—As I understand it, these guilds or companies are formed as a sort of mutual protection societies. The members have a strong feeling for their companies, and would be ready to obey any reasonable request, and sometimes any unreasonable request. They consider themselves as strictly amenable to the companies, and if these companies undertake to enforce any rule made by them they will generally do it.

Q.—If, in China, they respect their companies more than they do their government, they would be the same here, would they not?

A.—So I should imagine. I should explain those raids that I mentioned more fully. It is not an uncommon thing in Asia for raids to be made. On the borders of British India, for instance, individuals sometimes lose their crops; they are short of food and become hungry, and, as is natural in that stage of society, they go somewhere where they can get food; they therefore make raids into India, frequently on British subjects. Sometimes the English Government has felt obliged to go into the interior to punish persons making those raids. The Chinese Government has no power to suppress these raids, and punishment must come from other sources, if at all. The natives raid when they are hungry and want food, and these hungry spells come on whenever they are desired, it seemed to me. In Singapore the condition of the Chinese was a subject of constant reflection and observation to me. In that city, at the time I was there, there was, as I was told, over eighty thousand Chinese. They were given a portion of the town to inhabit, and that portion swarmed with them. I was assured that sometimes they became exceedingly troublesome to the government owing to their being liable to get into quarrels. When they got into a quarrel they would be destitute of reason and would be like wild beasts, rushing through the streets stabbing and killing others. In Java, several years ago, the Dutch prohibited their immigration into that country, they were feared so much, because of their influence over the native population.

Q.—In what respect?

A.—In trade; they were so much more unscrupulous, cunning, and selfish in making bargains than the natives of Java. The East India Malays are quite a different character of men from the Chinese. The Chinese are superior to them in cunning, and they take such advantages, especially in Java, that they found it necessary to prohibit altogether their going into the interior of the island. They have been used, however, to advantage in the tin mines of Banca. In that work they have been very serviceable.

Mr. Pierson—Do you understand that the Chinese Government favors or desires to repress Chinese emigration?

A.—It is understood that the government does not desire the Chinese to leave the country, but whether their leaving is or is not in violation of any regulations of that government, I do not know.

Mr. Evans—From what part of China do the Chinese, who come to this coast, come?

A.—From Canton, and from provinces bordering upon that part of China.

Q.—Under whose control is that part?

A.—Canton is under the Chinese. Hong-kong would be the place from which they would ship for California. That is a British colony. There would be no difficulty for any number of persons to leave Canton, where there is a constant connection by steamers, for Hong-kong, where they could ship for California. The mass of Chinese immigrants do not come from Hong-kong. They simply go there for the purpose of embarking. The mass go there, for that is the only place where they can leave the country for America.

Q.—Do you understand that these guilds or companies are in the relations of families?

A.—They are quite different. They are societies having no parental relations.

Mr. Haymond—How is the condition of the laboring men in that country to be compared with the condition of those here?

A.—It is undoubtedly going from misery to comfort. The amount of destitution in China is very serious. Pekin, in my opinion, is one of the filthiest cities to be found. There is what is called a Chinese City of Pekin and a Tartar city. The Chinese city is filthy to a degree almost beyond belief. I have seen tricks perpetrated in the streets of Pekin proper that would only be tolerated in brutes in a civilized country. When I was there I wondered how ladies could go into the streets at all, and I was told that they hardly ever did; that they never attempted to walk in the streets, but when compelled to go out used the conveyances of that country. When they wanted exercise they were carried to the walls of the city, where they could walk without seeing sights that would be disgusting. Those streets are filthy beyond what should ever be seen among human beings. The great mass of the people, it seemed to me, were ignorant, and not in a position to be removed from ignorance. They have, it is true, a system of education, but that system of education is confined to certain books written four thousand years ago. They think there is no knowledge anywhere that is not found in those books, and, as a consequence, their learning, from the highest to the lowest, must be very limited, according to our ideas.

Mr. Pierson—Do they read and write?

A.—They are taught to read and write in the common schools that are throughout the whole country. It is not a governmental system, but is kept up by their peculiar system of office-holding. A person cannot hold office except he have an education in the books I have described. Those books teach a high system of morals, and they learn them. About three hundred years ago there were persons who believed that all the knowledge of any value was embraced in the Bible, and that office-holders should be compelled to have a thorough knowledge of its contents. That is the rule in China regarding the works of Confucius. The consequence is, that although our people have the idea that the Chinese are very well. educated, they are possessed of only a very limited one. Although they are required to read and write, and to know Confucius, yet that knowledge in itself—all they have—is so inadequate to the demands of the present age, that we may say that they have no education at all.

Mr. Haymond—What was the received opinion among Americans, English, and other intelligent people in China, as to the character of emigration to this country, whether free or servile?

A.—With regard to that, I would not like to say. Regarding their honesty, I can mention this fact, which may interest the committee: I was assured by all the merchants with whom I conversed on the subject in the towns that I visited in China, where there are foreign merchants residing, that nobody hired a Chinese servant without taking a bond from some responsible person that he would be responsible for any thefts that servant might perpetrate. It was considered there, among those with whom I conversed on the subject, that Chinamen are so constituted that they must sooner or later steal something. It is their nature. Consequently they are not trusted in any house until they bring their bondsmen. When thefts are committed, and they are not of rare occurrence, the bondsmen pay for the things stolen. As far as I know and heard, no one thought of hiring a servant without taking a bond to meet any deficiency caused by theft.

Q.—Are the women considered to amount to anything?

A.—The women in China occupy the same position as in most parts of Asia—virtually slaves; mere creatures, to pandor to the wishes of the males, and promote their happiness.

Mr. Donovan—You have given us a description of the literature of the Chinese; now, take their architecture. How does that compare with other works dating back, say four thousand years—the pyramids, for instance, of Egypt?

A.—The architecture of the Chinese, if it deserves that name, is the most primitive of any now in use. In Pekin, for instance, although it is one of their largest cities, I did not see three houses two stories high, outside of the palaces, which are inclosed within the city by themselves. I only heard of one house in the city more than one story high. I was told by a Father of the Catholic Church that, when they were erecting the church, they unwittingly erected a steeple. After that steeple was up, they were notified that they must take it down. Then they found that there was a law prohibiting any one from building a house more than one story high, the reason given being that they should not be high as to enable the occupants to look over into the Emperor's palaces, and see his grounds. In that case, the Fathers compromised by agreeing not to put up a stairs or ladder to get into the steeple.

Mr. Pierson—Of what are their buildings mostly constructed?

A.—Of brick. There are some structures in Pekin—as, for instance, the Temple of Heaven—that are quite commendable. It is made of white marble, and the architecture is good. Here the Emperor, when he is a man grown, sacrifices animals. The place is very pretty, the roof is tiled; and as regards architectural beauty, the temple will compare favorably with similar buildings in other countries. The dwellings, however, are far inferior.

Mr. Donovan—Is the architecture equal to that of any of the great nations dating back four thousand years, or those of the present time?

A.—I think not. It is quite inferior to that of the Egyptians, the Latins and Greeks, and other nations of antiquity. Their literature is better than their architecture. I have the works of Confucius and Mensius translated into English. I have examined them with some attention, and regard them as works of great credit. The morals they teach are certainly very commendable, and will compare favorably with the moral teachings of other books of that age. Outside of those works I have never read any works of the Chinese. The Chinese, so Dr. Williams says, are almost destitute of imagination. They have no poets, as we understand them. What they have is of the most inferior, commonplace character. Their music is quite destitute of wit and harmony. Their novels are exceedingly simple stories, such as our little boys and girls read here.

Mr. Pierson—Are their officers elected or appointed?

A.—They are appointed by the government. They have competitive examinations; but they are only in the works I have mentioned, so that the choice is confined to persons educated according to the government method.

Q.—Do you know of any diseases peculiar to China?

A.—I do not.

Q.—Is there a great deal of leprosy there?

A.—There is said to be a great deal in certain districts.

Mr. Haymond—How long have you resided in California?

A.—Ever since June, eighteen hundred and forty-nine.

Q.—What positions have you held in California?

A.—I have never held any except what you gentlemen now hold. Besides that, I was District Attorney here in this city (San Francisco) in eighteen hundred and fifty. I was in the State Senate twice. That is all.

Q.—From what you have seen of those people, and from what you know of your own knowledge, what effect do you think a large emigration from that country to this would produce on our social and political condition?

A.—It would have the most deplorable effects. It seems to me that a large Chinese immigration would cheapen labor to such a degree, as that white labor could not compete with them.

Q.—Why would they cheapen it? Why can these people work cheaper?

A.—For the reason that the Chinaman, from his birth, is educated to live cheaply, to live on the smallest amount possible to be conceived of. I suppose that a penny a day would feed a Chinaman in China very comfortably, indeed. Those habits of living he brings with him to this country; and he can live here for so much less than can men of our own race, that with even one-half the wages he can obtain sufficient living, and an equal amount of profit with free labor.

Q.—Do they bring their families with them?

A.—They do not. I am told that there are some Chinese merchants here who have their wives; but, as a rule, the women will not leave China at all. When their husbands want to leave China, they tell them to go; but they will not go with them.

Q.—Every steamer that comes here from China brings a number of Chinawomen. Do you know from general repute the character of those women?

A.—The general understanding here is that they are of the lowest kind; that these women are, as a rule, prostitutes.

Mr. Lewis—About what proportion of the people in China are what you call people of rank?

A.—It would be impossible for me to say. I suppose that nobility there is hereditary, although men on passing examinations are entitled to hold office. There is caste in China to certain extents. The guilds have employments of various kinds, and they make their members adhere to those employments. This amounts, to a certain extent, to caste.

Mr. Evans—You said, awhile ago, speaking of the women, that as a rule those coming here are prostitutes. How is it regarding the married women? Are they chaste or lewd?

A.—As I understand it, they are entirely chaste. They are not permitted to be otherwise. They are never allowed to be placed in a position where they can be tempted, for they are always confined to their residences.

Q.—How is infidelity in the wife looked upon in China?

A.—It would be considered as a serious offense. With concubines it would be quite a different thing. If with the consent of the man, the concubine could do as she wished. Her offense would be in doing it without his consent.

Mr. Donovan—Then a man has one wife and a dozen concubines?

A.—Yes, sir.

Q.—These latter can do as they like and go where they please, but it is an offense for the mother to be "irregular"?

A.—Yes, as I understand it; they are his slaves and do his bidding.

Q.—Then a man could have his wife here and bring over a dozen concubines and let them out for purposes of prostitution?

A.—I suppose that there would be no domestic difficulties about it.

Q.—It would not be opposed to any moral ideas the Chinese have?

A.—No, sir.

Q.—The first effect of Chinese immigration would be to degrade labor. What effect would it have on the manufacturing interests of the country, and the commercial interests, if all the labor were performed by Chinamen instead of by white men? Would it have the effect of discouraging and preventing manufactures, and decreasing the amount of wages paid the white men employed in manufactories?

A.—I have never been engaged in mercantile pursuits or manufacturing, but would so imagine. They would destroy some branches of labor; but I understand that there are many branches of industry which demand low-priced labor in order to be successfully carried on. I have been informed that Chinese labor is necessary to carry on some kinds of manufacturing business. The Chinese can do certain kinds of inferior work as well as anybody else, and being obtainable so much cheaper, are preferred, and are even necessary.

Q.—If the Chinese were employed generally would the market for productions not be necessarily destroyed, owing to the difference between their wants and the wants of the white laborer displaced by them?

A.—I would rather not answer that question, because I am so imperfectly advised.

Mr. Pierson—In other countries do the Chinese assimilate? Would they intermarry and adapt themselves to the habits and customs of the people?

A.—I have known cases of that kind. The Governor of the Island of Ternate, one of the East Indies, had married a Chinawoman. He told me that he found her exceedingly attentive to all his wants, and he rather liked it. They told me also that there were several cases where the Dutch had married Chinese, and I was also told that it was not a rare occurrence for the English girls to marry Chinamen, but of that I have no information further than hearsay.

Mr. Lewis—Do you know anything about any inducements that this people have, other than their own volition, for coming to this country?

A.—That, I do not know. I believe that they regard it as desirable to come here—those who are laboring people. They have a different idea of this country from what they have of most countries.

Q.—Do you know, from your own observation and experience, how Chinamen, who have been here and returned to China, regard it?

A.—I am told that they speak more kindly of the Americans than of any other nation.

Q.—Then the sentiment is a favorable one, and the inducement to come here great?

A.—I should say that up to the time of the recent agitation they were more friendly disposed towards Americans than towards any other nation.

Mr. Evans—Is not one of the greatest inducements the wages they get here—ten cents there and fifty and seventy-five cents here?

A.—Yes, sir. There is one other fact that occurs to me at this moment; it is a fact that their treatment here has probably been rather too good for their own interests. When they first came here in considerable numbers, they never thought of getting into a street car, but would ride on the outside—either on the front or rear platform. They did not feel themselves at liberty to sit on the inside, especially in close contact with ladies and gentlemen. On my return here, after an absence of several years of travel, I was greatly surprised to find not only the increase in numbers, but to see the great change in their customs towards the white people. I daily find them

—those of the lowest class, and, sometimes, I fear, not clean—inside the cars in close juxtaposition to ladies. On the streets, they are more aggressive and more independent than they were some years ago. I think, myself, that we are very much to blame, because there are men amongst us who encourage them to "assert their rights," as they call it, and make themselves of importance, and they are not so much to blame as these persons who have miseducated them.

Mr. Lewis—Have you discovered in China admiration for our institutions, or was it our wealth they admired?

A.—They have no knowledge of our institutions. They simply want to come here to get money to take to China in order to be better off than they otherwise would be.

Q.—You do not know of any of them speaking favorably of our institutions?

A.—I do not think they have any knowledge of them, or if they have they believe that nothing can be compared to China and her institutions.

Mr. Rogers—Did you hear any reason given why they are so anxious to have their bones returned to China?

A.—The Chinese are an exceedingly superstitious people, and they have very extraordinary customs. During the lives of their parents, they literally worship them. When they die, they believe that if they do not take care of the remains of their parents and relatives they will suffer in consequence of it. That is my understanding of it. It is entirely a religious matter, and that is done to please the spirits of the departed. The bones are therefore taken back to their own country and buried, that the spirits of the dead may be propitiated.

Mr. Donovan—Do you know anything about contracts that they must go back, and if made with the government, company, or with individuals?

A.—I do not. I presume that they must come here under such contracts, as the bones are returned by the respective companies. When these Chinamen come here, they do so as perfect strangers, and, being without means, would become lost were it not for the presence of these companies or associations, which look after them. They are taken care of as soon as they arrive, and are maintained until employment is found for them.

Mr. Lewis—Do you know anything about the inducements on the part of the Chinese Government that led to this Burlingame treaty?

A.—I was here when Mr. Burlingame arrived, and it so happened that I was in China when the treaty reached there. From Tien-tsin there is no regular mail, and the Consul asked me to carry up the mail for him. In that mail was the Burlingame treaty, and in one of the newspapers which I took from here was a printed copy of the treaty. They did not have any copy of the treaty except this newspaper, and it was sought after. It immediately became the topic of conversation in Pekin, and it was there a matter of surprise that it had been made. It was understood that Burlingame did not have the power to make the treaty. From that I infer, and I presume that the inference is correct, that the Chinese Government did not make any effort to get the treaty, and, for a time, did not know whether they would confirm it or not. I got the impression that it was quite a voluntary thing on the part of Mr. Burlingame.

Q.—What is your impression as to the effect the abrogation of that treaty would have? Would you regard it as a public calamity?

A.—Not at all.

Mr. Evans—Suppose it were abrogated; could it prevent immigration?

A.—Not unless some other steps were taken. I don't think they came in consequence of the treaty. They were coming before the treaty was made, just the same as now. I don't think that the abolition of that treaty would change their coming in the least.

Mr. Lewis—Some people say that the abrogation of the Burlingame treaty will injure our commercial relations. Don't you think that if these relations are necessary they will go on, treaty or no treaty?

A.—Decidedly.

Q.—You think that the passage of laws to prevent their coming here would be unwise?

A.—It can be accomplished in a friendly way, I think. What is known as the Burlingame treaty has had nothing to do with immigration. It would have been just the same had the treaty never been made. To abolish the treaty for the especial purpose of preventing their coming here would not only not accomplish its object, but would turn the Chinese against us. In that view such a step would be impolitic. If there was a simple abrogation of the treaty it would have no effect one way or the other. It is highly desirable not to offend the Chinese Government. They are a numerous people, and we have a good trade with them. I think that we can quietly accomplish everything desired without offending them in the least. We can accomplish much by asking them to prevent the emigration of the lowest classes—the coolies. That is very likely the only objectionable feature in this immigration. Tell them how it affects us and I think they will act.

Mr. Haymond—Do you regard this whole immigration as coolie immigration?

A.—The mass of it; by no means the whole. There are a great many Chinese who come to this country for the purpose of learning the English language. That portion, however, is very small when compared with the great mass.

Mr. Lewis—Do you know whether their term of servitude extends over all time, or is it to last only until a certain amount of money is paid?

A.—I do not know the details.

Mr. Donovan—Are there any Chinese shipped here from China proper, or are they all shipped from Hong-kong?

A.—They must take the steamer at Hong-kong. There is no other place where they can come from.

Q.—What is your belief as to the association or mixture of an inferior and a superior race? What is the effect upon the superior?

A.—It tends to degrade that race.

Q.—Does it tend to elevate the inferior race?

A.—It is most likely that the inferior race would be benefited by contact with the superior race.

Q.—Then the result, as you understand it, is, that contact with the Chinese benefits them and deteriorates the race to which we belong?

A.—Mere contact of the two races would not necessarily deteriorate the superior race, because the superior race will not allow that contact to become too close.

Mr. Lewis—Do you know whether it is the law and custom of that people to discourage any sort of improvement in China?

A.—It is habit. It is their education. They believe they have now all knowledge, and will not countenance innovations. It amounts to a law; it is custom. They believe the books of Confucius contain everything, and having mastered them, there is nothing more to learn.

Mr. Donovan—Then, while we benefit them, they will do us as much injury, will they not?

A.—I am not aware of their having been of any great service, except to persons desiring cheap labor. There are, of course, certain enterprises in this country that have been benefited by Chinese labor.

Mr. Haymond—Take it as a whole, what is the effect of Chinese immigration upon the State?

A.—At the present time, I would hate to say that they produced greater injury than benefit, but if continued to any considerable extent it might injure our country.

Mr. Lewis—When we consider that there are four hundred million of them, and their inducement in coming here is our money, would not an immigration under such circumstances work serious injury to American labor?

A.—It seems to me that there is danger of it.

Committee adjourned until to-morrow, April twelfth, eighteen hundred and seventy-six, at eleven o'clock A. M.

SECOND DAY.

SAN FRANCISCO, April 12th, 1876.

Rev. OTIS GIBSON sworn.

Mr. Pierson—What is your profession?

A.—A clergyman.

Q.—How long have you been such?

A.—Since eighteen hundred and fifty-four.

Q.—Have you ever resided in China?

A.—Ten years—from eighteen hundred and fifty-five to eighteen hundred and sixty-five—at Foo-chow. It is one of the five ports open, and is half way between Canton and Shanghai. It is the largest seaport in China for the export of tea. It is about fifty or sixty miles from Hong-kong.

Q.—Did you pursue your profession there?

A.—Yes, sir; I was a missionary to the Chinese of the Methodist Episcopal Church.

Q.—Do you know anything of Chinese immigration?

A.—I have seen a great deal and heard a great deal of it.

Q.—From what part of China does most of the immigration come?

A.—These Chinese here are nearly all from the Canton province. They come down the river, and are shipped from Hong-kong—a British port.

Q.—How long has it been such?

A.—Since the result of the opium war of eighteen hundred and forty-four. It was a part of the settlement of that war.

Q.—Do you know upon what terms the Chinese are imported into this country?

A.—They come free. I think all Chinamen come free, except the women. Many come under some kind of an engagement. I have never seen engagements made; but constant intercourse with Chinamen, and the knowledge I have of them here, leads me to believe that Chinamen who are poor and wish to get here, make a promise with some one who will advance them enough money for passage, to repay this money with a large percentage of interest. The advancing party runs the risk of non-payment. I know one case of a young man in my school. Forty dollars was advanced him for passage, and for this he had to return one hundred dollars. When Chinamen come here in that way, they are taken charge of by one of the six companies, and kept until work is found for them. Sometimes they have to keep them for three or four weeks. Sometimes these men run away, and the company loses whatever was advanced.

Q.—Is there any sort of a contract by which service is pledged for any specified time—during life, or until the money is repaid?

A.—I understand the contract to be, that they are under obligation to pay this back out of the first money they get, but in an amount double or treble the amount advanced for passage.

Q.—Do you know what means the Chinese companies have for enforcing that sort of a contract?

A.—The Chinese companies at the present time, and since I have been in this country, so far as I know, have no criminal power, and do not exercise any. The six companies, so far as the people are concerned, are arbiters. When they cannot arbitrate the case, they go into our Courts. The six companies derive a large portion of their power from the fact that the Pacific Mail Steamship Company will not sell tickets to Chinamen unless they have a permit from the companies or from the missionaries. The price of a passage to Hong-kong is, I think, forty dollars; but the Chinamen can't get the ticket unless he is a Christian, or has the stamp of the six companies. That, I understand, is the extent of the power which the companies have over the Chinamen here. Some years ago, when there was opposition between here and China, the fare was only twelve dollars. Two men of my mission applied for tickets, but were refused, the contract being, that unless they had the stamp of the six companies, they must pay one hundred dollars. It was finally agreed that any person having my name and belonging to my church could go for the ordinary price.

Q.—So that even now a Chinaman who has not paid his debts to the various companies cannot go back unless he is a Christian, or has your sanction?

A.—He must have my name, or that of any one of the missionaries. I suppose there are one thousand Chinamen in this country who would return to-day if they could return on paying the passage money.

Mr. Lewis—What is the character of these companies—associations of capital, for the purpose of making money, or for the protection of Chinamen?

A.—It is very difficult to tell entirely what those six companies are. When Chinamen leave home, and go to other countries, the first thing they do is to form a guild, and build a temple. The temple is the hall where they meet to talk over matters, arrange business matters, and settle differences and difficulties among themselves. They are a great people for arbitrating, and are extremely clannish. The six guilds here are formed of men from different parts of China. As

I understand it, there is no contract with Chinamen who come here to belong to a company; for many come by steamer who know nothing of the companies until the interpreter meets them at the steamer. He asks them from what place they come, and that fact determines to what company they go. There is no initiation fee, and no annual or stated installments to be paid. It is simply that when he goes home he shall pay a fee. That is my understanding of it.

Q.—They are societies, then?

A.—They might be so called, but they are not political or doctrinal societies. They elect officers, a President and Interpreter, yearly.

Mr. Pierson—What do you understand by the term "coolie"?

A.—That is a word brought to us from India, and it means a low servant or laborer. The terms "coolie trade" were applied to the importation of coolies into Cuba and South America. In China the word "coolie" means the chair-bearers, the earth-diggers, the street-cleaners, and hod-carriers, etc.

Q.—Not meaning servitude?

A.—No, sir. Among the Chinese, in their own country, there is no such thing as slavery, according to our notions of slavery.

Q.—Is there any system of servitude whatever?

A.—There may be a system of binding a boy out for a term of years; nothing more.

Q.—Is there servitude for crime?

A.—There is punishment for crime, but I think there is no servitude. I never heard of it. The women I do not include, for they are bought and sold. Among the highest classes dowries pass, and that, though real bargain and sale, is not called such. The poor folks sell their girls outright.

Q.—From what class is our Chinese immigration?

A.—From the lowest class.

Q.—By that you mean laborers?

A.—Yes, sir.

Q.—Do you mean degraded in a moral sense?

A.—I think they are the lowest class of people. Most of the Chinese who come to this country are ignorant—very. I do not think there is one in five that can read a page of a book, and not one in ten that can read a small tract, or book, or newspaper through intelligently. Nearly all of them can read the signs over the stores; nearly all can do that much reading, but to take a book and read it they cannot do it.

Q.—What is the average rate of wages in China?

A.—At Foo-chow, ten to twenty cents a day, when I went there. When I came away, twenty to thirty cents, cash, a day. Common laborers are hired by the month for four, five, and six dollars, boarding themselves.

Q.—Have you any means of knowing how many Chinamen there are in San Francisco?

A.—I had a conversation with some of the officers of the six companies about two months ago, just before this excitement occurred in this city. They gave me the names on the books of each company, and I judged that the number in the State was about one hundred and fifty thousand, or rather that number on the coast. In this city (San Francisco), thirty thousand. That is my approximation.

Q.—How many of those Chinamen have become Christians—Roman Catholic as well as Protestant?

A.—I could not give you statistics of that, exactly. I don't know what the statistics of the Roman Catholic Church are. They have very few proselytes. We have a very healthy mission. There the Chinese come, read the Christian literature, listen to Christian teaching, and learn to renounce idolatry as they learn the English language.

Q.—What do you suppose your converts amount to? Can you approximate how many?

A.—I suppose that in this city there may be, in all, one hundred. I do not know. There is this about it: they sometimes go to one place and sometimes to another. If you take one hundred at Dr. Stone's church and fifty at Dr. Lathrop's church, in those figures you will count some twice. I can't tell the exact number here. Many have been baptized and have gone to China as missionaries.

Mr. Lewis—What is your experience as to their sincerity?

A.—Just the same as among other people.

Mr. Pierson—Haven't they rather lax ideas on the subject of honesty?

A.—American merchants in China tell us that in mercantile honesty they are equal to any other nationality. In San Francisco it is good. I am not now speaking of the laborers, but of the merchants.

Q.—What are their habits of life in China, in regard to cleanliness?

A.—The Chinese are not a cleanly people. They are not what we call a cleanly people.

Q.—How are they here?

A.—They are not cleanly here.

Q.—Do you know anything about their domestic life here?

A.—There is very little domestic life here; almost none at all.

Q.—Do the wives of the Chinamen come to this country?

A.—Very few. There may be one hundred. I doubt if there is one hundred.

Q.—Are these of the higher classes?

A.—They are the richer ones.

Q.—What are their ideas of marriage in China? Are they limited to one wife?

A.—No; they are not limited to one wife. They can have as many wives as they please. A man marries, if he is able, till he gets a boy. If his first wife produces a boy, he don't care for more wives.

Q.—Do all the wives stand on an equal footing? Is one a wife, and the rest concubines?

A.—They are married, and the children are all legitimate.

Q.—What is the relation of man and woman in China?

A.—They have an idea that the man is the head of the house.

Q.—Is the woman anything more than a slave to the man?

A.—I guess it is about the same in China as it is here. I once had a Chinaman speak to me on that subject. He was an intelligent man and an officer of the government, who has sent three or four of his sons to America to be educated. He said: "Many Chinamen laugh at you and the English people because women rule in your country; but women rule in China, too. Women rule the world. The Chinese women rule the same as in your country, only we have the name of ruling them; but we don't."

Q.—Have you any means of judging as to the proportionate number of Chinamen engaged here in various occupations?

A.—I could not give it from memory. A year ago I employed a Chinaman to gather for me statistics of how many were employed in this city. I spent some time and money in it, as I thought of writing a book on the Chinese in America; but, like all good works, it was not completed.

Q.—In your opinion, is this Chinese immigration productive of more injury than benefit, or the contrary?

A.—That is a political question. The Chinese have brought some evils; but I think, after careful study, that, as a matter of political economy, they are a benefit; for there are more white people at work in California to-day than there would have been, or could be, if the Chinese were not here.

Q.—Suppose they were to increase in the same ratio during the next ten years, what would be your opinion?

A.—Unless our existing laws are executed with more honesty than they are now, I think it would be unfortunate. I think we have sufficient law, if executed honestly, to check a great deal of it. That has been my experience. I mingle with the Chinese in their quarters a great deal, and I know that this Chinese gambling is simply a matter of buying the privilege to violate the law. The same is true regarding the women. There is a percentage of the profits that goes to persons other than the Chinese, for the purpose of carrying on prostitution.

Q.—Is prostitution in China regarded with the same idea of degradation that it is in this country, or is it a sort of profession by itself?

A.—The standard of morals in China is different from what it is here, for the civilization is lower. I think there is as much chastity among the Chinese as a people, as among our people. Among the people who have families it is a great crime for a woman to betray her chastity to a man, and family chastity is a great virtue in China. Prostitution there is regarded the same as it is here. In the cities where they live, they have separate quarters, and are not allowed to go anywhere else. They are under quite as strict, or perhaps stricter, regulations there than they are here.

Q.—Have you been with the Chinese ever since you resided in this State?

A.—I have been a missionary on this coast since eighteen hundred and sixty-eight.

Q.—Do you go into their houses to any extent?

A.—Yes, sir.

Q.—What is their mode of life? Take the Globe Hotel, on Jackson and Dupont Streets.

A.—I have not been there very much. There were three or four gambling places there, and a great many Chinamen used it to bunk in. It is like camp life in a mining town or the lumbering regions?

Q.—Do they board and lodge in the same house?

A.—They, perhaps, merely lodge there, and eat in the eating-houses. The rooms are of different sizes. These men who own these buildings, and rent them to the Chinese, divide them up into rooms, some eight by twelve, some ten by fourteen, some six by ten, etc. In rooms of that kind four or five men sleep; for they spend a great deal of money for opium, in gambling, and at brothels, and are forced to live as cheaply as possible.

Mr. Haymond—What do you understand by coolie?

A.—A common laborer.

Q.—At the time of the making of the Burlingame treaty, how was that term understood in China?

A.—Contract labor. About that time, what was known as coolie importation was taking place to South America and Cuba. Those men were induced to come to the ports on certain promises, and they were kept in large halls there, called barracoons. They contracted to serve a certain number of years for a certain price, at the end of which time they were to get their liberty. The contracts, however, were not kept, and many failed to get free. As a result, the Chinese Government sent a Commission to look after them.

Q.—It means, then, the importation of common laborers?

A.—Yes, sir. That is, however, not practiced in China now, I think.

Q.—This immigration to California is about the same thing, is it not, only under private auspices instead of the government?

A.—I think not.

Q.—It is of common laborers?

A.—Yes; but they come of their own desire.

Q.—They are coolies?

A.—They are common laborers. They come of their own free will. As I said before, they make arrangements with some person who has capital to pay for their passage, they agreeing to return the money with interest—double or treble the amount advanced.

Q.—It is that class you call coolies?

A.—No, sir. I would never use that word as it is used in our country. I do not understand that these people are here in servitude—are slaves. I do not use the word "coolie" in that sense. If you ask me what the Chinese here are, I would say that the most of them are common laborers. The word "coolie" is not a Chinese word. It is an Indian word, which was introduced there.

Q.—What is the meaning of the word in India?

A.—A sort of low laborer. In Hindostan or India, it is a common or low laborer.

Q.—You do not know of any country, except California, where they use the words "coolie" and "slave" as synonymous?

A.—No, sir. It simply means the lower class of laboring people. A man understanding the meaning of the word will never use it in the sense of a slave. In China, there is the chair coolie, who carries your chair for five or ten dollars a month, the house coolie, etc.

Mr. Evans—Can you give us any information about the number of American citizens living in that country?

A.—It is ten years since I came away. At that time there was a large American settlement at Shanghai, probably more than at any other port in China, outside of Hong-kong. Also, in Canton, Amoy, Swatow, Pekin, and such places. I suppose there were four or five hundred in Shanghai, and one thousand in each of the other places.

Q.—Was the number increasing or decreasing?

A.—Increasing, but not so rapidly as the Chinese do here. Speaking approximately, I should say there are five or six thousand Americans residing in China. If you include persons on board ships in the ports and harbors, I should say from ten thousand to fifteen thousand.

Mr. Pierson—Have you any means of judging as to the number of Chinese coming under contract to work, and the number coming free from it?

A.—No, sir. I don't think, however, that all come under contract. Take a family of four or five boys and an old man. They hear stories about this country, and the ease with which money is made fast. They get their earnings together and send one of the boys. He comes here and sends money back as fast as he can send it. I think half the people come in that way. It is only when large firms go to the companies to get laborers that they are imported, the companies finding they can make more by importing now and advancing the passage money than they can otherwise. It is only in such a case that the companies send to China for men.

Q.—Did you ever read the Burlingame treaty?

A.—Yes, sir; but not lately.

Q.—The term "coolie" is used in that treaty. In what sense? Is that term used as you use it?

A.—Is that in the treaty?

Q.—Yes. The importation of coolies is prohibited.

A.—I think it is used, then, in the sense of servitude. It was caused, probably, by this barracoon system, where the people were used as slaves.

Mr. Haymond—These coolies were all of the lower working classes?

A.—Mostly; not altogether. A few men were induced to go on board ships at the last moment—merchants and business men—and carried away. The word "coolie" in the treaty probably refers to them.

Q.—Burlingame lived at court a long time. What would have been his understanding—the same as yours?

A.—I should think so, but I don't know. I would use the word in no other sense than as relating to the laboring classes. The coolie trade was caused by a professed demand for laborers in Cuba and South America. The Chinese went there under contract, but these contracts were violated, and the men enslaved. Men were stolen in China by these traders, assisted by Chinamen whom they employed. They took these stolen men to the barracoons, and kept them there until they could be shipped off. That is the coolie trade.

Mr. Donovan—Are not these Pacific Mail Steamship Companies now actually engaged in this coolie trade?

A.—No, sir. I would not think that could be said. You might say that they are engaged in coolie immigration, with the definition of common laborers given, but not in the coolie trade; not in its offensive sense. They are only interested in the passage money.

Mr. Lewis—These companies pay the expenses of the men that come here. Is that at the instance and expense of the companies, or the persons themselves?

A.—I suppose the men pay it back. I do not believe that the six companies import a man here. I have had a great deal of study to find out what the six companies are. Last year I had a very intelligent Chinaman teaching. He was a literary man, and is now President of one of the companies. Through him and some others I learned little by little, and I am satisfied that the six companies, as such, do not import a man. When a firm wants to employ a large number of Chinese, say one thousand, the manager goes to one of the companies, tells them he wants so many men and agrees to pay a certain price. If the company think they can do better by sending to China, they do so, and induce men to come out.

Q.—Have Americans anything to do with the affairs of these companies?

A.—I think not. The six companies do a great deal in the way of settling cases. Some time ago one of my school boys came to me, and said that he wanted I should settle a case in the Courts, imagining I had great power with our Courts. He said that he and his companions had had fishing grounds near Redwood City for three years. Last year some men belonging to another company went down, and took a part of the ground. They had had a quarrel, and the case was in the Courts at Redwood City. After proof was heard, the original parties were sustained. On an appeal the case was reversed, and the Chinaman seemed to think that the American Courts were strange things. They first decide a thing to be right, and then wrong. They came to San Francisco, and called the six companies together to settle this thing. They met, and compromised the affair, each company putting its stamp to the compromise, except one company, and that the one to which the other parties belonged. Here was a difficulty, and they appealed to me to write to the Judge of the Court to tell him that they were right and the others wrong.

Q.—In China, is it considered a greater offense to take the life of a man than it is to take that of a woman?

A.—The general sentiment of the Chinese people is that the man is the more important animal. I don't know whether, when you come to the murder of a woman, they would make a distinction.

Mr. Haymond—How does it come that these six companies exercise any control over these people in the matter of settling their difficulties?

A.—That is very natural. Although their interpretations of justice are sometimes a little irregular, yet, when they consider the delays and uncertainties of our Courts, they prefer to compromise where they can.

Q.—How would a compromise judgment be enforced? In the case you mentioned, it appears that the judgment could not be carried out because one company refused to assent. Where the company refuses this concurrence, what is done?

A.—It is left with the men for settlement.

Q.—Do you know of any cases of resistance to the orders of the six companies?

A.—I have never heard of any case where there was any resistance. They have some way of carrying them into effect, but how, I can't say.

Q.—Don't they pretend to divide this city into districts, and farm out the washing, for instance, to those people?

A.—I do not understand that the six companies have anything to do with that. It is the Washing Guild, composed of men belonging to the washing business.

Q.—Are their orders enforced by punishment upon violation of orders?

A.—I don't know. I think there is something of that kind.

Q.—Do the six companies levy taxes?

A.—I do not know. I think they have sometimes undertaken to do that, but it is all voluntary. They cannot get anything except the men are willing to give it. The Hop-wo Company undertook to build a temple on Clay Street, and the money was raised by subscription. Most of the Chinamen would give four bits to have their names on the temple.

Q.—What is your knowledge of their compromising criminal cases —interfering with the administration of criminal justice?

A.—I have no knowledge on that point. They are exceedingly clannish, and if a man of one clan kills a man of another clan, each man will do all he can for his own clan.

Q.—Has not money often been paid to withdraw prosecutions?

A.—I believe so

Q.—Is it not a well-settled matter that a great many people are held in slavery here—bought and sold?

A.—Only the women. I don't think there is a man so held. The women, as a general thing, are slaves. They are bought or stolen in China and brought here. They have a sort of agreement, to cover up the slavery business, but it is all a sham. That paper makes the girl say that she owes you four hundred dollars or so, passage money and outfit from China, and has nothing to pay. I being the girl, this man comes up and offers to lend me the money to pay you if I will agree to serve him, to prostitute my body at his pleasure, wherever he shall put me, for four, five, or six years. For that promise of mine, made on the paper, he hands him the four hundred dollars, and I pay the debt I owe you according to contract. It is also put in the contract that if I am sick fifteen days no account shall be taken of that, but if I am sick more than that, I shall make up double. If I am found to be pregnant within a month, you shall return the money and take me again. If I prove to have epilepsy, leprosy, or am a stone woman, the same thing is done.

Q.—Are these contracts regarded as moral among the people who make them?

A.—Well, there is a certain class of knaves among Chinamen who have no morals at all.

Q.—These contracts are sustained by the great mass of Chinamen here, are they not?

A.—I think there is in existence now—there has been—a company of men engaged in this traffic of women; not the six companies, but a guild like the Washing Company. They have their rules and their regulations, and they stand by each other. One of those companies is called the Hip-ye-tong. When a Chinaman runs away with a woman from one of these brothels and marries her, he is followed by these companies, and asked to pay them her value, or look out for the consequences. It is a common thing for them to use the processes of our Courts to protect their interests—their assumed rights. If a woman escapes from a brothel, she is arrested for some crime, and possession is obtained in that way. Where she marries, the chances are that both man and woman will be arrested, or the man will be arrested and the woman run off to some other place. Sometimes Chinese come to me to get married. I don't care to marry them, and, to discourage it, have set my price at ten dollars, whereas the Justices' fees are only two dollars. They seem to have a sort of indefinite and unreasonable idea of protection when they come to me.

Mr. Pierson—You used the terms "stone woman." What do you understand by that?

A.—I did not know, and asked them. They said it was a woman so naturally disabled, that a man could not have any intercourse with her.

Mr. Haymond—Then, so far as the women are concerned, they are in slavery, with more hard features than have been known to white races?

A.—Yes, sir. And even after the term of prostitution service is up, the owners so manage as to have the women in debt more than ever, so that their slavery becomes life-long. There is no release from it.

Q.—When these people become sick and helpless, what becomes of them?

A.—They are left to die.

Q.—No care taken of them?

A.—Sometimes, where the women have friends.

Q.—Don't the companies take care of them?

A.—Not frequently.

Q.—Is it not a frequent thing that they are put out on the sidewalk to die, or in some room without water or food?

A.—I have heard of such things. I don't know. I don't think they are kind; I think they are very unkind to the sick. Sometimes the women take opium to kill themselves. They do not know they have any rights, but think they must keep their contracts, and believe themselves under obligations to serve in prostitution.

Q.—What is their treatment? Is it harsh?

A.—They have come to the asylum all bruises. They are beaten and punished cruelly if they fail to make money. When they become worn out and unable to make any more money, they are turned out to die. A portion of the profits arising from this business goes to the Chinese, and a portion to men not Chinese. There is collected for each woman imported as a prostitute, forty dollars. Of that, ten dollars goes to white men. Twenty-five cents a week or month—I forget which—is levied on each woman, and part of this goes to these white men. Gambling-houses pay five dollars a week to certain policemen for the privilege of keeping them open. Last year thirteen dollars a month were given to some party around the City Hall. I am under bonds of secrecy, and cannot give the names of my informants.

Q.—If Chinese prostitution should be stopped in this city and in the State, would there be any use or employment for these women?

A.—I think most of the women would get married according to the American law, and live with the Chinese.

Mr. Donovan—Is it possible that the Chinese are so degraded, that they would marry this class of people?

A.—Very few of the Chinamen here are married. In China the rule is that all respectable women shall be married; but a large class of men are not married. In some provinces there is a system of infanticide of girls, particularly among the poorer classes, and women become scarce. I have seen proclamations in China from the authorities, against infanticide, because there were not enough women for wives for the men.

Mr. Rogers—I would like to have you give us your experience as a missionary with this people?

A.—Our success with this people has been slow. They begin by going to school, and we gradually teach them to have a disgust for idolatry. That is the first point to be reached. During my labors I have baptized thirty-five or thirty-six persons.

Q.—In how many years?

A.—Since eighteen hundred and seventy-one, properly speaking.

I was here some years before, but was lecturing up and down the coast.

Q.—What is the Chinese religion?

A.—Idolatry. All the Chinese are Confucians, but that is no religion. They are very much attached to their faith. Confucius does not teach religion; it is more of a system of state politics.

Mr. Donovan—Are these Chinamen affected with syphilitic diseases before or after coming here?

A.—I suppose they must be—especially the women.

Q.—Don't they keep houses open for the accommodation of boys who are willing to go there?

A.—I think there is a good deal of that. I am told that white boys are accommodated cheaper than Chinamen.

Charles Wolcott Brooks sworn.

Mr. Haymond—You have heard the testimony of Mr. Gibson?

A.—I have.

Q.—In your own language, go over the ground and tell us what you know of the subject under investigation?

A.—I first went out to Asia in eighteen hundred and fifty-one. I have been there several times, and have seen a great deal of the country, and have given the subject some thought.

Q.—How long were you in China?

A.—Different times; I never staid there any great length of time. I suppose I have been all through Asia—perhaps was in China two years altogether. I have been there five or six times.

Q.—Have you occupied any official positions at any of those times?

A.—Yes, sir; in the Japanese Government. I was agent of the Japanese Government at this city; about sixteen years Japanese Consul here. I was a diplomatic attachê of the Japanese Embassy that went around the world. I have prepared some notes of what I desire to state, and will tell what I know by referring to them. Our first treaty with China was made by Mr. Reed in eighteen hundred and fifty-eight. Subsequently Mr. Burlingame, in Washington, then acting as Ambassador for China, made a supplemental treaty. That was, supplemental articles of agreement relating to specific things. They became thereby a part of the original treaty, so the Burlingame treaty is not a separate treaty at all, but merely an addenda to the original Reed treaty of eighteen hundred and fifty-eight. The abrogation of one part would work an abrogation of the whole. Most of the privileges that Americans enjoy in China are not derived so much from the specifications of the treaty as from the "favored nation" clause of the treaty. This clause is to the effect that the power making the treaty shall be entitled to all the privileges enjoyed by any nation having a more favorable treaty with China. If you were to abrogate that treaty entirely you would still be governed in your relations with China by international law. By so doing, therefore, nothing would be gained, while our citizens would lose their protection which they now enjoy in China. The Federal Government would then have the power to prevent immigration altogether, but the abrogation of our treaty would effect nothing.

Q.—The treaty opens only six ports to Americans, while all of the United States is open to Chinamen?

A.—That is a mistake. Americans have access to all parts of China

—they go anywhere they please. We get privileges not mentioned in the Burlingame treaty, by virtue of the "most favored nation" provision, and we have to examine all those treaties to know exactly to what we are entitled. Americans in China are under the rule of the American Consul. They wander around the country at will, and in case of their breaking a law they are tried by their Consul, and not by the Chinese authorities. The Burlingame treaty provides for trade; then the right to appoint Consuls—Chinese Consuls in America, and American Consuls in China; then the agreement on both sides to respect liberty of conscience; next, prohibiting the coolie trade.

Q.—What was understood by the coolie trade at that time in China?

A.—Merely a laborer. In eighteen hundred and fifty-one I studied Sanscrit, so that I spoke it. The word "coolie" is an old Sanscrit word, and means, in India, a laborer. The word "walla" refers to the next highest grade; then "baboo," which means the business man. The meaning of the word "coolie" is the same in China as in India. In the Burlingame treaty it refers to the coolie trade—a trade in labor—the common laborers. The importation of Chinese here would literally come within that definition, though I think this different from the coolie trade as contemplated in the treaty.

Mr. Donovan—If this is the coolie trade, then the Pacific Mail Steamship Company is engaged in it, is it not?

A.—Yes, applying that definition in that manner. They are really engaged in bringing here coolie labor, but whether in the sense of a coolie trade or not I cannot tell.

Mr. Haymond—Is not this the way it is done: A, a laborer, contracts with B, a contractor, to pay his passage to some foreign country, agreeing to work there a certain number of years for a certain sum of money? That is the coolie trade which is prohibited by the Burlingame treaty, is it not?

A.—Yes. I think any contract labor would be forbidden by it. It was the abuse of that trade, however, which called the attention of the civilized world to it, and demanded its prohibition. Instead of making or keeping such contracts, the contractors violated them, and the coolies were subjected to all the horrors of the slave trade.

Mr. Pierson—Is it not a fact that Americans in China will not leave the ports to go into the interior without first securing a permit from their Consul for their protection?

A.—It is customary to get permits. I don't know that they would be traveling entirely at their own risk; but I would take every precaution. A permit of that kind is a sort of security, and they are used in different parts of Europe by travelers. Some time ago I made inquiries among some of the leading Chinese houses as to the amount of money Chinamen living here send back home; and I was told that those who send back any, send back, on an average, about thirty dollars a year. Some of them do not send back any money at all. A few send more than that; but thirty dollars is considered a very good sum to send in a year. The Chinese generally return to China in five years. Their average stay here is five years. In regard to correcting this coolie business—this contract labor business—I think it is the duty of the American Consul at Hong-kong to question these people. The law provides—British and American—that, when the people are ready for shipment, the Consul shall ask them certain questions—whether they go voluntarily or not. He must ascertain if there is any contract to labor; and if there is, he must forbid their coming. If they are all right, he grants clearance-papers to the steamer. I think the steamer folks are not to blame. I think the onus of the whole thing lies with the American Consul at Hong-kong. "By emigration regulations in force at the colony of Hong-kong, all laborers under contract to labor abroad must, before leaving, have their contracts read or translated to them personally and alone, and their distinct assent obtained, fourteen days before they can legally embark. After a fortnight, it is again read to them by an emigration officer, and inquiry made if they have changed their minds. If still anxious to go, they are sent on shipboard, where they are offered by the Consul a last opportunity of withdrawing, who certifies that they executed their contracts voluntarily; and thus having, after reflection, thrice publicly reaffirmed the fact, they clear legally from Hong-kong." [Witness reads from article in *Overland Monthly*, written by himself.] They have a right to make contracts, but it must be of their own free will. Then the Consul, having certified to the fact, grants a clearance to the ship. Where there is fraud it is the duty of the American Consul to put a stop to it, and he can do it if he does his duty.

Q.—Who is the American Consul at Hong-kong?

A.—Mr. Bailey. His predecessor was Mr. Allen.

Mr. Haymond—Suppose the Consul desired, in good faith, to make inquiries, and these people were brought there under duress—would not some influence there prevent them from disclosing the truth?

A.—I think it is as Dr. Williams says—what is needed in American foreign diplomatic service is educated interpreters or officers, with some kind of an understanding of their language, who can go among the people and explain to them their rights. Our Consuls are appointed from Iowa, Wisconsin, etc., and the first thing they do is to read about China. Then they go there, and hire a Chinese clerk, on whom they are entirely dependent.

Q.—There are thirty thousand Chinese in San Francisco, and yet, with the best interpreters, we cannot get at the truth.

A.—We have very few interpreters. Gibson is one of the best. They are more afraid here than they are in China, to tell the truth.

Q.—Why is there such a fear here—because they have their own system of punishments?

A.—I suppose they have, although I really know nothing about it.

Q.—That is the opinion among intelligent people—that truth cannot be ascertained because they themselves administer punishments if anybody acts otherwise than in accordance with the will of some governing power?

A.—That is, I think so. One of the great difficulties is the organization of a foreign hostile force within the territory of the United States. It is a very difficult thing, however, to tell how you are going to administer justice when Chinese tribunals of that kind exist. It is practically impossible. The Chinese are very deceitful, and that very deceit is an indication of a weaker race. A weak man makes up in lying what he lacks in strength. They feel that weakness, and they conceal it by strategy and deceit.

Mr. Pierson—Do you know anything about the organization of these six companies?

A.—Yes, sir. A few words, however, upon immigration: The United States, of course, goes with Great Britain to a certain extent, but the policy of Great Britain is different from ours. Her policy is an aggressive policy. She desires to find places to send her people to; she wants to get possession of territory, so she sends her emigration everywhere. The United States invites immigration. She wants to settle up her waste lands. The policies of the two governments are quite different. In regard to whether the Chinese coming to this country are a greater benefit or a greater detriment, I will say this: San Francisco is already, by internal revenue returns, the ninth manufacturing city of the United States. No doubt a portion of this prosperity is due to Chinese labor, and it is very probable that a larger number of white people find employment from the presence of the Chinese. A certain amount, therefore, may be good, but a larger amount will be bad. The Chinese are bad for us, because they do not assimilate and cannot assimilate with our people. They are a race that cannot mix with other races, and we don't wish them to. The Chinese are bad for us, because they come here without their families. Families are the centers of all that is elevating in mankind, yet here we have a very large Chinese male population. The Chinese females that are here make this element more dangerous still.

Mr. Haymond—I believe the term "hoodlum" belongs here?

A.—I think it is a local word.

Q.—Might it not be that boys in this country are out of employment because the Chinese work in the lighter trades?

A.—I have thought a good deal about that.

Q.—If the channels are already filled up with other labor, how is that?

A.—We look upon the Chinese as an inferior race, and in the great race of life mind wins. We could use them to do our inferior work.

Q.—They do the light work—the work that in other countries falls to the women and the boys, and fill up the channels that would otherwise be open to our boys?

A.—It may be.

Q.—It is the only white city in the world where they have Chinese in any numbers, and coming from the lower working classes, as they do, they necessarily degrade labor and debase the moral standard—injure the community, in many ways, do they not?

A.—That is undoubtedly true. There are, however, more whites employed here because of their presence here. If white labor were employed in making cigars we would have to send to Manilla for our cigars. If they did not make shoes we would have to send to Lynn. I was asked this morning to what I attributed the presence of hoodlums. I think it is owing as much to the lack of enterprise as to the want of honest labor. Our cities are filled with persons desiring to follow city callings. It comes from laziness, and a low moral standard. In regard to this subject of Chinese immigration, it should be taken hold of and settled in a statesmanlike manner. There is no doubt great abuses exist among our people in the administration of our laws. I believe that our laws are enough to check this immigration if they are honestly and faithfully administered. Outside of that, this matter of Chinese immigration is regulated by the law of supply and demand. As soon as they find out that their coming is unprofitable, they will cease to come. Their filth, and vice, and degradation can, in a great measure, be done away with, and it is hoped the labors of this committee will be successful in that direction.

Experience shows that the average gain of Chinese is about four thousand a year. A large portion come here at this season, and a large number return home in the fall; but as the demand keeps constantly increasing, the supply also must be kept up, leaving us a gain of four thousand a year about. About fourteen thousand arrive every year, and ten thousand go back. Each man remains about five years. I do not think there are over sixty-seven thousand Chinamen here, and they all come from Canton. We get only the lowest class of laborers here, because we get those without money. A man who has one hundred dollars we can't get. In China three hundred dollars is a competence, and the interest upon that will support a family comfortably, according to their idea of comfort. In regard to immigration, the Chinamen who come to this country, all come from the British port of Hong-kong, which is as much a part of Great Britain as is the Isle of Wight. The British statistics show that there are one hundred and seventy-five thousand Chinamen in the colony of Hong-kong, and nothing could prevent their coming to California except you destroy the demand for them here. We might end our relations with China, in the hope of stopping Chinese immigration, but there is nothing to prevent the Chinamen from acquiring a residence in Hong-kong, and that being a British colony, we could not stop immigration except by an understanding with Great Britain. I think we have sufficient law here to govern this whole thing, if it is only faithfully executed. If we can avoid a rupture with China, and complications with Great Britain, we had better do it. I believe somewhat with Herbert Spencer in relation to the survival of the fittest. In their own country they have developed into a lower order of the races. China is so surrounded by a barrier of mountains on all sides as to shut out improvement. The population have been isolated from all Asia, and for two hundred or three hundred years China has gone backwards. The opening of her trading ports was against her wish, yet, at the same time, it was giving her light. While our missionaries have done little indeed, they have taught the Chinese reading and writing, and some principles of philosophy. They have seen the steam-engine, the electric telegraph, steamships, etc., and have become convinced, in a measure, how immensely behind the rest of the world they are in knowledge. The Chinese are in about the same condition now that Europe was in the eleventh century, and they are coming up very slowly. Their standard of morals, of course, is much lower than ours.

Q.—What is the nature of their central government?

A.—It is a very weak government, indeed. It is composed of about seventeen provinces; but the Governors of those provinces are pretty nearly absolute in their districts. A certain amount of deference is paid to the general government, and by foreign powers it is held responsible for all damages resulting to foreign citizens. These provinces are practically independent of each other and of the central government. The rulers are appointed after a competitive examination in the Chinese classics; that is, the works of Confucius.

Q.—If the people come from Canton to California, and these other sixteen provinces have little interest in the question, nothing we would do here would affect our standing with them, would it?

A.—Not a particle. Canton is a southern province; and my impression is, that the men there are more lazy than they are elsewhere. It is a most undesirable class of the population.

Q.—What wages do workingmen receive there?

A.—When I was there the rate was about five or six dollars a month.

Mr. Evans—Do you know the area of the Island of Hong-kong?

A.—It is about, I should think, five miles across; and oblong, ten or twelve miles in length.

Q.—Barren or productive?

A.—It runs up to a peak, and is pretty steep. It is a rock rising up out of the sea, and is rather barren.

Q.—What is the population?

A.—I should say one hundred and seventy-five thousand—a little more, perhaps, and mostly Chinese. There may be three thousand others.

Mr. Haymond—Assuming that this central Chinese Government amounts to little, and that there are sixteen or seventeen independent provinces; that this immigration is from Canton, and from there alone—any action here regarding the Chinese would not affect our commercial relations or intercourse with other parts of the country, would it?

A.—No, sir.

Mr. Donovan—Have we any intercourse with China, other than through Hong-kong?

A.—Yes, sir; there are Foo-chow, Amoy, Shanghai, and other ports. Then going up the Yang-tse-kiang River, Americans are numerous there.

Mr. Pierson—At what do you estimate the American population of China?

A.—There is a large floating population in China on account of the bad climate. There are American firms which have been there for ten or twenty years. Partners come in and go out. They don't remain there a lifetime. The resident American population must be two or three thousand. The Chinese have lately commenced many improvements. They had commenced building a railroad, and were encouraging the construction of telegraph lines, and employing a great many Americans in that way.

Mr. Haymond—Your theory, then, is that we can leave China out of the question, except so far as the Province of Canton is concerned?

A.—Yes; except as it is part of the whole. It is so disconnected, however, that it would not be like striking a British province. The United States, I suppose, would take notice of any damage done to any State, and China would do the same. There is not so close a sympathy between China and her States that there is between our States and the general government; yet, at the same time, there is an equal political bond.

Mr. Donovan—Are not most of the lepers, and persons afflicted with elephantiasis and these other diseases, inhabitants of Canton—are they not as numerous there as in any other part of China?

A.—I should suppose so, for the reason that they are mostly found in southern countries and low lands. That being a southern province, we would be more likely to import diseased persons from there than from any other source. I have not, however, seen a great deal of elephantiasis in China; I have in India, on the Ganges, and low lands.

Mr. Haymond—How will the Chinese compare with the white races in morals? Take the Province of Canton?

A.—I would say that they are all about in the condition that Europe was in the eighth, tenth, or twelfth centuries—in the dark ages, when the morals were very low, indeed. I think, perhaps, that the families are as chaste as we are; but around the sea-port towns there is a floating or boat population, which is very bad, and it is from this class that we draw our immigration. The architecture of China is very rude, and far inferior to that of nations of the past. As regards magnitude, they have some large buildings; but the quality and style of the work is poor. A large portion of the people in China live on rice principally. Many around the sea-port towns are in the boats all the time. They are born there, and die there. This is the lowest order of the people. Then further from the shore are farmers who till the soil. They are a superior class. Going back into the mountains of China, you find the Maories, which are a better class still—an entirely different class of men. There is a peculiar kind of exclusiveness about the Chinese in the interior, which makes it difficult to reach them for the purpose of introducing changes of any sort.

Q.—How does the condition of the Chinese in this city compare with that of the Chinese at home?

A.—I have been very little in the Chinese quarters here, but I know it is filthy, indeed, and that they are very much overcrowded. They live in a filthy condition here, and in a filthy condition at home, in their own districts. The buildings here are crowded pretty much as they are at home. Buildings once occupied by Chinese are unfit for white occupation, but real estate dealers obtain from them double and treble the rent they receive from the whites. The streets —the business streets—are in a passable condition, probably because the Chinese are compelled to keep them clean by the municipal authorities. The alleys are terribly filthy. Ladies would not care to go on those streets or look into those alleys. I think there is a class of outlaws among the Chinese population here, who give us a great deal of trouble. There are also, as in every community, a great many good men who are made to suffer for the doings of the evil. Among our people, if John Brown does wrong, he suffers as an individual, but if a Chinaman does wrong, the whole race suffers for the act of the individual.

Q.—Are there any Chinese families in this city?

A.—I think not any to speak of?

Q.—Are there one hundred Chinese families in this city?

A.—That would be a large number, I should think.

Q.—Have you any idea of the number of Chinese women?

A.—No, sir; I have not.

Q.—What is the condition of these women?

A.—I don't know. I imagine it is very bad, indeed. I think that the principal or only remedy to be applied to that evil are stringent municipal regulations, thoroughly enforced.

Q.—That would be a remedy for those things, but would it be a remedy for the injuries which that race inflicts upon the race with which they compete?

A.—I think that would prevent the influx of the vicious class. If we were to make them live as Americans, I think we would very soon have no Chinese here. For instance, make men have fifteen or sixteen-feet rooms to sleep in, each, and compel the observance of sanitary regulations, and they could not afford to work for the wages they now receive. If they are forced to demand more pay, employers will not employ them.

Mr. Pierson—Have you observed any change in the character of the Chinese for the last ten or fifteen years—have they become more aggressive, more independent, more apt to assert their rights, as they term it?

A.—I think that is caused by the fact that a great many misguided Americans put them up to it.

Q.—Do you think that they have any particular love for our institutions?

A.—I don't think they have any at all. They come purely as a matter of gain—as a matter of dollars and cents. If it is profitable, they will come. If it is not profitable, they will not come. The very fact of their retaining their own dress and customs, and keeping themselves so entirely separate, as a people, shows that they have not. Contrast them with the Japanese. The Japanese who go abroad are persons who have money to spend, and they go for pleasure and information. They adopt the manners and customs of Americans. Our dress and our language they seek. The Chinese come abroad, not to spend, but to accumulate. They maintain their own customs and language. The Japanese like our institutions. The Chinese do not, but hate us most cordially, and hate the Japanese more than any other people—a hate which is as cordially returned by the Japanese. There is nothing in common between them. In eighteen hundred and forty-two, the population of China was four hundred and thirteen million two hundred and sixty-seven thousand and thirty. That is the latest census that I have any account of.

Q.—Is the population increasing or decreasing?

A.—I think it has been decreasing lately, caused, in a great measure, by the scarcity of women. They drown their females as we drown kittens. Opium has been a great influence in that direction, also. They import into China ten thousand five hundred tons a year, and the native growth is as much again. The importation was commenced by England, in payment for teas. To pay for the tea taken to England required a vast amount of silver, and the British Government viewed, with a great deal of uneasiness, the drainage of her country of forty million dollars or fifty million dollars a year. She forced them to take in payment opium, raised in India, and they soon learned to use this drug, until now it is a universal thing. Opium smoking in China is looked upon as a vice, just as drinking is in the United States, but the people have acquired the habit, and they cannot abandon it.

Mr. Haymond—Is the killing of female children a universal practice?

A.—It is among the lower classes. Nothing is thought of drowning a female child. It is rather like drowning kittens, when we have more than we want. The result is, there is a great preponderance of men, and the population cannot increase as rapidly as it otherwise would.

Q.—Japan is a young, growing country?

A.—Yes, sir. Compared with China, it is like comparing a young, growing nation with an old, dying one. It is generally supposed that they are the same race; but this is not so. They are of absolutely different origin, and there is no sympathy, no similarity between them. They are an enterprising people. I think that the

Japanese are of Turkish blood; of the same race as the Turks or Arabians. Regarding the solution of the Chinese immigration question, however, I have no doubt but that the Chinese Government would unite with us in stopping it if we asked. They are very fond of arbitration, and would willingly compromise the matter. We could thus do a great deal of good without friction. Commerce would not necessarily be endangered, for the law of supply and demand will regulate that everywhere throughout the world. If a man has anything to sell, and we will buy it, we can get it. The Chinese merchant will trade here if he can get his prices, or do better than he can elsewhere. We export to China articles of produce, and it is the great market for our silver. We have also a sort of three-cornered trade with Great Britain and China. We are exporting very much more in value than in import. Silver is the standard in China. Gold is an article of merchandise, like rice, tea, or anything else. It is the market for silver—by some called the "sink of the precious metals." As China has nearly one-third the population of the world, they require an immense amount of money to carry on their ordinary business.

Q.—They could spare enough of their people to overflow this whole country, and scarcely feel the difference, could they not?

A.—Yes, sir. But all their ideas are against it. They are an exclusive race, and it is only by determined effort that that exclusiveness has been, in a measure, broken down. It seems to me that if our government would send there a statement of facts and grievances, and ask the Chinese Government to coöperate with us in stopping this immigration in a friendly way, they would be willing to do it, because they want their people to stay at home.

Q.—Do you think it possible for the two races to live in this country without, sooner or later, coming into a collision which will result in one becoming subject to the other?

A.—No, sir. One will have to be subject to the other.

THIRD DAY.

San Francisco, April 14th, 1876.

STATEMENT OF HON. E. J. LEWIS,

On behalf of the sub-committee appointed to visit the Chinese quarter.

Mr. Lewis, in answer to questions, stated that he had resided in California twenty-seven years; in Tehama County twenty-three years; had served in the Assembly of the State and in the Senate two terms; a member of the Chinese Investigation Committee, and of the sub-committee appointed to make an examination of the Chinese quarter, and continued:

We went through the various quarters inhabited by the Chinese, for the purpose of getting whatever information we could concerning the moral, physical, and social condition of the Chinamen, and more particularly to ascertain if there was collusion between the officers of this city, as had been intimated by persons upon the witness stand, and persons violating the law; whether money was paid by the Chinese to have tolerated the crime of gambling. In going through the several parts of the city we were, of course, known, from the fact that the interpreter was well known. They were also informed who we were, and what our mission was. They appeared to be a little afraid of what they called the "City Hall fellows," but when it was explained that we were not their enemies, but were there seeking information regarding their condition, they appeared to be willing to give us whatever information was in their power. In going through the several parts of the city occupied by Chinese, we saw signs, which the interpreter informed us were gambling-house signs, but the houses were closed, in consequence, probably, of our visit to that portion of the city. They read "Open night and day;" "The table is spread night and day;" "Riches and plenty," etc. We then visited the Chinese Mission, on Jackson Street, where we saw a Chinaman preaching to seventy-five or one hundred others. We then visited the Globe Hotel, a structure, I think, four stories high, and about one hundred feet square, on the corner of Jackson and Dupont Streets. It would be impossible to approximate the number of Chinamen we saw there, with anything like accuracy. It is used as a Chinese lodging-house, and these people swarm there. In one of the rooms we found a white woman, teaching a class of Chinese youths—about twenty in the class. She said she was making some progress with them, and they appeared to be getting along about as well as white children of the same ages. In that house there were rooms eight by ten feet, and smaller. In a room of that size fifteen Chinamen had shelves, or bunks, where they turned in at night—and they must have been packed something like sardines in a box, clear up to the ceiling. I suppose the ceilings are about ten feet high. We then went to Dupont Street, and visited several places of business in what appeared to be the more respectable portion of Chinatown. We then went to the office of one of the companies—the Sam-yup Company—where we met the heads of these six companies. We had a long conversation with them, first, as to the number of Chinamen that belonged to each company, with a result as follows:

Sam-yup Company	10,100
Yung-wo Company	10,200
Kong-chow Company	15,000
Ning-yeung Company	75,000
Yan-wo Company	4,300
Hop-wo Company	34,000
Total	148,600

That, I understand, is the number now on this coast belonging to those companies. There are some Chinamen not belonging to any company. The companies, I think, are societies for the protection of Chinamen coming from some particular locality in China, or in the province of Canton. Each company represents a separate district. Their custom is, whenever a ship lands here, an interpreter or inspector goes on board and finds out the locality from which each Chinaman came. His answer determines the company to which he shall go, and he at once is enrolled as a member thereof. So far as we could gather from the Chinese, they do not pay any dues. The Presidents deny having exercised any criminal jurisdiction, or to have punished offenders. We could get nothing from them in relation to their contract with the Pacific Mail Steamship Company. They said that no man could go home if he owed any debts to the merchants, because that was the agreement among themselves. The steamship company being interested in shipping them, agreed not to let them go. That is all we could get.

Mr. Pierson—In what way do the companies protect Chinese?

A.—By affording them means of employment—to see that they get something to do. They see that they are provided for until they get work. The only restrictions, as far as we could understand, was that none could go home to China without paying the debts they owed Chinese merchants. I understand that it is impossible to get in debt to the companies, because they advance nothing. There is some sort of a contract with the Pacific Mail Steamship Company by which no Chinaman can get a ticket without the consent of the companies, unless he pays one hundred dollars for it. They say that the reason Chinese come here is, that those who are in California write back glowing accounts of this country and its wealth, thus inducing others to come. Where they have no money to come, and they cannot raise enough from their families or relations, some friend will advance the money and take a contract that the borrowing party shall refund the amount loaned, with heavy interest, as soon as he can earn it. There is no company contract, as I understand it. There is no immigration here that does not come from Canton, or within two or three days travel of it. Coming to a strange country, ignorant of our laws, language, and customs, they find these companies an absolute necessity. In answer to our question as to the inducements the Chinese have to come here, they said that they were the same as actuated everybody principally to better their condition financially. They said that they supposed the antagonism to their coming here was because of the competition between Chinese and white labor. They had no observations to offer on that point. We asked them if they had the power to suppress gambling-houses and houses of prostitution, and to compel the people to keep clean. They said they had not. They could advise but could not compel. They said they had sent home proclamations saying that there was no labor here for any more of them, and advising them to stay at home. They had as many here now as could be made useful. They said that further Chinese immigration would be injurious to all concerned. We left the Presidents and continued our walk through Chinatown. We went into places so filthy and dirty I cannot see how these people live there. The fumes of opium, mingled with the odor arising from filth and dirt, made rather a sickening feeling creep over us. I would not go through that quarter again for anything in the world. The whole Chinese quarter is miserably filthy, and I think that the passage of an ordinance removing them from the city, as a nuisance, would be justifiable. I do not understand why a pestilence has not ere this raged there. It is probably owing to the fact that this is one of the most healthy cities in the world. The houses would be unfit for the occupation of white people, for I do not see how it would be possible to cleanse them, unless you burn up the whole quarter, and even then I doubt whether you can get rid of the filth. The Presidents said that there were thirty thousand Chinamen in the city, and thirty thousand more in the State outside the city. From one thousand five hundred to two thousand five hundred Chinese women are in the State.

George W. Duffield sworn.

Mr. Haymond—How long have you resided in California?

A.—Twenty-four years, in San Francisco.

Q.—What has been your occupation?

A.—I was connected with the police force in eighteen hundred and fifty-three–four, and for the last eleven years.

Q.—Have your duties called you into the Chinese quarters of this city?

A.—Yes; for the last nine years.

Q.—Can you give a description of the extent of those quarters? What streets are occupied by them?

A.—A great many Chinamen live on Pacific, Jackson, Dupont, and Sacramento Streets. Those are the principal streets.

Q.—What is the area occupied, in blocks—about how many blocks of this city?

A.—About six or seven blocks. The whole Chinese population is confined to six or seven blocks.

Q.—At about what do you estimate that population?

A.—From twenty-five thousand to thirty thousand in this city and county. A great many work in factories outside the city, mostly at Black Point, and these come in about once a week, sometimes oftener.

Q.—Do you know the building called the Globe Hotel?

A.—Yes, sir. That is on the northwest corner of Jackson and Dupont Streets.

Q.—About what is the size of that building?

A.—About one hundred by one hundred and twenty-five feet, five stories high, and a basement. There are about two hundred and seventy-five or three hundred Chinese living in it.

Q.—How is it occupied?

A.—The basement and the ground floor, the floor on the level of the street, by stores. The upper stories are occupied by rooms of men making collars, tailoring, etc., and sleeping apartments. The sleeping rooms are some twelve by fourteen, some smaller, and fourteen or fifteen feet high. Of such rooms they make two stories out of one, each about six or seven feet high. In some of these little rooms there are only two Chinamen, and in some four or five; in some, more.

Q.—What is the condition as to cleanliness?

A.—It is very dirty indeed—filthy. The Chinese quarters, as a whole, could not be much filthier and dirtier.

Q.—Do you know anything about the number of Chinese women in this city? Can you approximate?

A.—I should think there are from one thousand to one thousand two hundred.

Q.—What occupations are they following?

A.—Principally prostitution.

Q.—How many Chinese women living in the Chinese quarters are not prostitutes?

A.—There may be one hundred, but not over that. The balance are prostitutes.

Q.—Describe the situation of the houses of prostitution, their general appearance, and the habits of those people?

A.—One class of these Chinese women go with white men, and another class go with Chinamen. They live in very small places, some of them in holes six by six and six by five. The Chinese prostitutes who go with Chinamen are of the better class. Their places are cleaner and they have more room. Where Chinawomen go with Chinamen they will not allow white men at all. I don't think there is any doubt about the women being bought and sold like sheep. Sometimes Chinese women escape and get married, but when they do get away the owners try to get them back, or make the man pay them her value. Sometimes they have him arrested for kidnaping or crime, and then steal the woman. Sometimes they resort to our Courts for the purpose of getting possession of her, and then send her back to her life of prostitution. The women are treated now a great deal better than they used to be. They used to receive very rough treatment. They have not been beaten much lately, because the police watch them and arrest them for beating. When they become sick and helpless they send them to the hospitals or leave them to die. Sometimes they leave them with a cup of rice, to die without attendance. They take no care of them when they get sick. I have caught Chinese in the act of turning the sick out to die—leaving them on the sidewalk and in the street to perish.

Q.—Can you approximate the number of Chinese houses of prostitution in this city?

A.—There may be in the neighborhood of forty or fifty. I don't know that there are so many now, because a great many have been broken up within the last five or six weeks. This excitement has tended to do that. I don't think we can find in this city one house resorted to by white men but what has been broken up. The result is, these women must go into the country.

Mr. Pierson—What particular streets do they occupy?

A.—Principally alleys—Stout's Alley, Spofford Alley, Washington Alley, and Sullivan Alley.

Mr. Haymond—What is the condition of those alleys?

A.—Very dirty and filthy.

Q.—Are there many Chinese in this city that are married?

A.—Very few. Sometimes a Chinaman will get a Chinese woman out of a house of prostitution, go to a Justice's Court, and get married.

Q.—Taking the Chinese quarter as a whole, is it as filthy as it can be?

A.—Yes, sir. It cannot be much dirtier.

Q.—Were you ever in New York City?

A.—Yes, sir.

Q.—Was there any part of that city, as it existed twenty years ago, that could be compared with the Chinese quarter?

A.—No, sir. The Five Points could not be compared with it. The Chinese quarter is dirtier and filthier than the Five Points were.

Mr. Evans—How many gambling-houses are there?

A.—Very few. There used to be a great many. I don't think you can find one now.

Q.—How many were there six weeks ago?

A.—Forty, fifty, or sixty.

Q.—As many gambling-houses as houses of prostitution?

A.—Yes, sir. They had the reputation of being gambling-houses, but the policemen could never catch them. I have not seen a game of tan played in three years. In early days there use to be tables for white men—as many white men played as Chinamen. There are no gambling-houses running now.

Mr. Donovan—Can you read the Chinese characters?

A.—No, sir.

Q.—Can you read gambling signs in the Chinese language?

A.—No, sir. I can't tell a gambling sign from any other.

Q.—The heads of the companies told us that the gambling-houses had been in the habit of raising and paying money to men at the City Hall, to secure themselves from interference—and the same thing regarding the houses of prostitution. They said that if we could get honest American officers, there would be no more gambling and prostitution in Chinatown; but until that time, they will continue to exist. This was told us by the heads of the companies, the six Presidents being present.

A.—In answer to that, I will state that all those men talking to you were interested in those gambling-houses.

Mr. Haymond—How is this population as to criminal propensities?

A.—They are a nation of thieves. I have never seen one that would not steal.

Q.—What is the proportion of criminals to the whole number? What is the proportion of men who follow crime for a livelihood?

A.—I call a man who will steal a criminal.

Q.—Then nearly all will be criminals?

A.—Yes, sir.

Q.—Do you know anything of their spiriting away witnesses and compounding crimes?

A.—Yes, sir. They will do it all the time—from the Presidents down.

Q.—Have they some means of settling cases outside of Court?

A.—They all do it.

Q.—And there is no means of getting testimony outside of the Chinese?

A.—No, sir.

Q.—And they settle crimes whenever they can do so?

A.—Sometimes one company will prosecute another, but where they can settle for money, they will do it.

Q.—Have they any regard for justice here?

A.—No, sir; not a bit.

Q.—How does their testimony stand in the Courts?

A.—They think no more of taking an oath than they do of eating rice. They have no regard for our oaths at all. Their own oaths they regard as sacred, and the only way you can get them to tell the truth is to cut off a rooster's head and burn China paper. They followed that system here in early days, but not lately.

Q.—Is it not often the case that on a preliminary examination there is testimony enough to convict a man, but when you come to the trial these same witnesses testify exactly the reverse, or else will not testify at all?

A.—Yes, sir.

Q.—Do you know anything of parties being held in slavery?

A.—No men are held, but the women are all slaves. The women are in slavery of the most revolting kind.

Mr. Pierson—What proportion of the convictions in the Police Court are Chinese?

A.—I can't exactly tell, but a great many Chinamen are convicted in the Police Court.

Q.—Do you know of the existence of any Chinese opium-dens.

A.—Yes, sir; every house is one. Ninety-nine Chinamen out of one hundred smoke opium.

Q.—Do white people frequent these opium dens?

A.—I think there is one on Pine Street, and one on California Street.

Q.—Do you know of any white people being interested in the business of Chinese prostitution—receiving any part of the profits?

A.—No, sir.

Mr. Haymond—What, in your opinion, is the effect of the presence of the Chinese here on the industrial interests of this city?

A.—I think it is bad. They are the worst class of people on the face of the earth.

Q.—Why are the gambling-houses closed now?

A.—Because the police officers made raids on them. This excitement has had a great deal to do with it. How long it will last I can't tell.

Q.—Have you any special instructions from the head of the department as to your duty in closing them up?

A.—No, sir.

Q.—Have you had any instructions in regard to closing up houses of prostitution?

A.—Since Mayor Bryant has been in office he has given me instructions. I never received any before.

Mr. Rogers—Are you a regular officer?

A.—I am a special officer.

Mr. Evans—How are the special policemen paid?

A.—The same as regular officers.

Q.—Who pays them?

A.—The Chinese. We draw nothing from the city treasury. We have no regular salary, but we depend on the voluntary contributions from the store-keepers. A part of our duty is to employ men to keep the streets clean.

Q.—How many special policemen are there in the Chinese quarter?

A.—Five or six.

Mr. Haymond—Are these special policemen all paid by contributions from the people living on their beats?

A.—Yes, sir.

Abram Altemeyer sworn.

Mr. Haymond—How long have you lived in California?

A.—Since eighteen hundred and fifty-eight.

Q.—What business are you engaged in?

A.—I am a member of the firm of Einstein Bros. & Co. We manufacture boots and shoes.

Q.—How many hands have you employed?

A.—From three hundred to five hundred, according to the season.

Q.—For how long a time have you employed Chinamen, and how many?

A.—For the last four or five years we have employed from two hundred to three hundred and seventy-five.

Q.—Do they work at all portions of the business?

A.—Different portions of the business.

Q.—What wages were you in the habit of paying?

A.—Most of them were contracted for. They were engaged when they didn't understand the business, and taught what to do. At first we gave them fifty cents per day, and as they advanced we increased their wages, until about the eighth month they got one dollar a day. We contracted for them, for two years, with Yu-chuy-lung Company. We made contracts with them to furnish us so many men for a certain price, and we paid the money to that company. They furnish us as many men as we want, and we have nothing to do with the Chinamen, except to work them. The first month I think we paid them fifty cents per day; the second, I think, sixty cents, and so on, until in the sixth month they got seventy-five cents, and in the eighth month one dollar, for each man. One dollar a day is the contract price for two years, and they work ten hours a day.

Mr. Donovan—Suppose the company gives you a man who don't know anything about the business, what guarantee have you that you will have the same man for two years?

A.—In the first place, the company is responsible, and in the second place, we hold back from each man's wages a certain amount to secure fulfillment of their contract. Our contract provides that when a man goes away the company shall furnish us another, and we start him at the same price that we give green men. When they violate the contract, we appropriate this deduction which we have made from their wages.

Q.—How do they hire men—as agents, owners, or controllers?

A.—We tell them that we want a certain number of men, and they get them for us. We cannot go directly and hire these fellows, because we can't speak their language and cannot explain what we want. We save much time and trouble by having all our dealings with one company.

Q.—Have you any contract for recompense for anything they steal?

A.—Yes, sir. It is to the effect that in case a man is dishonest, or steals anything, the agent shall be responsible.

Q.—Have you found them dishonest?

A.—I have, in several instances.

Q.—Are they honest or dishonest, as a rule?

A.—They will bear close watching. I think they will take things whenever they can get a chance.

Q.—Has not your company compelled the Chinese company to make up losses amounting to four thousand dollars or five thousand dollars, from your Hayes Street establishment?

A.—Yes, sir; we made the contractors pay for all the goods we did not find. I think we made them pay one thousand dollars. They found a good many of the goods themselves and returned them to us. The goods were found in the boarding and lodging-houses.

Q.—From what you know about Chinamen would you, under any circumstances, be willing to trust them without watching?

A.—No, sir.

Mr. Haymond—Do you know what wages are paid Eastern men for work which you pay one dollar a day for?

A.—They are making from seven dollars to eight dollars a week there now.

Q.—Do you find any of these Chinamen who speak English?

A.—We have only one man who speaks English, and he is the interpreter.

Q.—Is the employment of Chinese labor here detrimental to the employment of white labor?

A.—Yes, sir; there is no question but that it keeps white men from coming here, while those who are here cannot get work.

Q.—Is it not true that the lighter branches of trade and manufactures, which in other places are filled by boys, are here filled by the Chinese?

A.—Yes, sir.

Q.—This deprives both boys and girls of occupations?

A.—Yes, sir.

Mr. Evans—Suppose there were no Chinese here, could you find white boys and girls to take their places?

A.—We have tried it, and find we can. We find no difficulty whatever in getting all the workmen we can employ.

Q.—At the same price?

A.—No, sir. We are willing to pay white men double as much. We pay white people by the piece, and they can make as much as they can. A white man will do twice as much work as a Chinaman, and will produce work of a better quality. The difference in cost will be very little, and that is one reason we are changing to white labor. We are paying white men two dollars and fifty cents, three dollars, and four dollars a day, the wages depending upon the quality of the workmanship.

Mr. Haymond—What do the Chinamen you have had employed live on?

A.—I went into their boarding-house, and all I saw them eat was rice.

Q.—Imported from China?

A.—Yes, sir.

Q.—How do they dress?

A.—Just the same as you see them on the street—Chinese clothes altogether. They wear none of our manufactures, except the hat.

Mr. Lewis—What factory is this on Clay Street?

A.—That is a place where the Chinese make shoes. There are forty or fifty such places here.

Q.—Are they skillful?

A.—They are quick at imitation. They learn soon by looking on. Then they go off in business for themselves. For business men to employ Chinese, is simply putting nails in their coffins. Every Chinaman employed will be a competitor. The result must be the driving from the country of white business men and white laborers. White laborers could not live as they do, and the result would be a ruinous competition for the whites. The Chinese merchant can live as much cheaper than the white merchant, as can the Chinese laborer live cheaper than the white laborer. When such a thing gets full headway, the whites will be displaced. I have made this thing a very careful study, and my experience teaches me that these views are correct.

Mr. Evans—Why did you employ Chinese labor at all?

A.—When we first employed the Chinamen, white labor was very scarce. Besides, in those days existed the Crispin Society. They demanded extravagant wages, and manufacturers were compelled to employ Chinamen; but those days are all gone by. There are plenty of white laborers here now, willing to work at reasonable rates. When we put an advertisement in the papers this week for white labor, we must have had one thousand applications from men, boys, and girls. Another fact is, that when Chinese were first employed, there were few boys in the community. They have grown up since, however, and at the present time there are a great number of them.

Q.—Is it not a fruitful cause of hoodlumism that the Chinese are driving boys out of the legitimate avenues of employment?

A.—Yes, sir.

Q.—How many boys have you employed now?

A.—I think about fifty.

Q.—How many do you employ altogether—men and boys?

A.—About four hundred, I think.

Q.—How many Chinamen?

A.—We have about one hundred left.

Q.—Did you discharge your Chinamen before or after this excitement?

A.—We had discharged about seventy-five or eighty before this question was broached at all, and put white men in their places. We have discharged about one hundred since. We shall dispense with Chinese labor altogether as soon as we can do so. The only Chinamen we have employed now are those engaged in making misses' and children's shoes—light, cheap work, to which we must train up boys.

Q.—Where did these Chinamen who have factories learn the business?

A.—They all learned in the white factories?

Q.—Then it is your opinion that white labor can be used here with as much economy as Chinese labor, if not more?

A.—Yes; if light machinery is brought into play.

Q.—How about the woolen mills and tanneries?

A.—I do not think the tanneries employ anything but white labor; but if they do, I should judge they could change with advantage. With machinery especially, white men are better than Chinamen. We have replaced some Chinamen at our machinery with little white boys, twelve years old, and they are much better than the Chinese.

JOHN L. DURKEE sworn.

Mr. Haymond—How long have you lived in California?

A.—Twenty-seven years.

Q.—What is your business?

A.—I have been Fire Marshal here for twelve years.

Q.—What are some of the duties of your office?

A.—To attend fires, look after parties arrested for arson, carry out the orders of the Board of Supervisors in regard to fire ordinances.

Mr. Donovan—What has been your experience with fires in the Chinese quarter?

A.—Very bad.

Q.—Do fires, generally, burn much there?

A.—They burn pretty badly. A fire in the Chinese quarter is very troublesome for the reason that there are so many partitions. Out of an ordinary room they will make two and three stories, and when a fire gets in there it is hard to get at it. They are the most careless people with fire that I ever saw in my life. There are as many fires there as in the balance of the city, and it is a miracle that there are not more.

Q.—You have been through a great many of these buildings, have you not?

A.—Yes, sir.

Q.—How do they conform to the laws and ordinances of the Board of Supervisors in relation to the fire ordinances?

A.—They don't conform at all. They are more trouble than all the white people put together.

Q.—Have you found them to have had much influence in getting orders in relation to fire revoked?

A.—Yes, sir.

Q.—I will call your attention to a particular instance—the building leased to the Chinese by the Rev. Otis Gibson, on Jackson Street, north side, between Kearny and Dupont. Have you had any trouble there?

A.—Yes; I have had. They were putting up a two story frame-building in an alley-way there, and I notified them to stop it. Mr. Gibson came before the Board of Supervisors and got a permit and resolution allowing him to build. It was vetoed by the Mayor, but passed over his veto. There is where we get checkmated, and the Chinese are exempted from our ordinances.

Q.—Do you know who controls that property, and leases it to Chinamen?

A.—I know from hearsay—the Rev. Otis Gibson, Chinese missionary—and he is the one who got that permit.

Mr. Haymond—From what part of the United States did you come?

A.—New York.

Q.—How does the Chinese quarter here compare with the worst parts of New York of twenty-five years ago, in point of cleanliness?

A.—I could not make the comparison—this is so infinitely filthier. I never saw a place so dirty and filthy as our Chinese quarter.

Q.—Do you know the Globe Hotel, and its condition?

A.—I have not been in it for some time, but when I was there, it was like the balance; probably a little worse, if possible.

Q.—How near to the City Hall have the Chinese extended their quarters?

A.—They are within sight and hearing distance all around here, and very close to the business part of town. Property around here is constantly depreciating in value, because of the approach of the Chinese. The whites cannot stand their dirt and the fumes of opium, and are compelled to leave their vicinity. This part of the city has grown very little in eight years, while other portions have grown very much. Houses occupied by Chinese are not fit for white occupation, because of the filth and stench. Chinamen violate the fire ordinances, and unless we catch them in the act we cannot convict. They all swear themselves clear. The only way I can account for our not having a great fire in the Chinese quarter is, that the wood is too filthy and too moist from nastiness to burn. It has too much dirt on it to catch fire.

Rev. A. W. Loomis sworn.

Mr. Haymond—How long have you resided in California?

A.—Since September, eighteen hundred and fifty-nine.

Q.—Where were you prior to that?

A.—I was five years in Illinois and Missouri; previous to that, two years in the State of New York; and previous to that, in China—from eighteen hundred and forty-four to eighteen hundred and fifty. I was most of the time at Ning-po; resided for a few months at Macao, Hong-kong, and Canton. I was a missionary there.

Q.—Give, in your own language, a description of their condition, morally, socially, and politically; the manner in which they live; what they work at; the wages they receive; their religion, etc.

A.—They are all idolaters. The laboring classes and the literary classes are the worshipers of Confucius, heaven and earth, the sun, moon, and stars. Most of the people are, in a measure, Buddhists. They worship all the gods, and they have household gods. Their gods are many in number, and are mostly deified heroes. The Buddhist religion is imported from India, and was brought to China perhaps one hundred or two hundred years after Christ, and is particularly prevalent in Mongolia and Tappan. There are some temples here devoted to the Chinese worship, and are usually well fitted up, constructed as private ventures. A great many people who worship in them pay so much money, others subscribe, and subscriptions come in from all over the country. They are less attached to their religion here than they are at home, and a great many become very careless in this country after being here awhile. This is the case especially with those who attend our school; many of them become nominally Christians, and give up the worship of the gods. They declare that their gods are no more than senseless things, and they have found a better one. There are some here professing christianity who are living in a very commendable manner. I am connected with the Presbyterian Mission, corner of Stockton and Sacramento Streets. It has been in operation since eighteen hundred and fifty-two—Dr. Speer commencing the work, I succeeded him. Rev. Dr. Condit has been attached to the mission. We have received eighty members—deducting those who have been dismissed, and we have sixty-three. They are not all here now. Some are in China, and others are scattered over the country doing work, and reporting to us frequently.

Q.—That dates from your administration in eighteen hundred and fifty-nine? Nearly twenty years ago?

A.—Yes, sir; seventeen years. We have had a school that length of time. The Chinese come and go. The population is constantly moving. A large immigration comes here in the spring, and many return in the fall. Many go home to visit and return here again. They go back in the fall so as to arrive in China in time for the Chinese New Year. They have a great attachment for their homes, in China, rarely going out of sight of them. You find the Chinese almost everywhere; many here have been in Australia, many in Victoria, etc.

Q.—What is the condition in China of the class we have here?

A.—Those who are here largely represent the agricultural class. At first the immigration was confined principally to shop-keepers and small farmers in and around Macao, Hong-kong, and Canton. Latterly the common laborers have flocked here. There are not many scholars among them, because, being away from the cities, they have no educational advantages.

Q.—What wages are received in China?

A.—I think from three dollars to five dollars a month.

Q.—And board themselves?

A.—Well, I don't know about that. I think servants in Hongkong, Canton, and Macao receive three dollars or four dollars a month, where they are employed in families. Then they board with the families, I think. On the farms they board themselves.

Q.—How much will it take to support the family of a laboring man in China, where he has a wife and two or three children?

A.—Three or four dollars a month. Some live on less than that. Everything is very cheap. A man who acquires three hundred dollars or four hundred dollars is rich—esteemed comfortably well off. There are large land holders and heavy merchants there who are very wealthy.

Q.—What is their moral condition in their own country?

A.—In some respects they are very commendable. As regards virtue and faithfulness between man and wife, the Chinese will compare favorably with the white race of San Francisco. These Chinawomen that you see on the streets here were brought for the accommodation of white people, not for the accommodation of Chinese; and if you pass along the streets where they are to be found, you will see that they are visited not so much by Chinese as by others—sailors and low people. The women are in a condition of servitude. Some of them are inveigled away from home under promise of marriage to men here, and some to be secondary wives, while some are stolen. They are sold here. Many women are taken from the Chinese owners and are living as wives and secondary wives. Some have children, and these children are legitimate.

Q.—These women engaged in prostitution are nothing more than slaves to them?

A.—Yes, sir; and every one would go home to-day if she were free and had her passage paid.

Q.—They are not allowed to release themselves from that situation, are they?

A.—I think they are under the surveillance of men and women, so that they cannot get away. They would fear being caught and sold again, and carried off to a condition even worse than now.

Q.—Are not the laws here used to restrain them from getting away—are they not arrested for crime?

A.—Oh, yes. They will trump up a case, have the woman arrested, and bring people to swear what they want. In this way they manage to get possession of her again.

Q.—Have they at any time interfered with the women brought to your mission?

A.—We have not at our mission, but I think Mr. Gibson has had interference from them.

Q.—Do you know what they do with the women when they become sick and useless?

A.—I do not know. I have seen some on the street that looked in bad condition, and I have heard of their being abandoned to die, but I have never seen any case of that kind.

Q.—Do you know how they treat these people?

A.—I understand they treat them very badly. Women have come to the Home with bruises and marks of violence on their persons. I think their condition is a very hard one.

Q.—Then it is a slavery which, from the very first, destroys body, soul, and everything else?

A.—Yes, sir; and the women will be glad to escape from it if they knew they would be protected.

Q.—When you were in China—from eighteen hundred and forty-four to eighteen hundred and fifty—did the term "coolie" have a recognized meaning?

A.—The term "coolie" was introduced into China from India. In India it is the name of a caste. In China it simply means a servant. There are no men slaves in China, but the menial work is all done by these coolies or servants.

Mr. Donovan—What wages do Chinamen receive at home?

A.—Three, four, or five dollars a month.

Q.—It has been testified before this committee that a Chinaman in China has one wife and as many concubines as he pleases?

A.—A man has one wife, and she is mistress of the family. The children all acknowledge her as mother, and the secondary wives acknowledge her as such. They are her servants or associates.

Q.—Has the husband a right to hire out the secondary wives for any purpose he may deem fit—for instance, for the purpose of prostitution?

A.—I don't think he would. I have never known of instances of that kind, but I have known of instances like this: A man who had no male issue by a certain woman has offered her to another man, for a certain time, for a consideration.

Q.—Would you consider that a very respectable standard of morality?

A.—I don't think so.

Q.—Is it not a fact that, in China, they destroy the female children in a great many instances?

A.—I understand they do. I always have understood that, but it is more prevalent in the southern portion of the country than in the northern.

Q.—Do you know that the Chinese Government has issued proclamations, forbidding the killing of female children, the principal reason being that they want sufficient women in the empire to satisfy the men?

A.—No; I don't know that. The system of morality taught in China is equal to any that we find anywhere.

Q.—Do you consider that a man who will sell his wife in order to get a male heir is a good man?

A.—I do not indorse that.

Q.—About how long were you in the Province of Canton?

A.—Four months at Macao, and a few weeks in Canton.

Q.—Do you know anything about how these people come here?

A.—I think they all come voluntarily.

Q.—Do they make contracts to serve a certain length of time in consideration of their fare being paid?

A.—When men are too poor to come here themselves they get some one to advance the money, and they agree to return that money with a certain advance. When contractors here want many Chinamen they go to some Chinese broker. This broker rushes about town to get laborers at the rates agreed upon, but if he does not succeed he sends to China, contracting with the men to work as cheap as they can. He advances their passage-money and retains from their wages this amount, with heavy interest. I do not think the six companies have anything to do with it. I don't think there is any coolie traffic carried on in the same way that it is in Peru and the West Indies. I have known the same thing amongst Americans. In early days white men came to California under such contracts. There is no denying the fact that they do come under contract to perform certain labor to repay passage-money. They always keep these contracts, but I have known of cases where white men, under similar contracts, have failed to keep them.

Q.—Are not the Chinese compelled to keep their words by the missions, the six companies, and the Pacific Mail Steamship Company?

A.—There is an arrangement with the steamship company, that no Chinamen can get a ticket without a permit.

Q.—Then no Chinamen can go out of this country without your permission, the permission of Rev. Otis Gibson, or the permission of the six companies?

A.—That is the arrangement with the steamship company.

Q.—Do you know whether they have any Courts in which they try crimes?

A.—No, sir; I do not know of any such arrangement. When trouble arises, the companies get together for consultation and do all they can to settle difficulties; but I have never heard of a criminal Court amongst them. Of course, friends will try to assist friends and get them out of trouble.

Mr. Evans—Haven't you found it to be the rule that people of any particular nationality, going to a new country, go to their own people for information?

A.—Yes, sir. The Irishmen, the Frenchmen, the Italians, or any people, especially when they cannot speak English, go to their own people; and it is the same way with the Chinese.

Q.—Are there not mercantile associations in this city that fix prices and rates among themselves?

A.—Yes, sir.

Q.—And the man who violates their rules is considered an immoral man?

A.—Yes, sir.

Mr. Donovan—You don't know anything about their tribunals?

A.—No, sir.

Q.—You don't know of any other way they have of controlling Chinamen—other than that of preventing them from going to China?

A.—No, sir.

Q.—What do they charge them for commission?

A.—I believe it is two dollars a ticket.

Q.—How is your mission sustained?

A.—It is sustained by voluntary contributions from the East. It is connected with Presbyterian Church.

Q.—By American people, or by Chinese?

A.—By American people. Our contributions from this coast are small. We have a system of contribution in all our churches. We depend upon contributions for our support, and would be glad to receive them from any source. That is the case with all churches and with all creeds.

Q.—You are employed by your church as a missionary?

A.—Yes, sir.

Q.—And you are expected to elevate and christianize the Chinamen?

A.—Yes, sir.

Q.—So you try to elevate them, and if they have any shortcomings you try not to see them?

A.—The work of the missionary is, of course, to try and do good by preaching the gospel, by establishing Sunday-schools, and by visiting among the people. We read the Bible to them, and tell them what is a Christian life. Of course, they are not easy to teach christianity, for they come here idolators. In morals, I think they compare favorably with any heathen nation in the world, and in many respects very favorably with ours. Any nation having a grade of morals superior to those taught by Confucius and the Chinese classics cannot be found; and if the Chinese would live up to the teachings of their sages, there wouldn't be a more moral people on the face of the earth.

Q.—How does their practice compare with their theory?

A.—There is the trouble; and the same thing exists among our own people. The Americans go to church and hear good things, but they don't mind them. Moreover, in San Francisco, there are a great many ministers working amongst our own people, while there are only a few of us amongst the Chinese.

Q.—Are you in any way interested in Chinese immigration?

A.—No, sir. In regard to immigration my own position has been this from the beginning: if they would stay away it would be better for them, because coming here they learn many bad things that they would not learn at home. I think contact with the low class of Americans and foreigners is damaging; and these excitements which are started up periodically are very uncomfortable to us as missionaries.

Q.—Then the people who come from China are better than the people of our own race—of our own nation—and those who come from other nations?

A.—I did not say so.

Q.—You said they are damaged by contact?

A.—I think we have people in this city who are worse than any Chinaman that can be picked up. Don't you?

Q.—I don't know about that. I think our people are better.

A.—I think if you visit our Police Court you will find among our own people and other nationalities examples as bad as you can among the Chinese. You will find they can swear as hard, if not harder, than any Chinaman.

Q.—As a race are the Chinese honest or dishonest?

A.—Honest.

Q.—Were the servants you employed Christian Chinamen?

A.—No, sir; not always.

Q.—Were they influenced by your teachings?

A.—I hope so.

Q.—Governor Low testified, the other day, that no man will hire a Chinaman in China without requiring of him a bond to guard against loss by theft, because it is considered that every Chinaman must necessarily steal some time or other. How is that?

A.—I never required bonds, nor have my missionary friends. I don't think there are more thieves among them than there are amongst our own people, in proportion to the population.

FOURTH DAY.

San Francisco, April 15th, 1876.

Jas. R. Rogers sworn.

Mr. Haymond—How long have you resided in California?

A.—Twenty-seven years.

Q.—How much of that time has been spent in San Francisco?

A.—Six years.

Q.—What has been your occupation?

A.—During the last four or five years, a police officer.

Q.—Are you acquainted with the Chinese quarter of this city?

A.—Yes, sir.

Q.—About how much territory does it cover?

A.—About six to eight blocks, I think.

Q.—What is its condition in relation to cleanliness?

A.—Filthy in the extreme, so far as the inside is concerned. There are some stores on Sacramento Street that are clean.

Q.—How does it compare with the worst portions of Eastern cities?

A.—I never saw any part of New York, where I was born, that would compare with anything we have in Chinatown. It is worse than anything there. I don't think they would be allowed to stay in New York an hour. You can't see Chinatown in passing through the streets; you must go through the alleys and the houses.

Q.—To what purposes are the alleys devoted?

A.—Partly devoted to prostitution. There is a part which are the rendezvous of thieves—Cooper's Alley, for instance.

Q.—How are these women held?

A.—As slaves—bought and sold. They are held as prostitutes, and are obliged by what they call their mother, the head woman or boss of the institution, to stand at the windows and doors and solicit prostitution. Most of the Chinese houses of prostitution are patronized by whites, by young men and old ones. I have taken boys of not more than ten or twelve years of age out of these houses. The schedule of prices is such that the boys can afford to go there and patronize them. The women are treated according to their behavior. If they solicit prostitution, and make money pretty well, they are treated pretty well; otherwise they are fearfully beaten. When they become sick and helpless, they are taken care of according to the Chinese fashion. About three years ago Chief Crowley detailed me to shut up houses of prostitution in Chinatown. On one occasion I caught a woman soliciting, and told her to come with me. She said she had the ——. I thought she meant the venereal disease, but she pulled up her clothes and showed me that she had the small-pox; yet she was sitting there soliciting prostitution from white people. These women dare not leave their places, they are so filled with fear of their owners. There have been attempts made to escape, but the women have been so badly beaten that they have rushed to the police officers for protection. The women are sold for from four hundred dollars to six hundred dollars, and receive a red paper certifying that they shall be free, but by the time they have served out their time they are snatched up and run off to some other place, where they are forced to go through the same course. There is really no escape from the life. The owners of these women will invoke, indirectly, the aid of the law, in order to regain possession of escapes.

They have them arrested for larceny, or some crime, and as soon as they get the females the cases drop through.

Q.—Do you know the Globe Hotel here?

A.—Yes, sir.

Q.—Is that a fair type of the manner in which the Chinese live?

A.—No, sir; it is an improvement. It shows not the best phase, but it is above the average. The lower portion of that building is a restaurant, and two gambling halls, a short time ago, and a pawn shop. The upper stories are rooms which are pretty thickly filled. They hire out each room as a separate habitation, and fill it with Chinamen. Where the rooms are eighteen feet high, they put in three floors, sometimes four. Then they build bunks or platforms all around, and up to the ceiling of each little room. In Cooper's Alley they have rooms six feet wide, six feet long, and six high, where five or six Chinamen regularly sleep, and a stench arises from them which it is impossible to describe. I cannot tell how many occupy the Globe Hotel now. On one occasion I took seventy-five from one room, and locked them up for violating the "cubic air" ordinance. That was from a garret, the ceiling so low that I could not stand upright. During two months I arrested eight hundred Chinamen for violating that ordinance. The Globe Hotel has been referred to as a sample of Chinatown, It is not. Chinatown is worse every way than is that building. The underground dens are fit samples, places where only three, four, and five Chinamen can possibly sleep. Such places we find in Bartlett and Cooper Alleys, where filth reigns supreme.

Q.—The population of Chinatown has been estimated at thirty thousand. What proportion of that population lives on the fruits of crime—prostitution, gambling, etc.?

A.—I cannot tell. The money in the houses of prostitution is collected by bosses, and paid to men occupying higher positions among the Chinese. The merchants own these places; some merchants own three and four of these houses. That has been stated to me by Chinamen.

Q.—How many houses of prostitution are there in the Chinese quarter?

A.—I should say two hundred; all the alleys are full of them. There are from two to four women, and more, in each house.

Q.—How many gambling-houses?

A.—A great many. The number has decreased lately. I should judge that, before this excitement, there were from one hundred and fifty to one hundred and seventy-five, and, including lottery ticket houses, fully five hundred. They draw their lotteries twice a day—at four o'clock in the afternoon, and at eleven o'clock at night, and are patronized by many white people. Eight hundred people would be a fair estimate of the number engaged in and about houses of prostitution. There is not a Chinaman but what gambles. I believe there are very few Chinamen but what are thieves. I know some six or eight Chinamen in this town that are reliable; but they are, as a nation, thieves. That judgment is based upon my experience as an officer. I have been called into families where larcenies have occurred, and have nearly always found the thief to be the honest, trusted Chinese servant. The whole Chinese population may be regarded as being criminal. In Court, we cannot believe their testimony. They will swear to anything. I have had them come to me to ask me how many witnesses would be required to convict men. They will produce enough witnesses to either convict or acquit, as the case may be.

Q.—Is it not understood that there is some sort of a Chinese tribunal here which settles matters, and determines whether Chinamen, arrested on criminal processes emanating from our Courts, shall be acquitted or not?

A.—I do not know of my own knowledge that such a tribunal exists. I only know that when a Chinaman swears differently from what they want him to, his life is in danger. A Chinaman has just returned here after an absence of three years. A man was killed by accident, and he was notified that he must pay twelve hundred dollars. His partner had a knife stuck in his back on Jackson Street, and he was told he must pay twelve hundred dollars. He asked me what he should do, and I said not to pay it. He said they would kill him, or get Chinamen to swear him into State Prison. They sometimes, in that way, use our Courts to enforce their orders, just as policy may direct. They have no regard for our laws, and obey them, so far as they do, only through fear.

Q.—Did you say that you suppressed houses of prostitution?

A.—I did not suppress them; I kept them closed. I could not turn the inmates into the street; but I watched, and notified men and boys going there, that if they went in, I would arrest them.

Q.—Would they not open when you were away?

A.—Yes, sir. It is almost impossible to entirely suppress them, for they naturally will open; but they can be kept closed, and the business made unprofitable. There is no ordinance that cannot be enforced, and I presume the ordinances we have are sufficient to keep these houses all closed. They have all been closed since Mayor Bryant has gone into office. I believe he issued an order for the closing of gambling-houses, too; and so far as I can see, they have been closed—for the present, at least.

Mr. Pierson—Are you a regular or local officer?

A.—Regular.

Q.—How are local policemen paid?

A.—By residents on their beats. In the Chinese quarter they are paid by Chinese. They have no regular price, but get all they can, as is natural.

Mr. Haymond—When did you close up these houses?

A.—During the latter part of Chief Crowley's administration. I was detailed by him to look after gambling-houses and houses of prostitution in Chinatown, and was on that duty until the Chief went out. When there was a change, I was detailed to other duties. Upon the advent of Chief Cockrill, I was placed on the detective force. It don't require a large force to close these houses. I can do it all in one night. Arrest the inmates of one, and it travels like electricity from one to another; and in ten minutes every one will be shut up, and the doors will be barricaded.

Q.—If the houses of prostitution were broken up, and these dens cleaned out, what effect would it have upon the Chinese people? Would it increase or diminish them?

A.—Decrease them, because if locked up in prison there will be so many out of the way. When turned out they would either have to go to work or leave this part of the country. If we take away all their temptations to commit crime, we might make them more honest than they are. It might not keep many from coming here, but it would stop the importation of vile creatures and criminals.

Q.—Do you know what wages local policemen get on an average?

A.—They get all they can. The exact amounts I cannot tell, but they are all good beats. The officers are all thorough, first-class officers. I consider them as fine police officers as there are on the force. I have had them to assist me several times, and have always found them up to the mark. The local system is pretty good in some respects—it furnishes a guard for the Chinese quarter when the regular police could not do it. They make a great many arrests, and recover much stolen property.

Q.—Suppose there were officers, regular policemen, on those beats, receiving no pay. Don't you think they could stop gambling and prostitution?

A.—Yes; if they did there duty. There is hardly an ordinance that is not violated by the Chinese, and not one that cannot be enforced. They have an idea that money is at the bottom of the whole thing, and if they want they can buy privileges—they don't understand the city treasury. I have had them ask me how much I got, how much the Chief got, and how much the Judge got.

Mr. Pierson—Do you know of the Chinese paying money to persons other than special policemen, for the purpose of protecting themselves in their business?

A.—I have been told so by Chinamen. Chinese who collected the money told me of its payment. The Chinaman was Ah You, a keeper of a store and gambling-house.

Q.—To whom did he pay money?

A. ———, five hundred dollars one month.

Q.—For what purpose?

A.—He said he paid it from the gambling-houses to secure freedom from interruption. He said so much money was paid per month. It was collected from the games and stores—one hundred dollars went to the store, and the balance to ———.

Q.—For what purpose?

A.—Allowing gambling-houses to run.

Q.—How many Chinese are there in this city?

A.—Thirty thousand scattered all over town. In Chinatown there are from twenty-three to twenty-five thousand.

Q.—How many Chinese intelligence offices?

A.—Eight or ten. They are rather independent of the companies. There is one on Bush Street, kept by Sam Kee. He has been letting out a lot of thieves lately, but I told him he would have to quit and find the thieves. He did find them. I took steps to have his license revoked, and he then found the thieves.

Mr. Haymond—In your opinion, what influence does the presence of this population have upon the morals of this community?

A.—It is disastrous. In the first place, it depreciates the value of property. At the lottery-houses boys are allowed to purchase tickets. That is the first step in the direction of gambling. Boys frequently visit the Chinese houses of prostitution. I have seen small boys go into those alleys occupied by Chinese women and talk with them in the most filthy and disgusting manner imaginable.

Mr. Donovan—Do you know if the Chinese companies have inspectors who go down to the steamers whenever they arrive and take charge of the Chinamen who land here?

A.—They have told me so. I should judge that their object was to get the men consigned to each particular company.

Q.—If the ordinances were enforced, and these people driven out of the city, wouldn't it be simply scattering them over the State and making the thing almost as bad as it is now?

A.—I think a great many would go home. They could not live in small communities. Criminal classes always seek large cities.

FIFTH DAY.

San Francisco, April 17th, 1876.

Alfred Clark sworn.

Mr. Haymond—How long have you resided in California?

A.—Twenty-five years.

Q.—What has been your occupation?

A.—Been connected with the police force nineteen years. For the past seven or eight years I have been Clerk of the Chief of Police.

Q.—What do you know about the issuance of orders for the suppression of vice in the Chinese quarter?

A.—There have been orders issued to the captains of the watches, to instruct the officers to be vigilant and diligent in the suppression of prostitution and gambling. It is very difficult to suppress gambling, because they resort to so many devices to evade, and Chinese testimony cannot be obtained. They play with buttons and strips of paper, and it is hard work to convince a jury that these represent coin. In regard to the vice of prostitution, I have here a bill of sale of a Chinawoman, and a translation of the same.

Witness submits a paper written in Chinese characters, and reads the translation, as follows:

An agreement to assist the woman Ah Ho, because coming from China to San Francisco she became indebted to her mistress for passage. Ah Ho herself asks Mr. Yee Kwan to advance for her six hundred and thirty dollars, for which Ah Ho distinctly agrees to give her body to Mr. Yee for service of prostitution for a term of four years. There shall be no interest on the money. Ah Ho shall receive no wages. At the expiration of four years, Ah Ho shall be her own master. Mr. Yee Kwan shall not hinder or trouble her. If Ah Ho runs away before her time is out, her mistress shall find her and return her, and whatever expense is incurred in finding and returning her, Ah Ho shall pay. On this day of agreement Ah Ho, with her own hands, has received from Mr. Yee Kwan six hundred and thirty dollars. If Ah Ho shall be sick at any time for more than ten days, she shall make up by an extra month of service for every ten days' sickness. Now this agreement has proof—this paper received by Ah Ho is witness.

TUNG CHEE.

Twelfth year, ninth month, and fourteenth day (about middle of October, eighteen hundred and seventy-three).

The Chinese women are kept in confinement more by fear than by anything else. They believe the contracts to be good and binding, and fear the consequences of any attempt at escape. An ordinance was made to cover this kind of a contract. See municipal ordinances, section forty-two: "It shall be unlawful for any person to sell, or attempt to sell, propose, threaten, or offer to sell any human being; to claim the services, possession, or person of any human being, except as authorized by law; to solicit, persuade, or induce any person to be or remain in a state of servitude, except as authorized by law, whether such person receives partial compensation or no compensation; to be, enter, remain, or dwell in any brothel or house of ill-fame, except for a lawful purpose; on account of any real or pretended debt due, or pretended to be due, by any person, or any passage money paid for, or money advanced to any person, whether in this State or elsewhere, to hold or attempt to hold the person, or claim the services or possession of any human being, except in cases authorized by law; to exercise or attempt to exercise any control over any human being, except as authorized by law; to demand or receive from any person, any human being, or any money, or thing of value, for or on account of any real or pretended claim to the person, possession, or services of any person who was bought, sold, held, claimed, or attempted to be held or claimed in violation of this section; to threaten any person for receiving, harboring, assisting, or marrying any person who was bought, sold, held, claimed, or attempted to be held or claimed in violation of this section; to threaten any person for not paying or promising to pay any demand for money, or any thing of value, made in violation of this section; to threaten any person for not restoring or delivering, or promising to restore or deliver, to the claimant, or his agent, any person who had been bought, sold, held, claimed, or attempted to be held or claimed in violation of this section." Under that ordinance we have taken several convictions, and sent the parties to jail.

LEUNG COOK sworn.

Charles Jamison sworn as interpreter.

Mr. Haymond—How long have you been in California?

A.—About four years altogether.

Q.—What is your business?

A.—Keeping—occupied in store of Tung-ching-lung Company., on Commercial Street.

Q.—Do you know anything about the organization of the six companies—are you a member of either one, and if so, state which one?

A.—I am employed in the Ning-yeung Company as officer. I have general charge of that company—write letters, send letters for my countrymen, take charge of their mail, etc. I am President of that company. When Chinese first came to this country, knowing nothing of the language, they found it difficult to get along, and the company was organized to assist them in getting employment and in going from place to place. It has been in existence since the fourth year of the reign of Ham-fung—about twenty-two years.

Q.—Has this company any office in any part of China?

A.—No, because it don't need it. Its sole object is to look after Chinamen here.

Q.—How many members have that company?

A.—Since the reign of Ham-fung, the fourth year, till the reign of the present Emperor, twenty-two years, there were seventy-five thousand members. There are thirty thousand or forty thousand here now; the rest went back to China.

Q.—How many head men have the company had since it has been in existence?

A.—I do not remember exactly. I think in the neighborhood of twenty. There is a change of President every year. The merchants do the voting—the merchants who belong to the Ning-yeung Company.

Q.—How do Chinese laboring men get here?
A.—They come of their own accord and pay their own passage.
Q.—Where do they get the money to pay?
A.—They are industrious and save their wages.
Q.—Is not the money used by some of these people advanced to them and then collected here by these companies?
A.—No, sir; the company has no passage to pay for them.
Q.—Are there not men in China who contract to pay passage here and the Chinamen here have to pay the money back to them?
A.—I don't know about that.
Q.—Do the women who come here pay their own passage?
A.—About the women I don't know at all.
Q.—Is there a separate company for bringing women here?
A.—About that I don't know at all.
Q.—Did you ever see a contract like that. [Shows witness contract submitted by Mr. Clark, relating to the woman Ah Ho.]
A.—No, sir.
Q.—Do you know that there are Chinese prostitutes in this city?
A.—There are Chinese prostitutes here; how many, I don't know, because I ain't in that line of business. You can find that out by inquiring of the officers on that beat. [Witness was handed contract referred to, which he read, and which being at the same time interpreted, read substantially the same as the translation as above set forth in the testimony of Mr. Clark.]
Q.—Don't you know that all these prostitutes come here under such contracts as this?
A.—I do not know about such business.
Q.—Have you ever heard of this business here?
A.—No, sir; not at all.
Q.—Who is it that makes up the company to which you belong?
A.—Myself, inspector and cook—three members, officers.
Q.—Who pays the expenses?
A.—Subscription among the Chinese merchants.
Q.—Do you know what a coolie is in China.
A.—No, sir.
Q.—From what part of China did you come?
A.—From the State of Kwang-tung (Canton), in the District of Sung-ning.
Q.—Do the Chinese here come from there?
A.—Most of the Chinese here come from Kwang-tung (Canton).
Q.—Why do they send the bones back to China—the bones of dead Chinamen?
A.—It is a custom to do so. They think a good deal of the remains of deceased persons, and when a person finishes his life, they take his remains back to China to show to some of his relations in order to have them remember and do honor to them.
Q.—Who pays for sending them back?
A.—Subscriptions from the Chinese merchants.
Q.—Do you know anything about gambling?
A.—No, sir.
Q.—Do you keep a book of the names of the members of your company?
A.—Yes, sir.
Q.—Why is it that the Pacific Mail Steamship Company refuses to

sell tickets to Chinamen unless they have the stamp of the companies?

A.—When my countrymen come to California, my company takes care of them, pays their boarding and lodging expenses. For this they collect, afterwards, from each man, five dollars. That is considered to pay back the amount due the company for its advances, for expense, and its trouble. When they pay it they get a paper or permit, and can then buy tickets. Where men are sick, poor and unfortunate, they remit the five dollars and give the permit anyhow. Where men are in debt to anybody, and the company finds it out, it will not give the permit. If the debtors are too poor to pay, they are allowed to go.

Q.—Is any part of Canton as dirty as it is here in the Chinese quarter?

A.—In Canton it is clean. It is not dirty like it is here. In the interior of China, it is not so clean—in the villages.

Q.—Do you know of any villages in China so dirty as the Chinese quarter in this city?

A.—Some places are clean and some dirty.

Q.—Why don't they keep clean here, when they have plenty of water to do it with?

A.—The workmen occupy all their time in labor, and do not have any time to keep their places clean.

Q.—Is not half that population around the streets during the day?

A.—I do not know; I did not notice particularly. Very likely there are some.

Q.—Do you know anything about these Chinamen converted to christianity?

A.—Some are Christians.

Q.—Do you discover any difference in those men from other men, in business transactions, or the social relations?

A.—I don't see any difference.

Q.—How many Christians are there?

A.—I don't know.

Q.—Do you know twenty?

A.—I only know one person—Chin Quay. He is in San José, preaching.

Q.—How do the Chinese, generally, regard those who have turned Christians?

A.—I don't know whether they regard them in a friendly way or not.

Q.—Don't they consider the Christian Chinamen as thieves and hypocrites?

A.—I don't know.

Max Morgenthau sworn.

Mr. Haymond—How long have you resided in this city?

A.—Since eighteen hundred and fifty.

Q.—What has been your business?

A.—Principally manufacturing. I am interested in three or four factories—the Mission Woolen Mills, Pioneer Woolen Mills, jute factory across the bay, and the candle and soap factory.

Q.—How many men do you employ?

A.—In the neighborhood of two thousand.

Q.—How many Chinamen?

A.—Nearly half.

Q.—How do the wages of the white men compare with those of the Chinamen?

A.—They are from two hundred to three hundred per cent. higher.

Mr. Pierson—How does their labor compare with that of the whites?

A.—It depends upon the kind of labor. In weaving, the Chinaman gets very little until he learns the business; then we give him from ninety cents to one dollar twelve and a half cents per day. If we had to employ only white men, we could not run our factories—we would have to stop them. The whites do more work than the Chinese, and even where the experience is the same they do more. We have women who run two looms. Some Chinamen are good weavers, but many are not. We pay by the hour, so the ones who do the most work earn the most money. When we want Chinamen, we go to some company and say we want so many men, and we get them. Their wages we pay to the company, or the man who gets them for us, taking his receipt.

Q.—What effect do you think the presence of these Chinese laborers has had upon the working classes?

A.—I have come to the conclusion that this immigration will, in the course of time, be a very serious thing for this State. My opinion up to this time is, that they have been of great advantage to this coast. I know what difficulty we had with this white labor. We started with white labor. One day, some three years ago, we concluded to put some boys to work; so, put in eighty-five sewing machines, and employed that many boys. One day I found all the sewing machines empty. I asked the superintendent what was the matter—where were the boys; and he said that they had all left him. I asked on what grounds. He said that they generally stopped at twelve o'clock, but the boys did not come back when their hour was up. Some came at two o'clock, some later, and some not for two days. They nearly all came back at last, and were asked why they acted so. They said they were off on a pleasure trip around the bay. He said that they must not do so again, for if they did we could not go on with the work. Two or three expressed themselves as dissatisfied with this, and said: "Boys, let's take our hats and jackets, and let them go to hell." So the boys left. I have no love for the Chinamen, but we can have no control over the white boys.

Q.—When you first employed Chinese labor, there were very few boys in the country, and very little female labor?

A.—Yes, sir.

Q.—So that Chinese labor was a make-shift, in the first place?

A.—Yes; and we were glad to get it. I will say now, that if this immigration keeps up, it will affect the country disastrously. I have read the newspapers, and listened to a good many speakers, but have not been able to see my way out. A few years ago some gentlemen came here from the Eastern States, and I gave them money to start a candle and soap factory. For ten or eleven months we did not hire a single Chinaman. Men would come to me and ask for work, and I would give it to them—paying green hands one dollar and fifty cents per day. Before they learned they generally caused much damage in waste of material and breakage of machinery. I engaged ten or eleven girls to do easy work, paying them at the start ninety cents a day. I made it my business to go out there every morning at half past six o'clock to see that steam was up, and one morning found all the girls gone. I was told they had taken a holiday on account of somebody. I said "I know what holidays are; we have Sundays, Fourth of July, Christmas, New Year, and even St. Patrick's Day, but this man I never heard of. Didn't the girls give you some notice?" "They did not give us notice," I was told, "they simply did not come." He told them they would have to stop that, and they wouldn't do it, so we were compelled to discharge every one of them. They thought it was better fun bumming around in the street instead of earning an honest living. I came from Bavaria, and there every boy must learn a trade, no matter whether his father has five dollars, or fifty millions of dollars.

Q.—Don't the Chinese fill the places in the lighter employments usually filled by boys and girls—and is not that a cause of hoodlumism?

A.—That is their own fault, if it is so. I don't know.

Q.—Suppose the Chinese should start to work in Bavaria, as they have here——

A.—I don't think that government would submit to it. If the Chinese flowed in upon them it would compel them to take care of their own people.

Mr. Haymond—Don't you think it is bad to have a class of immigration into any country, where they come for the purpose of acquiring a little money, bringing no families, and never buying land?

A.—I have hoped for the last six or eight years that the Chinese would come here with their wives, raise children, educate them as our own children are educated, cut off their queues, and dress like us, but I think that cannot be. They consume much of our produce, and a large portion of our manufactures are used by them, however. During certain months of the year we make nothing but cassimeres for the Chinese. Whatever wages they can save they send to China, yet they necessarily spend considerable here. If we could not employ Chinese we would have to stop work for the present, and people would have to send abroad for these goods. That would be as bad as sending the money to China.

Mr. Donovan—Would it not be better for the American people to have goods made East, by whites, than by the Chinese, in California?

A.—My principle is, that charity should commence at home.

Q.—Your idea is, that we should make a few men who own stock in these companies rich, while we would ruin the country?

A.—The manufacturers would not get rich. Our superintendents have received instructions to put white people to work wherever it can be done to advantage. There is no reason why we should go elsewhere for our goods, for we have here all the materials for making better goods than we can import profitably. A great deal of raw material is exported East, and imported in the shape of manufactured articles; but the competition is such as to cause goods to be as cheap here as elsewhere. Of course, we get what we can. We must do it to keep up business. If we had no factories here, we would have to pay more for the goods than we do now. The fact that we make these goods forces Eastern men to put things down to the lowest prices. A short time ago I started a burlap factory. Last year I lost fifty thousand dollars, because I had to give the farmers bags for nine and a half cents, where it cost eleven cents to produce them. If the factories were not here, commission men would put up the prices; and preventing that, lost us fifty thousand dollars. All the other burlaps used are made at Dundee.

Mr. McCoppin—Have you visited the Chinese quarter at all?

A.—Yes, sir.

Q.—Have you observed the habits of the Chinese?

A.—I have.

Q.—Are they cleanly?

A.—No, sir; the way they carry on is a great shame. They are here in the heart of the city, and are a great nuisance. I have lived near here for nineteen years; but if they come closer, I will have to leave my home. They live crowded together in small rooms, on filthy alleys. I don't believe many places that I know have been dry or clean for ten years—never clean. I have mentioned the thing to the Chief of Police; but he explains to me how he has no control over them.

ALFRED CLARK recalled.

Mr. Haymond—Mr. Clark, anything additional that you have to state we will now hear.

A.—I wish to state regarding Chinese women.

Q.—Suppose a Chinawoman escapes, what do the owners do?

A.—Follow her, and take her back. If they fail, they generally have her arrested for larceny, and get possession in that way. They use the processes of our Courts to keep these women in a state of slavery. They do not let them get out of their clutches, however, if they can help it, for they know that there is no legal way of reclaiming them. When they become sick and helpless, there are instances where they have been turned out to die. The bones of women are not returned to China, as are the bones of the men. The six companies do not control this woman business; it is under the management of an independent company, called the Hip-ye-tong. Whether they import the women or not, I don't know, but they look after affairs here. A Chinaman married a woman at Gibson's, and after the marriage received notice that he must pay for the woman or be dealt with according to the Chinese custom. He was made to believe that he would suffer personally if he did not comply with their demands. Acting upon information, we arrested a number of them, and got some of their books, which we had translated. On the rolls, I think there were one hundred and seventy women. Seven or eight Chinamen were arrested, but all the witnesses we could get for the prosecution did not exceed three or four, and no conviction was had. I think at about that time this ordinance which I read in my testimony before, was passed.

Q.—Assuming the population of the Chinese in this city to be twenty-five thousand or thirty thousand, what proportion belongs to the criminal class?

A.—Those violating the laws by gambling, prostitution, and thieving will be more than ten per cent. The total number of arrests for the year ending June thirtieth, eighteen hundred and seventy-five, was sixteen thousand eight hundred and twenty, of which number the Chinese were one thousand one hundred and eighty-four. Nearly every Chinaman breaks the laws and the ordinances of the city, but we cannot catch them so as to convict. In relation to the sale of women, in searching amongst the papers in the office, I found another bill of sale, drawn to get around the ordinance above referred to. It was translated, and reads as follows:

AN AGREEMENT TO ASSIST A YOUNG GIRL NAMED LOI YAU.

Because she became indebted to her mistress for passage, food, etc., and has nothing to pay, she makes her body over to the woman, Sep Sam, to serve as a prostitute to make out the sum of five hundred and three dollars. The money shall draw no interest, and Loi Yau shall serve four and one-half years. On this day of agreement, Loi Yau receives the sum of five hundred and three dollars in her own hands. When the time is out, Loi Yau may be her own master, and no man shall trouble her. If she runs away before the time is out, and any expense is incurred in catching her, then Loi Yau must pay the expense. If she is sick fifteen days or more, she shall make up one month for every fifteen days. If Sep Sam shall go back to China, then Loi Yau shall serve another party till her time is out; if, in such service, she should be sick one hundred days or more, and cannot be cured, she may return to Sep Sam's place. For a proof of this agreement, this paper.

Dated second, sixth month of the present year. LOI YAU.

This prostitution is carried on under just such contracts as that. We got that contract from a Chinawoman brought in. I think there was a prosecution and conviction in this case, under the ordinance.

Q.—What is the condition of the Chinese quarters?

A.—Very dirty. The dirt is taken from the streets by scavengers paid by the Chinese for that purpose. In the buildings, however, we find much filth and dirt. Regarding lotteries, they draw them frequently. Tickets are sold for five cents and upwards, and the drawings are twice a day. We have made arrests, but the accused have demanded jury trials, and made their trials difficult and tedious.

Q.—Have you ever heard of the bribery of officers by the Chinese?

A.—I have heard of such things, but investigations always failed to fasten the crime on anybody. The special police system has its evils, but it does much good. It would be impossible to keep down crime, and secure the partial administration of justice in the Chinese quarter, if we had to depend upon our own regular force. That is small enough now. To suppress crime, there would require a force which would cost the city much money. The specials make a great many arrests, but our best reliance would be on regulars if we could spare them from other parts of the city. It is possible to arrest a great many offenders, but to convict them is another thing. Crime cannot be entirely suppressed in the Chinese quarter without having a largely increased police force, and an additional number of Courts. The business of prostitution can, even now, be made unprofitable to a considerable extent. But when the officers would leave their beats these houses would all open again. After all, so many of these people are law-breakers that it would require a small army of police to look after them, were we to try to weed out crime altogether. The effect of this large criminal population is very injurious on the morals of the community. There is ten per cent. of the Chinese population that makes up the gamblers, prostitutes, and thieves.

LEE MING HOWN sworn. Charles Jamison interpreter.

Mr. Haymond—How long have you been in California?

A.—Four years.

Q.—What is your business?

A.—Been teaching for Gibson. Am now President of the Sam-yup Company.

Q.—How long?

A.—Almost a year.

Q.—How many members have that company?

A.—In the neighborhood of eleven thousand. Some live in San Francisco, and others in various places.

Q.—How did they come here?

A.—They heard that everybody in California made a fortune, so they came here. If they have means, they pay their own passage; if not, they borrow from others. They sell their farms and property to get here. If they have no property, and can't borrow, they don't come.

Q.—How long do they stay here?

A.—They go back when they make a fortune. Some have been here ten and twenty years.

Q.—How much is a fortune?

A.—No limit. Some make a few hundred, and some a few thousand, and call it a fortune.

Q.—What were you doing at Gibson's?

A.—I am not there now. I am in the company. I was at Gibson's when I landed, and staid there until last year.

Mr. McCoppin—What are Gibson's relations to the Chinamen?

A.—Teaching them English and telling them about christianity—making Chinamen Christians.

Q.—How many Christians has he made?

A.—About more than ten. (Over ten and under twenty.)

Q.—Out of sixty thousand Chinese in California?

A.—He has taught a good many to be Christians, but only more than ten (over ten and under twenty) have become Christians.

Q.—How long has Brother Gibson been preaching the gospel to the Chinese?

A.—About ten years, I think, in San Francisco. Whether he preached anywhere else or not, I don't know.

Mr. Haymond—How many of the See-yup Company are Christians?

A.—Most of the Christians belong to the See-yup Company.

Q.—How many?

A.—More than ten. (Between ten and twenty.)

Q.—Are you a Christian?

A.—No, sir.

Q.—What wages do workingmen get in China?

A.—Superior situations get eight dollars to ten dollars per month, and the inferior kind two dollars or three dollars a month.

Q.—Do they board themselves?

A.—Boarded by the employer.

Q.—How much does it take to support the family of a laboring man per month?

A.—At least one dollar for each individual.

Q.—How much does it take to support the same class here?

A.—In San Francisco the lowest is about six dollars each, for boarding alone.

Q.—How many Chinamen bring their wives to this country?

A.—There are a few hundred married women here.

Q.—How many prostitutes?

A.—I imagine about one thousand, or a few hundred more.

Q.—Who own these women.

A.—Don't know. I imagine some belong to themselves, but others are owned by some one else.

Q.—How do they get these women?

A.—I don't know much about this kind of business, but I imagine some come here by their consent, while others are bought.

Q.—Are any stolen?

A.—I think not.

Q.—What do they do with those women when they get sick and unable to make more money, and are about to die?

A.—Taken care of by the owner.

Q.—Do any of these women go back to China?

A.—Yes, sir.

Q.—What becomes of these women when the police close up the houses of prostitution?

A.—I don't know.

Q.—How many Chinese gamblers are there in this city?

A.—I do not know.

Q.—Is any part of Canton as dirty and filthy as the Chinese part of this town?

A.—It is about the same.

Q.—Do you rent houses of prostitution?

A.—No, sir.

Q.—Where does your company get its money?

A.—By subscription from the stores.

Mr. McCoppin—How long have you been at the head of your company?

A.—About one year.

Q.—How often do they change?

A.—Once a year. Sometimes a man is chosen for a second and a third term.

Q.—Who elects officers?

A.—The merchants—members of the company.

Q.—How much salary do they pay the President?

A.—Eighty dollars a month.

Q.—What does the President do?

A.—Attends to new comers, persons not acquainted with the language of this country, and assists those who want help—such as the sick and disabled.

Q.—What must a Chinaman do before he can go home to China by steamer?

A.—He can go by letting the company know of it. He must have the permit of the company. But some go without permits—such as actors, sailors, etc.

Q.—When was this arrangement made with the steamship company?

A.—Since the first voyage of a China steamer.

Q.—What does the Sam-yup Company do with one of its members that commits a crime?

A.—If they found it out they would deliver him to the authorities at the City Hall. We don't deliver him up ourselves, but get an officer to take possession of him.

Q.—When have you done that?

A.—That is the rule, but my company has not done anything of that kind yet.

Q.—When do you propose to commence?

A.—Can't tell.

Q.—If one of that company steals from another, or whips another, don't they settle it with money—make him pay for the injury?

A.—No, sir.
Q.—Do any gamblers belong to your company?
A.—I don't know. Very likely there may be some.
Q.—Do you know of Chinamen paying anything to Americans to be allowed to gamble?
A.—Don't know. That kind of gambling business the people don't dare to let the company know anything about.
Q.—Why?
A.—They belong to the inferior classes, and will not let the company know. If they told us we would advise them to discontinue.

AH YOU sworn. Charles Jamison interpreter.
Mr. Haymond—How long have you lived in California?
A.—About twenty-eight years.
Q.—From what part of China did you come?
A.—Canton.
Q.—What is your business?
A.—I occupy a place where they manufacture jewelry.
Q.—Have you ever collected any money, and paid it to anybody in order to get leave to keep gambling-houses open?
A.—No, sir.
Q.—Do you know of anybody that has?
A.—No, sir.
Q.—How do the working classes of Chinamen get here?
A.—Some come here by their own money, and others by borrowing from their friends and relatives. When they make the money here, they send it back in a letter to the friend that lent it.
Q.—What are coolies in China?
A.—Men employed to carry things. When there is nothing to carry, they do farm-work.
Q.—Are there any of that sort of people in California?
A.—Maybe once in a while you will come across two or three.
Q.—Who does the carrying here?
A.—Men that have no particular business. Sometimes they do their own carrying, and sometimes they hire Chinamen.
Q.—How many Chinese women here are married?
A.—Good many.
Q.—About how many?
A.—How many I don't remember exactly. A few hundred.
Q.—How many women are in houses of prostitution?
A.—I don't know—two or three hundred.
Q.—Are there not one thousand?
A.—Some have gone up to the mountains.
Q.—Who owns these women?
A.—Don't know.
Q.—Are they bought and sold here?
A.—Don't know.
Q.—Have you ever heard of anybody being sold?
A.—No, sir.
Q.—Do these women come of their own will?
A.—By their own consent; and do you suppose they were forced to come here?
Mr. McCoppin—Have you told anybody that you raised money to pay for the privilege of carrying on gambling?
A.—No, sir.

Q.—Did you tell officer Rogers that?
A.—No, sir.
Q.—Did you tell Rogers you paid ——— five hundred dollars a month?
A.—No, sir; I told Mr. Rogers, if I had any trouble, I would get ——— to attend to it.
Mr. Haymond—What did you expect to have trouble about?
A.—Gambling-houses.
Q.—What would the Sam-yup Company do if they found a Sam-yup man conducting gambling?
A.—Tell him to quit.
Q.—Suppose that he wouldn't quit.
A.—The company has no power to stop it. The company have posted notices on the street, telling gamblers to stop.
Q.—When were those notices posted?
A.—A little over a week.
Q.—And it was stopped?
A.—Yes, sir.
Q.—Are you a Christian?
A.—No, sir.
Q.—About how many Christian Chinamen have you known in the last twenty-eight years?
A.—A little over one hundred. Some of these were false Christians, and some true. Some only pretended.
Q.—Why do they pretend?
A.—Sometimes so they can kidnap women easier. They have better chance then.
Mr. Donovan—Did you ever take a woman away?
A.—No, sir.
Q.—Did you ever sell a woman?
A.—No, sir.
Q.—Did you ever keep a house of prostitution?
A.—No, sir.
Q.—Were you associated for months with persons in a house of prostitution?
A.—No, sir; I have a wife.
Q.—Do you know that man (officer Thomas Kennedy)?
A.—I have seen him.
Q.—Did you ever tell this man that the house in which prostitutes were living belonged to you?
A.—No, sir.
Q.—Did you ever tell officer Kennedy that you were paying officer Duffield money for guarding his house, and could not pay him any?
A.—I was interpreting for another person. It was not my statement, but that of some other person.
Mr. Haymond—You never told officer Rogers that you paid somebody five hundred dollars, or any amount of money, to protect gambling-houses?
A.—No, sir. Sometime Mr. Rogers was collecting money for this kind of business, but he was going to not attend to it. Some parties paid him three hundred dollars. Three Chinese persons gave it to him. Two gave it and three were present—Ah Hung, Ah Chune, and myself.
Q.—When was that?
A.—About twenty-three months ago. It was given to him in the

rear of Gum Wo's store. I was not there as owner of gambling-houses, or ——— houses, but as a witness, to see that money paid. Mr. Rogers himself came to me and wanted me to be a witness that the money was paid. He told me to tell the Chinamen to subscribe a few dollars for his benefit and he would stop arresting.

Q.—Did Rogers get that money then?

A.—No, sir; they put it away then, but came and got it.

Mr. Donovan—Do you know Mr. ———?

A.—He is my counsel.

Q.—Did you ever give him five hundred dollars?

A.—Yes, to work up murder cases, for the Yu-chuy-lung. They employed him to convict the murderers. Four men are under arrest for murdering one man, and these men are the ones they wanted convicted. Deceased belonged to the Kwo-ye-tong, or shoemakers. Three of the murderers are bailed out in fifteen thousand dollars, but one is in jail.

THOMAS KENNEDY sworn.

Mr. Donovan—Do you know the Chinaman who last testified (Ah You)?

A.—Yes, sir.

Q.—What occupation or business has he been in, to your knowledge?

A.—I always took him to be boss of a house of prostitution. My beat used to run from Dupont Street and Jackson——

Q.—You are an officer?

A.—Local policeman. There was a small house of prostitution started on the north side of the Globe Hotel. I went there to secure my pay, and met this man. He told me he paid George Duffield, and could not pay me. He claimed to be the proprietor of this house. He was always around there. There were three women in that house.

Q.—He claimed he was not running that house. Did you hear him?

A.—Yes, sir.

Q.—Is that a specimen of Chinese swearing?

A.—Yes, sir; when it is to his interest, a Chinaman will swear to anything.

Q.—Are you on the force, now?

A.—No, sir; not for two months.

JAMES R. ROGERS recalled.

Witness—It is impossible for any man to tell what are the emoluments of the office of special policemen. They collect all they can and that amount varies. During the "cubic air" excitement, I arrested from seventy-five to one hundred Chinamen nightly. They tried then to have me let up on them but I could not. I had the jails and the Court crowded day after day, until there were so many that business was hopelessly behind. Ah You offered me three hundred dollars, as he says, but I refused to accept it. I pronounce his statements an utter falsity.

Mr. Haymond—Do you know who own the buildings used as houses of prostitution in the Chinese quarter?

A.—White people, partially.

Mr. Donovan—Did you hear Ah You swear just now?

A.—Yes, sir.
Q.—Is he a fair criterion of the Chinese witness?
A.—Yes, sir. They all swear as their interests may dictate.

SIXTH DAY.

San Francisco, April 18th, 1876.

Captain R. H. Joy sworn.

Mr. Haymond—What is your profession?
A.—Master mariner.
Q.—Of what place are you a native?
A.—Liverpool. I am a British subject.
Q.—Have you been in China?
A.—Yes, sir. The last time, I was there nine or ten months. I was master of the steamer Crocus, and am now.
Q.—In your business, were you often brought into contact with Chinamen?
A.—Yes, sir; very often.
Q.—Have you ever been in the City of Canton?
A.—Yes, on pleasure trips.
Q.—How does the social and moral condition of those people compare with that of the same classes in other countries?
A.—What I saw was not very high.
Q.—When did you arrive in California?
A.—Two days ago. I came here in command of the British steamer Crocus.
Q.—Did you bring any Chinese passengers?
A.—Yes, sir; eight hundred and eighty-two.
Q.—What is the character of these people?
A.—They do not hold a very good character in their own country. They were not so much trouble, however, as the papers have represented. The accounts as published were highly embellished. We had a little trouble at first, but very soon stopped that.
Mr. McCoppin—Is this class a desirable one for any country to have?
A.—I don't think it is, because of the low moral condition of the people.
Q.—Have you been in Australia?
A.—I have.
Q.—How are the Chinese treated there?
A.—Not very well. The inhabitants found that they were being crowded out by the Chinese, and have commenced driving them from the country. Large numbers are leaving. I brought two hundred and forty from Singapore, where they came from Australia in the Brisbane. I left them at Hong-kong.
Q.—In Australia, were separate quarters assigned them?
A.—They generally congregate together. There are no rules and regulations requiring them to occupy a separate quarter of the town, but they do so, naturally.
Q.—In the papers you are credited with having said that all the Chinese that you brought here were of the very worst classes—the criminal classes.
A.—No doubt many of them are very bad. All the Chinese around

Canton are very bad. They are generally fishermen, and when they can take advantage of anything, they do it.

Q.—Will they steal?

A.—Yes, sir.

Q.—Do those people come here voluntarily?

A.—Yes. They have an idea that this is a sort of El Dorado, where they can obtain plenty of money with little work.

Q.—Do they pay their own passage?

A.—I think they do. My steamer is a chartered one, and I bring it here safely, receiving therefor a salary. I don't know how the passage money is paid.

Q.—Have you any connection with the Pacific Mail Steamship Company?

A.—No, sir. This is a separate company.

Mr. Haymond—In their own country, what was the occupation of most of these people?

A.—On the passenger lists they are called laborers. Of course that is all we know about them.

Mr. McCoppin—As an Englishman, what would you think if they were to overrun your country?

A.—It would behoove the Englishmen to drive them out.

Q.—Why?

A.—They work for low wages, and they are not the class of people that we would like to have in our own country.

Q.—Why is it they can work for lower wages?

A.—They can live cheaper. A handful of rice, with water, will suffice for their meals.

Mr. Haymond—How do their morals compare with those of the English working classes?

A.—They are very much lower in every way.

Q.—What effect, do you think, the introduction of thirty thousand or forty thousand Chinamen into an English city would have?

A.—Their standard is so much lower, I don't think they would be allowed in any English city, and I hope never to see that happen.

Q.—In the vicinity of Canton, does an immense number of people live on the rivers?

A.—Yes. A great many live in boats, following the occupation of fishermen, and working around the ships.

Q.—What is the character of that people as law-abiding citizens?

A.—The Chinese Government is very rotten, and exercises but little control over these men. The mandarins levy as much tribute as they can on the people around them. I suppose they must pay, in their turn, to some higher authority.

Q.—Are any of them engaged in piracy?

A.—I would not like to say.

Q.—What is the prevailing impression among seamen who visit that port, as a rule?

A.—There are very many different opinions. The general opinion is not very favorable.

Q.—How do these people compare with the same classes of English or German, about their homes?

A.—They are very much lower—far inferior.

Q.—Are their cities and towns clean or dirty?

A.—Very dirty, indeed. When one has been in a Chinese city once, he has no ambition to return to it again.

Q.—Have you visited the Chinese quarters in Australia?

A.—Yes, in Melbourne.

Q.—How are they there?

A.—Very dirty. Of course they are compelled to keep the streets clean, but that is as far as their cleanliness goes. I think the people are driving them out, now. It is being done by the people themselves, not by the government.

Q.—Are there many women imported to that country?

A.—I never saw any women there at all.

Q.—Do you think they would permit the landing of a ship load of prostitutes?

A.—I think it is most certain that they would not. Four or five women came on board my ship when I was about to leave, but the American Consul had them taken on shore. I did not like the looks of the women, and took their photographs to the Consul. At a glance he saw what they were and ordered them on shore.

Q.—How did they come on board?

A.—They came in a boat. They had passenger tickets stamped by the American Consul, or his deputy. That is required, and in addition each one is personally examined. These women spoke good English, and said their husbands were in San Francisco. They were evidently improper characters, and were sent ashore.

Q.—You think that great injury would be caused by the introduction of these people into England, or a country like this?

A.—Of course it would in England, but I do not know much about California. This is my first visit here, and I cannot tell much about how they would affect you.

Q.—You think that a country must be a very bad one to be improved in morals by the addition of Chinamen?

A.—Decidedly, I think it would.

Q.—Have you met with many converted Chinamen—Chinamen converted to christianity?

A.—I have seen some who pretended to be converted, but I would not vouch for their earnestness. I took some missionaries out with me from London—two ladies. I took them to Shanghai, where they were going to try to convert the heathen.

Q.—So far as your knowledge goes, what success has attended missionary labors in China?

A.—I do not think it has had any success. If you pay the Chinamen they will believe anything you desire, so long as the money lasts. Take away that incentive, and they relapse into heathenism and idolatry. I think that attempting to convert Chinamen is a piece of most foolish nonsense. I don't think there is any possibility of their becoming converted to christianity.

Mr. Lewis—Are the Chinamen whom you have seen "converted," of any better morals than the unconverted?

A.—I saw one who appeared to be improved, but whether he was sincere or not, I do not know.

Q.—Was he engaged in missionary work?

A.—He was preaching.

Q.—And got pay for it?

A.—I believe he did.

Q.—Do they measure morals, generally, by interest?

A.—I believe that is so.

W. H. KINSELLA sworn.

Mr. Haymond—What is your occupation?

A.—Chief officer of the Crocus.

Q.—Have you ever been in China?

A.—Yes, sir. The last time ten months.

Q.—You are a British subject?

A.—Yes, sir.

Q.—Do you know the class of Chinese who emigrate to this country?

A.—I received them on board ship and looked after them afterwards, keeping them in good order.

Mr. McCoppin—Where were you born?

A.—Liverpool.

Q.—What would your fellow-citizens think if eight thousand or ten thousand a year of these fellows were placed on your docks?

A.—They wouldn't find room.

Q.—Liverpool is a large city, is it not?

A.—Yes; it has over five hundred thousand people, but is so well filled up that I don't think there would be any room for Chinamen.

Q.—Would the people permit such a thing?

A.—I hardly think so. There is just about room for the whites there now.

Q.—Would such people have any injurious effect on the morals of England?

A.—The Chinese morals are very low, but I cannot say that an old established country, like England, would be affected much.

Mr. Lewis—Suppose a great many of them were to be introduced into the manufacturing establishments, displacing white boys and girls—would that be injurious?

A.—Most certainly.

Mr. Haymond—Have you ever seen any Chinamen who had been converted to christianity?

A.—The one whom the captain mentioned.

Q.—Is he the only one you saw in ten months?

A.—Yes, sir.

Q.—Are there many missionaries in Hong-kong?

A.—That is a British port, and has about as many missionaries as any European town ordinarily has.

Q.—It has a large Chinese population?

A.—Yes, sir.

Q.—How does the Chinese city of Canton compare with Liverpool, in point of cleanliness?

A.—I was there only four hours.

Q.—What is the reputation of the class of people who come here?

A.—I do not know much about that, and cannot give you any positive information on that point.

Q.—What is the received opinion of seamen?

A.—I cannot say. They are generally supposed to leave nothing that they can carry away.

Q.—How would they treat a merchant ship, lying unarmed?

A.—They would try to get the best of it and make what they could. Where a ship goes ashore she is stripped in very short order. They stripped a boat a year ago in that way.

Q.—Would the introduction of many thousands of these Chinese injuriously affect the morals of a country?

A.—Not those of a very old country. How it would affect a new country I can't say. In Australia they needed cheap labor to develop the place.

Q.—Have the Chinese any such thing as moral restraint?

A.—No, sir; not so far as I have observed them. If they can get the best of you in anything they will do it. When caught committing crimes they are very severely punished, though no especial effort is made to ferret out wrong-doing. Beheading is a favorite punishment with the Chinese Government.

Q.—Would not such a class of Chinese as come here find England rather a warm place for them?

A.—Well, yes.

Q.—How do you treat these fellows on board ship when they become obstreperous?

A.—Put a few in irons, and the rest become meek.

David Supple sworn.

Mr. Haymond—How long have you resided in California?

A.—Twenty-seven years next May. I have lived in this city all the time.

Q.—What is your occupation?

A.—Previous to coming on the police, I was a stevedore.

Q.—How long have you been on the police?

A.—Seven years.

Q.—Do you know anything about the Chinese quarters of this city?

A.—I have had a little experience with the Chinese.

Q.—What is the condition of that part of the city, in regard to cleanliness?

A.—Beastly.

Q.—How do the people live?

A.—They live in small places, more like hogs than human beings.

Q.—What proportion of the people belong to the criminal classes—engaged in prostitution, gambling, violating city ordinances, and laws relating to health?

A.—About the whole of them.

Q.—How many families are there among the Chinese?

A.—Very few. I have never seen a decent, respectable Chinawoman in my life.

Q.—What is the understanding here in regard to the manner in which these women are held?

A.—They are held in bondage, bought and sold. I have had bills of sale translated by Gibson.

Q.—Is it possible for these women to escape from that life, even if they desire it?

A.—Sometimes the Chief of Police can give some protection, but it is customary for the owners to charge them with crimes in order to get possession of them again. Sometimes they kidnap them, and even unscrupulous white men have been found to assist them.

Q.—Do you know what they do with them when they become sick and helpless?

A.—They put them out on the street to die. I have had charge of the dead myself, on the street. I have seen sick and helpless women turned out in that way.

Q.—What is the general reputation of the Chinese in regard to truth and veracity?

A.—I have never yet seen a Chinaman that I would be willing to believe under oath. That is their general reputation. They will testify whichever way their interests may require. That has been my experience, and the experience of everybody with whom I have had any conversation, whether private citizens or officers.

Q.—Do you know whether they are accustomed to interfere with the administration of justice?

A.—I understand that they do. Each of the different companies has rules and regulations for the government of its members.

Q.—If these regulations are violated, how are the offenders punished—how do they enforce their rules?

A.—I cannot tell. The general understanding is, that they punish men in some way or other. All our efforts to find out their secret tribunals have failed. We don't understand their language, and that makes it hard work for us to learn anything definitely.

Q.—Do you know anything about boys of twelve and fourteen years of age visiting houses of prostitution in the Chinese quarter?

A.—Yes, sir; we have them fairly crippled—going about the city, hardly able to put one foot before the other.

Q.—Then the moral effect of the presence of this population is very bad?

A.—It is ruinous to the community.

Q.—Do you know anything about any Christian Chinamen in this community?

A.—I have seen one—a Catholic clergyman—but he was the only one I ever knew. I have seen others on the street corners, singing and praying, but I could not say how sincere they were.

Q.—Can the city ordinances be enforced in the Chinese quarter?

A.—Yes; with a sufficient police force.

Q.—Do you know anything about the number of Chinese engaged in the manufacture of clothing, cigars, etc.?

A.—No, sir. I have seen the prostitutes sitting in their houses working button-holes for the business houses. They generally work on cheap slop-clothing. Even the young girls in these houses of prostitution are engaged in this work.

Q.—How many are engaged in this business?

A.—All the prostitutes.

Q.—How many men are engaged in making shoes, cigars, etc., in this city?

A.—I suppose they must number fifteen thousand men.

Q.—You don't know how many in each trade?

A.—No, sir. I know that we have eighteen thousand or twenty thousand boys and girls in this city who are growing up for the State Prison and houses of prostitution for want of employment, because the Chinese have filled all the places.

Alexander Badlam sworn.

Mr. Haymond—What is your business?

A.—Assessor of San Francisco.

Q.—For how long?

A.—A little over a year.

Q.—What is the total value of the property assessed here?

A.—Not far from three hundred million dollars.

Q.—How much property is assessed to the Chinese?

A.—I think their personal property amounts to about five hundred thousand dollars. The real estate probably amounts to one hundred and fifty thousand or two hundred thousand dollars. The population of this city is probably two hundred and thirty thousand—from two hundred and thirty thousand to two hundred and fifty thousand. The Chinese number about thirty thousand, and pay only about one three-thousandths part of the tax.

Q.—Do you know who own this Chinese quarter?

A.—Yes, sir. [Witness submitted a list of property owners.]

Q.—What is the general character of this population—is it good or bad?

A.—Bad, I think.

Q.—Do you know whether rentals are high in the Chinese quarters?

A.—The Chinese pay better rents because they can crowd so many into so small a space.

Q.—How long have you resided in this city?

A.—Twelve years.

Q.—How many Christian Chinamen have you seen?

A.—I don't know that I ever saw any.

Q.—In your judgment, what effect has this population on the morals of the youths of this community?

A.—I think the effect is bad upon young and old. They are a very undesirable class of people. Their statements cannot be depended upon. They pay little tax, and endeavor in every way to evade even that.

Q.—Are they disposed to acquire property?

A.—I think that recently they have discovered that large interest can be made on their money by leasing land and putting up brick houses, and some are doing it. At present the real estate owned by them will not exceed in value two hundred thousand dollars.

D. J. MURPHY sworn.

Mr. Haymond—How long have you resided in this city?

A.—Over twenty-two years.

Q.—What is your profession?

A.—Attorney-at-law.

Q.—What official positions have you held in this city?

A.—District Attorney two years, and I am in my second term now.

Q.—In your official capacity, have you been brought into contact with Chinese?

A.—Yes, sir; I have looked on my docket for two years, and I find that of seven hundred cases that I examined before the Grand Jury, one hundred and twenty were Chinese, principally burglaries, grand larcenies, and murders—chiefly burglary. They are very adroit and expert thieves. I have not had time to examine for the last two and a half years, but the proportion has largely increased during that time.

Q.—Do you find any difficulty in the administration of justice, where they are concerned?

A.—Yes, sir. In capital cases, particularly, we are met with perjury. I have no doubt but that they act under the direction of superiors, and swear as ordered. In many cases witnesses are spirited away, or alibis are proven. They can produce so many witnesses as to create a doubt in the minds of jurymen, and thus escape justice. In cases where I have four or five witnesses for the prosecution, they will bring in ten or fifteen on the part of the defense. They seem to think that numbers must succeed, and it very frequently so happens. It frequently occurs that before the Grand Jury, or on preliminary examination, witnesses swear so as to convict, but on the trial they turn square around and swear the other way. I have heard it said that they have secret tribunals where they settle all these things, but I know nothing of that. It is my impression that something of the kind exists, and I think they sometimes use our Courts to enforce their decrees. I have had to appeal to Executive clemency for pardon for Chinamen sent to the State Prison by false swearing, under circumstances which led me to believe them to have been the victims of some organization of that kind.

Q.—Innocent men can be convicted?

A.—Yes; and I have no doubt innocent men are convicted through the medium of perjury and "jobs" fixed up on them. I have had doubts, during the last three months, in cases of magnitude, involving long terms of imprisonment.

Q.—Among reputable lawyers of this city, who have had experience with Chinese testimony in the Courts, what value has that testimony, standing by itself?

A.—By itself, and without being corroborated by extrinsic facts or white testimony, it is very unreliable.

Q.—That is the opinion of the better class of lawyers?

A.—That is my opinion, and I have had considerable experience with them.

Q.—Do you know any Christian Chinamen?

A.—The only one I saw was a clergyman—Father Tom—in years gone by. A great many go to Christian churches and Sunday-schools, but I have very little faith in them and their christianity.

Q.—Assuming that there are thirty thousand Chinese in this city, about what, in your opinion, is the proportion belonging to the criminal classes, including prostitutes, thieves, gamblers, and violators of the city ordinances?

A.—I should think seven-tenths or eight-tenths. I have done business with some Chinese merchants, and found them high-minded, fair, and honest; but, as a class, the Chinese here, I think, are naturally vicious, dishonest, and untruthful.

Q.—What dangers may be apprehended from the presence of a population like that in a city of this kind?

A.—I am not prepared to give an answer to that, although I think it is dangerous to the morals of the community, and there is great danger to be apprehended from admixture with them. I am fearful of it in the future. I see but very little good resulting to the community from the greater portion of this class. The charges upon which they are tried are generally of the higher grades, such as felonies of the various grades.

A. Schell sworn.

Mr. Haymond—How long have you resided in California?

A.—Since the sixth day of July, eighteen hundred and fifty.

Q.—Where do you reside?

A.—Knight's Ferry, Stanislaus County.

Q.—What is your business?

A.—I have been engaged in the practice of law. I am now engaged in grape and wool-growing and in stock-raising. My business is rather of a multifarious character.

Q.—Have you been in the habit of employing Chinese laborers to any extent?

A.—I have, since living at the ferry in eighteen hundred and fifty-six, employed all kinds of laborers—Scandinavians, French, Irish, and Chinese—employing eight or ten men, on an average, all the year round. I find that there are good and bad laborers among all classes. I prefer to employ white men when I can get them, but they cannot be had, and I am obliged to take Chinese. Were it not for Chinamen, much of my work would be left undone.

Q.—Did you hear the testimony of officers and the District Attorney relative to Chinese here?

A.—Yes, sir.

Q.—Have you been brought in contact with that class of men?

A.—We occasionally get criminals, but I am not speaking of them. I never met but one Chinaman who could not read and write his own language, and I have met a great many white men that could not do it. I have often, in the practice of my profession, been called upon to prosecute and defend Chinese, and would corroborate the testimony of Mr. Murphy, that there is not much credibility to be attached to their testimony. So far as their oath is concerned in a Court of law, I think very little reliance can be placed upon it. I think it is the prevailing opinion, among Californians, that they are not to be believed in Court, unless corroborated by white testimony; but, so far as the labor element is concerned, I think they are an important element in this State. How you may be affected in the city I cannot say, but I know in the country, if the Chinese element of labor was taken away from us it would be a great detriment. In the country there is no competition between Chinamen and white men, but I find this difference: the Chinamen will stay and work, but the white man, as soon as he gets a few dollars, will leave and go elsewhere. Once in a while I get a good white man, and he will work until he gets enough money to buy a farm for himself; then I have to go and get more laborers.

Q.—Do the Chinese ever save money and buy farms?

A.—No; I don't know that they do, but there is nothing to encourage Chinamen. The unfriendly legislation of this State is such as to discourage them. I believe the laboring man is an advantage to the country, whether Chinese or white men. There is room for all, and there is need for all the labor that can be brought to this country. I believe that if you exclude Chinese you will have to close up every woolen mill on the coast. The question is, whether we should encourage home manufactures or send money East for shoddy goods.

Q.—What class of immigration would you prefer—those who come here, live a short time and leave with their earnings, or those who come here to settle and build a home?

A.—The latter, of course; but you don't get that in the white men. I prefer white men in my place, but I have come here and tried to get them, but I have failed. With white girls it is the same way. They will not go to the country and do what work we want them to. There is not enough labor to carry on the industrial and manufacturing pursuits, so Chinamen are necessary.

Q.—Don't you think that this is so only because Chinese labor is so cheap?

A.—The white man's work is worth more than the Chinaman's, and he is better paid; but in the country we cannot depend upon him. I do not know how it is in the city.

Q.—Don't you think there is enough white labor in California to carry on the industrial pursuits?

A.—That may be. I do not know.

SEVENTH DAY.

SAN FRANCISCO, April 19th, 1876.

J. P. M. FRASER sworn.

Mr. Pierson—Have you ever resided in China?

A.—I have—fifteen years. I was in the British Consular service from eighteen hundred and fifty-nine to eighteen hundred and seventy-four.

Q.—Are you a citizen of the United States?

A.—No, I am not. I have only been in California for about three weeks.

Q.—Did you ever live in Hong-kong?

A.—No. I lived six years in Canton.

Q.—Do you know from what part of China emigrants to the United States come?

A.—Mostly from Canton.

Q.—To what class does the mass belong?

A.—To the laboring class—what we call coolies. The word coolie does not define anything at all. He can be called upon to do any kind of labor. By coolie we mean simply a laborer.

Q.—What was the coolie trade?

A.—Contracts by which Chinamen were sent to foreign countries to perform labor for a certain number of years, at the expiration of which they were to be returned to China. This trade was made objectionable from the fact that in eighteen hundred and sixty there was a great deal of kidnaping of Chinamen to supply the trade. The foreigners had Chinese agents on shore, who used to kidnap great numbers of Chinamen, and shut them up in barricoons, whence they were taken on board ships and taken to Peru and Chili, and other places. This trade, therefore, became so obnoxious that a stop was put to it.

Q.—Do you know anything about the terms on which Chinese are transported to this country?

A.—No, sir.

Q.—How are the Chinese emigrants taken from Canton to Hong-kong?

A.—Ships are chartered direct from Canton, but they must necessarily go to Hong-kong before they can clear. The vast majority of emigrants ship directly from Hong-kong.

Q.—Do you know how they get from Canton to Hong-kong?

A.—There is an immense junk traffic and steamer traffic, and any amount of vessels plying between the two places all the time.

Q.—What do you understand of the relative jurisdiction or power of the provincial governments and the Chinese Empire?

A.—The provinces are all subject to a central government, except Corea.

Q.—What is the head officer of the Canton Province called?

A.—Viceroy.

Q.—Is he appointed or elected?

A.—Appointed by the Imperial Government.

Q.—Have you been through the Chinese quarter of this city, to any extent?

A.—Yes; I have been in a good number of merchants' shops.

Q.—Have you been in the alleys and the lower places?

A.—No, sir. I have had too great an experience with Chinese cities to frequent these places.

Q.—Taking the Chinese quarter as a whole, you cannot say how it compares with Chinese cities in point of cleanliness, etc.?

A.—No. All I can say is, that there is not a clean city in China.

Q.—Are the people clean or filthy, as a whole?

A.—By no means cleanly.

Q.—Have the Chinese any governmental system of education?

A.—Yes, sir. All the men, as a rule, can read and write.

Q.—Is education compulsory?

A.—I think not; but it is expected that every man shall read and write.

Q.—What is the social condition or position of the female in China?

A.—She is supposed to take the position of general helper; not that of a companion. They are not thought much of.

Q.—How are they regarded by the men—as equals, or inferiors.

A.—Inferiors. You cannot buy a man; but you can buy a woman. A man can buy as many wives as he pleases; or, rather, I should call them concubines. There is only one wife really, who is at the head of affairs; but the children of all are regarded as legitimate, as the law allows them to have these concubines. The Emperor, for instance, has one wife and seventy-two concubines, but all the children wear the yellow girdle, that signifies imperial blood; and they are looked upon as a part of the royal family.

Q.—Do respectable Chinese women, as a rule, leave China?

A.—No, sir.

Q.—Does the Chinese Government encourage or discourage emigration?

A.—I do not think they encourage it. They rather like to have their people stay at home.

Q.—Have you lived in a Chinese village where there were no other English-speaking people?

A.—Yes, sir.

Q.—Were the Chinese orderly?

A.—Yes, sir. It was only eighteen miles from the Great Wall, and during an excessively cold winter, yet I heard of no robberies, or anything of that sort.

Q.—Judging the Chinese from a European standard, what can you say of their morality?

A.—They are not a bit worse than some European nations.

Q.—Do you think there would be any objection, on the part of the Chinese Government, to making a commercial treaty, and in that treaty to prevent the emigration of the lower classes?

A.—I think there would not.

Q.—Do you think, from your knowledge of the Chinese Government, that such a modification could be made?

A.—Yes, sir.

Q.—Do you know what they do with female children in China?

A.—As regards infanticide, that is not so wide-spread a calamity as is generally believed.

Q.—Is it criminal to destroy female children?

A.—It is criminal to commit murder of any kind. Their laws are as rigid as any in the Napoleon Code.

Q.—Have you ever met a Christian Chinaman?

A.—Yes—by name.

Q.—Why do you say "by name"?

A.—Because I don't believe you can get a Christian Chinaman, unless you pay him to be such.

Q.—What is your opinion of the labor of American and English missionaries in that country?

A.—It has been anything but successful. I do not think there are any strides being made towards the advancement of christianity. They will take what advantage they can of the free gifts of the white race, such as medicine, etc., and pretend to do such as you want as long as they are kept supplied.

Q.—From what part of England did you come?

A.—I am a Scotchman.

Q.—What effect do you think the presence of thirty thousand Chinese would have upon a city of two hundred and thirty thousand inhabitants?

A.—There would not be room for them.

Q.—Is there any part of England so thickly settled as the Chinese quarter of this city, where thirty thousand men live upon seven or eight blocks?

A.—I think not.

Q.—Have you ever seen in China any considerable number of Chinese when their passions were excited?

A.—Yes, I have.

Q.—How do they act under such circumstances?

A.—They talk a good deal, brandish their knives, etc., but when there is any show of resistance they are very quick at running away. They are arrant cowards, but so long as they have any kind of a foreigner to lead them, they will go where he will go. As soon as he falls, they scamper.

F. A. Gibbs sworn.

Mr. Haymond—How long have you resided in California?

A.—Since January, eighteen hundred and fifty—twenty-six years.

Q.—How long in the City of San Francisco?

A.—From eighteen hundred and seventy to the present time. The balance of the time I resided in Sacramento.

Q.—What is your official position?

A.—Supervisor from the Eleventh Ward, city government.

Q.—Do you know anything about hospitals in this city?

A.—I am Chairman of the Hospital Committee.

Q.—Are there any Chinese in the hospitals?

A.—In the hospital, one; in the almshouse, one; and in the pest-house, thirty-six. I think eight are afflicted with leprosy, and most of the balance with venereal diseases.

Q.—Do the Chinese contribute anything for the support of these persons?

A.—Nothing whatever.

Q.—What do they do with their sick and helpless?

A.—I understand they are turned out to die.

Q.—Have you ever been through the Chinese quarter of this city?

A.—Yes, sir; several times.

Q.—What is its condition as to cleanliness?

A.—It is in a miserable condition—a disgrace to the city and to the police for permitting it, and to the health department, too, I think.

Q.—In your opinion, what influence has the presence of this Chinese population on the morals of this city?

A.—A very bad one, indeed. The women have inoculated the youth with diseases. The prices are so cheap in Chinatown that young lads resort there, and as a consequence have all sorts of venereal diseases. There are many cases of young men in the hospital, suffering from syphilis, contracted in the Chinese quarter.

Q.—Have you ever seen any Christian Chinamen?

A.—No, sir; I have not. I have been told that the Chinese each pay five cents a day for the right to be doctored free when sick, but should a Chinaman fail to pay his five cents, he must look out for himself.

Mr. Rogers—You say a great many young boys are inoculated with these diseases—are many of them in the city institutions?

A.—I think there are some, but a great many more are cured outside. A large number of dispensations are given and filled at the city institutions.

ANDREW MCKENZIE sworn.

Mr. Pierson—What is your business?

A.—A local officer.

Q.—How long have you been such?

A.—Three years or a little over, for the Royal Chinese Theatre.

Q.—Where is that?

A.—On Jackson Street; and also, a year and a half on Jackson Street proper, and taking a portion of Bartlett Alley.

Q.—Do you mean by that that you have served four and one-half years as a local?

A.—Yes; but I have been on the police force since eighteen hundred and fifty-two.

Q.—Have you ever estimated the number of Chinese in the Chinese quarter?

A.—In the Chinese quarter itself there are about fifteen thousand or twenty thousand. Scattered on the outskirts and through the city there are about ten thousand more.

Q.—How large a space does this quarter cover?

A.—Seven or eight blocks.

Q.—What is its condition?

A.—The streets are clean and the fronts of the stores are pretty clean, but when you go underneath and back of the houses, it becomes filthy. The alleys are very unclean. The houses are from one to four stories high, and built mostly of brick.

Q.—Are there any considerable numbers of Chinese houses of prostitution on those alleys?

A.—There are quite a number, but I think just now they are all closed.
Q.—Are there gambling-houses on your beat?
A.—There have been, but they have all been closed within the last two weeks.
Q.—How many were there before?
A.—About twenty. We have never entirely suppressed gambling but generally managed to keep it under some restraint. We have driven it and prostitution to the back streets, and off the street itself.
Q.—How are Chinese women held here?
A.—I think Mr. Rogers can inform you on that point better than I can. He was employed by the Chinese up at the barricoon. There is more or less bondage in houses of prostitution—white and Chinese, too.
Q.—What do you mean by barricoon?
A.—A place where women coming from the ships are placed. It is underneath the joss-house or the old theatre fronting on St. Louis Alley, and running to Dupont Street. They are kept there until apportioned out.
Mr. Haymond—Do you remember the time an attempt was made to send Chinese prostitutes back to China?
A.—I do.
Q.—Do you know what officers were on duty and had charge of it then?
A.—I do not.
Q.—Is it not a notorious fact that these Chinese prostitutes are held as slaves, subject to the pleasure of their owners?
A.—Yes, sir.
Q.—Do you know how they are treated?
A.—No, sir.
Q.—Do you know whether they are made to work in the daytime?
A.—I have seen some of them sewing button-holes, sitting in their door-ways.
Mr. Pierson—Is that barricoon maintained there now?
A.—I think not, because no Chinawomen are coming now. They have stopped coming within the last year. In speaking of lepers, the Chinese told me they tried to get them away on the steamers, but could not. I used to bring in visitors to see them.
Q.—Do you know how many lepers there are in the Chinese quarter?
A.—I think, five or six. I don't know whether it is leprosy all through or not. It may be a sort of syphilitic disease.
Q.—Where are these lepers kept?
A.—Some in Cooper's Alley. They live in a small room by themselves, and when visitors go to see them they generally give two or four bits, and that supports them.
Q.—How do the Chinese treat their sick, disabled, and helpless?
A.—Those belonging to companies are taken care of. The others have to look out for themselves or go to the hospitals.
Q.—What has been your experience as to the honesty of the Chinese, as a class?
A.—There is a great deal of dishonesty, but I think there are some honest men. I don't look upon them as being as honest as white persons. The Chinese look upon us as rascals, and we look upon them in the same way.

Q.—Would you believe them under oath?

A.—A great many I would not believe. That is the rule. There are exceptions, of course.

Q.—Have you ever been in the Globe Hotel?

A.—Yes, sir.

Q.—How many people sleep there?

A.—I suppose between two and three hundred.

Q.—Is it difficult to enforce ordinances among the Chinese?

A.—Yes, sir.

Q.—You say that gambling-houses and houses of prostitution are now closed?

A.—Yes, sir.

Q.—And why?

A.—For the simple reason that they can get no business.

Q.—Is that caused by the enforcing of the city ordinances?

A.—I suppose it is.

Q.—Is it possible to enforce all the ordinances of the city?

A.—I do not think so. While I believe San Francisco to be the best governed city in the world, to enforce the ordinances in the Chinese quarter would require a police force so large as to bankrupt the city.

Q.—Is it difficult to enforce the fire ordinance?

A.—Yes, sir.

Q.—Do they habitually violate the health ordinance?

A.—Yes, sir.

Q.—And the laws regarding gambling and prostitution?

A.—Yes, sir.

Q.—So the great mass of the Chinese population is a criminal one, living in open violation of laws and ordinances?

A.—A great many.

Q.—And it is very difficult to enforce the laws?

A.—Yes, sir.

Q.—Do you know any city in the world where the laws are violated with the impunity they are in the Chinese quarter of this city?

A.—No; and I do not know of any people in the world who have the means to live better, yet will not live better.

Q.—Do you know the building on Jackson Street, near the theater—the building in which is Dr. Gibson's Sunday-school?

A.—Yes, sir.

Q.—Is it leased to Chinamen?

A.—Yes, sir.

Q.—Who leases it?

A.—The Rev. Dr. Otis Gibson, the Chinese missionary.

Q.—How does it compare, in regard to filth and dirt, with the Globe Hotel?

A.—It is filthier and dirtier. He has recently erected an engine there for pumping water for use in that house, and the water pumped is the seepage of all the sinks in the neighborhood.

Q.—Do you think it possible for any living being to live in a dirtier, filthier place than this house of Gibson's?

A.—No, sir; that house is as filthy as I have seen them. Had I not seen it with my own eyes I would not believe that any animal could exist in such a place.

Q.—Would you think a hog could exist there, unless you saw it?

A.—It would make very bad meat for butchers.

Q.—Do the Chinese live there?

A.—They do.

Q.—How many live in a room seven feet high by eight or ten feet?

A.—I suppose fifteen or twenty. They have bunks there like a ship's forecastle.

Q.—Will you give a description of the kind of filth they have there?

A.—It is almost indescribable. It is much of all kinds. There is rotten garbage there, seepage water—filth of all kinds. A steam engine has been constructed to pump water for the use of Chinese, and the water pumped is from the sinks and water-closets of the whole neighborhood. The Chinese use that water, for it is being forced upon them.

Q.—Who forces it upon them?

A.—The landlord.

Q.—Who is the landlord?

A.—The Rev. Otis Gibson. When Gibson was building that engine, and also a wooden house in there, I notified him that it was against the fire ordinance, and he got a permit from the Board of Supervisors. Regarding the enforcement of ordinances, I will say that among white people others will complain and assist the officers, but among the Chinese each one does all he can to defeat us. They assist each other in every way, and it is very difficult for us to enforce the law.

Q.—You are paid by the Chinese, are you not?

A.—Yes, sir.

Q.—And a large part of your pay comes from gamblers and prostitutes?

A.—Yes, sir.

Q.—Does the closing of these houses affect your salary to any great extent?

A.—Yes, sir. We do not make such big collections. There is a dark hour in all kinds of business, and this is our dark hour just now.

ALFRED CLARK recalled.

Mr. Haymond—Give us a description of the Chy Lung case.

A.—In eighteen hundred and seventy-four a number of Chinese prostitutes came here; and on the arrival of the Chinese steamer, the Chief of Police, with several officers, took the women to the City Hall. Mr. Gibson was used as interpreter, and the women examined. Some of them testified that they came under contract for service; but they did not care to fulfill the contract, if they could get out of it. Many of the women either would not talk, or swore they came to see their husbands. In September of eighteen hundred and seventy-four the Commissioner of Immigration caused the detention, on board the steamer Japan, of a number of women who came on that vessel—I think twenty-one—said to be prostitutes. It was so determined by the State Courts, and the women ordered sent to China. Under section one hundred and seventy-four of the Penal Code, these women were detained on board the vessel under direction of Commissioner Pietrowski. They were brought before the Fourth District Court on habeas corpus, but were remanded. The case was taken to the Supreme Court of the State at the July term of eighteen hundred and seventy-four, and there the opinion of the lower Court was sustained, and an order entered requiring the Pacific Mail Steamship Company to take them back to China, or give the bonds required under section one hundred and seventy-four. As the steamer was about to sail with them, they were taken by the Coroner of San Francisco on a writ of habeas corpus, issued from the United States Circuit Court. Upon a hearing, that Court reversed the decision of the State Courts, decided that the women were improperly detained, and the parties were discharged. The case was taken to the Supreme Court of the United States, and this latter decision sustained. Since that time we have done nothing in that matter.

Q.—It appeared in testimony this morning that the City of San Francisco, outside of the Chinese quarter, is the best governed city in the world. What is your opinion?

A.—I think that is correct. Our police reports compare very favorably with any other. In London the arrests average yearly seven to each officer; here it is one hundred and fifty. It is very difficult to enforce laws in the Chinese quarter, for reasons already given before your committee. It is almost impossible to get evidence against Chinese law-breakers, because they all swear together. To enforce the laws and ordinances, as we do in other parts of the city, would require a very large police force, and the city could not stand the expense. I suppose fifty officers stationed there all the time might preserve order and enforce the laws; but fifty officers for seven or eight blocks is something unheard of.

Samuel H. Cohen sworn.

Mr. Haymond—Of what country are you a native?

A.—England.

Q.—Were you ever in China?

A.—Six years, within a month.

Q.—What time.

A.—From eighteen hundred and forty-three to eighteen hundred and forty-nine. Since eighteen hundred and forty-nine I have lived here, in this city.

Q.—State what you know about the social, moral, and political condition of the Chinese people.

A.—I begin with the morals: I have lived in the south of China, in Hong-kong. We saw there very little of the Chinamen to know what they are, because the government gives them a certain part of the town. I saw enough, however, to convince me that the morals of the Chinese are worse than those of any people that I have met with. [Witness details series of unnatural, indecent, brutal crimes and offenses, which came under his own observation in China, and which are of such a character as to be unfit for publication.] They are very dirty people. I have seen them pick lice from themselves, and eat them. In Shanghai, in the public gardens, I have seen them sit down and perform that very interesting, but most disgusting, operation. In Hong-kong they have to be clean, because the police look after them particularly. The policemen are districted there in such a manner, that they are enabled to keep the place clean.

Q.—Do you know anything about the destruction of female children?

A.—I have heard of it up north, and also at the south. In the public streets they have large cess-pools. Everything is open and exposed, and these public water-closets are being used at all hours of the day and night; and women never dare to go upon the street, because of the indecencies which they would have to witness if they did. These places become filled up and flow over the streets, and then are scooped up in buckets and carried to a reservoir in the country. It is then used for manure, to assist the growth of vegetables. In traveling in the north of China, I have seen a great many Catholic Chinamen. The Catholics there seem to have done more towards christianizing the Chinese than all the rest. A Catholic priest told me their mission had converted sixty thousand in two years. The Chinese, as a class, are thieves, from mandarin down. While I kept store there, I have detected high officials and low Chinamen in the act of stealing from me. The punishments in some cases are excessively severe, even barbarous. They will lie. You cannot get the truth from them. Bribery is very common in official business.

David Louderback sworn.

Mr. Haymond—How long have you resided in San Francisco?

A.—Since eighteen hundred and forty-nine.

Q.—What positions have you held?

A.—From eighteen hundred and sixty-four I was prosecuting attorney for the Police Judge's Court until I was elected Judge of that Court.

Q.—What do you know about the habits, customs, and social and moral status of the Chinese population in this city?

A.—I think they are a very immoral, mean, mendacious, dishonest, thieving people, as a general thing.

Q.—What are the difficulties in the way of the administration of justice where they are concerned?

A.—As witnesses, their veracity is of the lowest degree. They do not appear to realize the sanctity of an oath, and it is difficult to enforce the laws, where they are concerned, for that reason. They are very apt, in all cases and under all circumstances, to resort to perjury and the subornation of .perjury. They also use our criminal law to revenge themselves upon their enemies, and malicious prosecutions are frequent.

Q.—Do you know anything of the tenure by which Chinese women are held?

A.—In cases I have investigated, parties have been convicted for dealing in this Chinese slavery—buying and selling women for purposes of prostitution. The women probably never realize that they are free agents, but act as though they were slaves.

Q.—Suppose a woman desired to escape from that life, what would be her chance for success?

A.—They very seldom desire to escape, they are so inured to prostitution and lewdness. Occasionally one of them gets married, but they know nothing of domestic life as we understand it. All these women here are prostitutes, or have been prostitutes. I have not met with a single decent Chinawoman.

Q.—Are all classes of Chinese engaged in this traffic in women?

A.—I think not. I have heard that the merchants were engaged in it, but there has never been any evidence to show that.

Q.—About what proportion of the Chinese population in this city are habitual law-breakers, violators of the city ordinances, thieves, gamblers, prostitutes, and living off the wages of crime?

A.—The proportion is very great.

Q.—Leaving out of consideration the Chinese part of this city, how are the laws generally enforced in San Francisco, as compared with other cities?

A.—I think they are enforced a little better than in other cities. It is difficult to enforce the laws among the Chinese, because of their mendacity and bad habits generally.

Q.—What is the effect upon the public morals, of that population, in a city like this?

A.—I think their presence is degrading to the white race.

Q.—Have you ever seen any Christian Chinamen?

A.—I have seen those who professed to be Christians. I never tested their sincerity. When Chinese are brought into Court I never think of inquiring into their religion.

Q.—What is your opinion in regard to the advancement of christianity by reason of the presence of the Chinese here?

A.—I don't think it amounts to much.

Q.—Do you think the presence of these people tends to the improvement of the morals of the community?

A.—No, sir; I think the reverse.

Q.—It does not tend to the advancement of Christian civilization?

A.—I think their presence is injurious to religion as well as morals.

Q.—What are the difficulties encountered in attempting to stop prostitution in this city?

A.—Inability to obtain sufficient evidence to justify conviction. We do not understand their language, and of course cannot go by general appearances. We must have legal evidence to warrant conviction for prostitution.

Q.—With a Chinese population confined to seven or eight blocks, would it not be easy to obtain evidence if the heads of the Chinese companies were to wish to stop it?

A.—They could render great assistance.

Q.—Do they do that?

A.—I never knew them to do that.

Yung Ty sworn. J. Millard interpreter.

Mr. McCoppin—How long have you been in California?

A.—Fifteen years.

Q.—From what part of China did you come?

A.—Three days' travel from Canton.

Q.—Are you President of the Hop-wo Company?

A.—Yes, sir.

Q.—How many members of that company are there?

A.—Our books show thirty-four thousand, but of this number ten thousand have returned to China, leaving twenty-four thousand here now. I do not know how many are in San Francisco, for I have been President only six months.

Q.—Are any of your company gamblers?

A.—I do not know. I am not acquainted with any.

Q.—Do any women belong to your company?

A.—Some families.

Q.—Are any of those houses of prostitution in the Chinese quarter carried on under the management of your people?

A.—No, sir; we do not have anything to do with them.

Q.—How do people belonging to your company come here?

A.—They raise money mostly at home. Some borrow from friends in China.

Q.—What do they do with their sick?
A.—If they have relatives they take care of them.
Q.—How is it that so many Chinese are in our hospitals?
A.—I don't know. All that belong to our company we take care of.
Q.—Are you willing to join the Presidents of the other companies to send back to China people afflicted with incurable diseases?
A.—We will consult together. If they are willing, I am.
Q.—How many of the thirty-four thousand belonging to your company are coolies?
A.—We have none of that class, for our men are mostly farmers at home.
Q.—Are they men who own the land?
A.—Most of them are working it on shares; some of them own the ground. Some of them are working for wages, while some work for themselves.
Q.—Are they called coolies?
A.—I don't know what you mean by coolies. They are not slaves; they are simply the lower class of men who work for a living.
Q.—What is a coolie?
A.—I do not know.
Q.—Do you know what a slave is?
A.—We have no such in our country.
Q.—Have you ever heard of the coolie trade?
A.—I don't know any such thing in China.
Q.—How many Chinamen in this city are Christians?
A.—I don't know.
Q.—Do you know one?
A.—No, sir. I have only been here in this city six months. I have been in this country fifteen years.
Q.—Have you ever heard of the Burlingame treaty?
A.—I have heard of it.
Q.—Have you ever read it?
A.—No, sir; I have only heard it spoken of.

Sin How sworn. J. Millard interpreter.
Mr. Haymond—How long have you been in California?
A.—Six years.
Q.—From what part of China did you come?
A.—Canton.
Q.—Of what company are you President?
A.—Kong-chow.
Q.—How many Chinese in this State belong to your company?
A.—A little over fifteen thousand.
Q.—How many of them are in San Francisco?
A.—I guess about five thousand.
Q.—Do you know any Christian Chinamen?
A.—I don't know anything about them.
Q.—Have you ever seen one?
A.—I do not associate with them. I don't know anything about them. If I have seen them, I do not recognize them as Christians.
Q.—Do any Christians belong to your company?
A.—If they do, I would not be apt to know it.
Mr. McCoppin—What do you do with your sick?
A.—If they have brothers or relations, they take care of them; if not, we take care of them.

Q.—Why is it there are so many Chinese in our hospitals?
A.—I don't know about that. I have only been President three months, and have not learned all these things.
Q.—Are you willing to join the other companies in sending back to China Chinamen afflicted with incurable diseases?
A.—I do not know what our company would do. We are not very well off, but I will consult with the others, and see what they say.
Q.—Do you know who own the women in these houses of prostitution?
A.—I do not associate with the men who have control of these women.
Q.—Do any of these men belong to your company?
A.—I cannot tell. If they do, they do not tell me.
Q.—Why don't you exercise your influence to discourage gambling and prostitution among the Chinese?
A.—We do discourage it, but they do not pay any attention to us. They do not let us know about these things.
Q.—Do you know that there are Chinese prostitutes in this city?
A.—I suppose there are.
Q.—Did you ever see one?
A.—I have seen plenty of women on the street, but which are prostitutes and which are private women I don't know.
Q.—Did you ever make any inquiry about it?
A.—No; I don't have anything to do with that kind of business.
Q.—Do you know any gamblers?
A.—There are gamblers here, I think, but I have never seen any.
Q.—How long have you been President of this company?
A.—A little over three months.
Q.—How often do you change?
A.—Sometimes once a year; sometimes once in two years.
Q.—Who elects the President?
A.—The merchants and members of our company.
Q.—How is the selection made?
A.—By voice. The merchants mostly get together and make it up who shall be President.
Q.—What is the salary?
A.—I get eighty dollars a month and board myself.
Q.—Do you know what a coolie is?
A.—No, sir.
Q.—Have you heard of the coolie trade?
A.—I don't know anything about that.
Q.—Have you ever heard of the Burlingame treaty?
A.—No, sir.
Q.—What induced you to come to this country?
A.—I came here to keep a store and to do business. There are a good many in this country who send back to China and praise it up, and that induces some folks to come.
Q.—Does the Chinese Government desire Chinamen to come to this country, or does it desire them to stay at home?
A.—We have no regulation as to that matter. Anybody can come and go back.
Q.—Were you a merchant in China?
A.—Yes, sir.
Q.—What would be considered a good salary for a clerk in Canton?
A.—It depends upon the kind of business. In the large houses,

three hundred dollars or four hundred dollars a year Small houses pay as low as twenty dollars a year.

Q.—Three hundred dollars or four hundred dollars for the very best?

A.—Yes; some pay as high as that. They pay that price only for expert labor.

Q.—How many people are living in Canton?

A.—Over a million.

SI QUON sworn. J. Millard interpreter.

Mr. McCoppin—What position do you hold?

A.—President of the Yung-wo Company.

Q.—For how long?

A.—Fourteen years.

Q.—What do they pay you?

A.—Sixty dollars a month.

Q.—How many people belong to your company in California?

A.—Ten thousand.

Q.—How many women?

A.—Not many.

Q.—How many Chinawomen are there in San Francisco?

A.—There must be over one thousand.

Q.—How many are not prostitutes?

A.—Several hundred.

Q.—Are these several hundred married?

A.—Most of them come here as wives, while some have been married according to American customs.

Q.—What do you do with your sick?

A.—Some are taken care of by friends and some by the company.

Q.—Why are so many in our hospitals?

A.—There may be some in foreign hospitals, but we take care of most of them ourselves. Each company takes care of its own men.

Q.—Are you willing to unite with the other companies in sending back to China Chinamen afflicted with incurable diseases?

A.—I think our company would be willing to do it.

Q.—How many Christian Chinamen do you know in this city?

A.—About ten or fifteen belong to my company.

Q.—How many among all the Chinese?

A.—I do not know.

Q.—Are they better or worse than other Chinamen?

A.—They principally talk as good, if they only follow it up.

Q.—Would you trust a Christian Chinaman as soon as any other?

A.—I have never had any business directly with them, and I don't know whether I would trust them or not.

Q.—Do you know any gamblers?

A.—No, sir.

Q.—Do you know how the men belonging to your company in this city are employed?

A.—Some are in business, and some do all kinds of work.

Q.—How many are servants in families?

A.—I don't know.

Q.—How many are at work making boots and shoes?

A.—We have men in the shoe factories, but very few.

Q.—How many are making overalls, shirts, and drawers?

A.—Very few. We have men engaged in a great many different things, but I don't know how many.

Q.—How many officers has the Chinese Government in this city?

A.—None, except one, who is in the East. We expect one this fall.

Q.—What is he coming for?

A.—I think he is coming here to go East to the American headquarters.

CHIN FONG CHOW sworn. J. Millard interpreter.

Mr. Haymond—From what part of China did you come?

A.—One day and a half travel from Canton.

Q.—How long have you been in California?

A.—Eight years.

Q.—What position do you hold now?

A.—President of the Yan-wo Company.

Q.—How many members of that company are there in California?

A.—Four thousand three hundred.

Q.—How many Chinamen are in California altogether, that do not belong to one of the six companies?

A.—About one thousand.

Q.—Are there not twice that many?

A.—No, sir.

Q.—To what company do the prostitutes belong?

A.—I do not know.

Q.—To what company do the gamblers belong?

A.—I do not know.

Q.—Do you know any Christian Chinamen?

A.—No.

Q.—Where do they live?

A.—I don't know.

Q.—Did you ever see a Christian Chinaman?

A.—I do not know. I would not know one if I should see him.

Q.—Who controls the Chinese joss-houses?

A.—Each company has a temple.

Q.—Who has charge of the one on Jackson Street?

A.—I don't know. It is not under the charge of my company.

Q.—Who supports them?

A.—I don't know.

Q.—Who pays the expense for keeping it open?

A.—I don't know.

Q.—Who bring Chinese women to this country?

A.—They come in various ways.

Q.—In what ways?

A.—They make arrangements themselves before they come here but who has charge of them here I don't know.

Q.—How many wives do Chinamen have under the law?

A.—All the way from one to four and five.

Q.—Do they lend their wives around to each other?

A.—No, sir.

Q.—Do they ever sell their wives?

A.—No.

Q.—Do you know what a coolie is?

A.—A laboring man.

Q.—How much does the Pacific Mail Steamship Company charge for taking Chinamen back to China?
A.—Fifty-three dollars.
Q.—How much of that does your company get?
A.—Nothing. It all goes to the steamship company.
Q.—Will the steamship company sell a man a ticket for China without the certificate of his company?
A.—I think they would sell it.
Mr. McCoppin—What do you do with your sick?
A.—We take care of the members of our own company.
Q.—How is it there are so many Chinamen in our hospitals?
A.—I don't know anything about that. We always take care of our own men.
Q.—Will your company join the other companies in sending back to China Chinamen afflicted with incurable diseases?
A.—I think they will.

EIGHTH DAY.

San Francisco, April 20th, 1876.

Wong Ben sworn.
Q.—How long have you been in California?
A.—Nearly thirteen years.
Q.—Where did you come from—what part of China?
A.—Canton.
Q.—What have you been doing since you came to California?
A.—Acting as interpreter, for a while, in the Police and County Courts.
Q.—How long is it since you learned to speak English?
A.—About ten years.
Q.—Where do you live now?
A.—I live here, in San Francisco.
Q.—Were you a witness in the Police Court yesterday, where some Chinese prostitutes were tried?
A.—Yes; we tried to break up that business. Last year I had two boys with me, and we tried to break up the gambling-houses and houses of prostitution. We tried to have the policemen arrest the keepers, but Charley Duffield kicked the boy in the head, and told him to go away. He would not let us go into the gambling-houses to see who were there, so that we could have them arrested.
Q.—Are you helping the police?
A.—Yes, sir. Charley Duffield told us we had no reason to go against the keepers of these houses.
Q.—Who are these keepers?
A.—Wong Woon, a big fellow, who keeps a house of prostitution. An Geo, another big fellow—every time a woman gets into trouble he gets her out. He goes and collects commission from women and makes them pay so much a month. He gets lawyers for the gamblers, too, and collects five dollars one week, and ten dollars a month.
Q.—Are these men merchants?
A.—No; they keep gambling-houses, and houses of prostitution. They buy women in China, and bring them here to be prostitutes—and they sell them again here.

Q.—What do they say if you testify?

A.—They put up one thousand five hundred dollars to put my life out. They tell me if that don't do it they will put up two thousand dollars, and then three thousand dollars. He told me last night he would give me one hundred and fifty dollars if I would not say anything, and that I must take it, or I would have my life put out. Wong Woon and An Geo collect thirteen dollars each month from gambling-houses, eight dollars a month from lottery-houses, then five dollars a week more from gamblers. They tell me I must not go against them, and they would give me money. If I would not take it they would put my life out. I won't take it, because young boys come here and spend all their money in gambling-houses and houses of prostitution, and by-and-by he hasn't got a cent. He can't go home. Why? Because he can't go, for he gambled off his money. When he sees that he works all the time and never has a cent, he thinks it is no use to work any more, and so becomes a loafer on the street.

Q.—Who bring the Chinese women here?

A.—Wong Fook Soi, Bi Chee, An Geo, and Wong Woon.

Q.—What do these men do?

A.—They keep gambling-houses and houses of prostitution.

Q.—To what company do these men belong?

A.—An Geo belongs to the See-yup Company; Wong Woon to the Sam-yup Company. That fellow has got lots of money. He buys women in China for two hundred dollars or three hundred dollars, and brings them out here and sells them for eight hundred or nine hundred dollars, to be prostitutes.

Q.—How do they get those women in China?

A.—In Tartary. They are "big feet" women, and are sometimes bought for ninety dollars. When they bring them out here they sell them for nine hundred dollars.

Q.—What do they do with them?

A.—They make them be prostitutes. If they don't want to be prostitutes they make them be.

Q.—Can they get away?

A.—No, sir.

Q.—What do they do with them when they get sick and cannot work any longer?

A.—They don't treat them well at all. They don't take as much care of them, whether they are sick or well, as white people do a dog. Chinawomen in China are treated first rate, but in California these "big feet" women are treated worse than dogs.

Q.—How many Chinese prostitutes are there in this city?

A.—Take in the high-toned prostitutes, those that live up-stairs, and I guess there are about eight hundred.

Q.—Do you know what the six companies are?

A.—Yes, sir.

Q.—Do they have anything to do with these women?

A.—No, sir.

Q.—How do Chinese come to this country—do the companies bring them here?

A.—No. The companies only take care of them when they come here. Then they don't know the place and the language, and the companies look after them. The women are taken care of and brought here by these big fellows I mentioned.

Q.—How many gambling-houses are there here?

A.—An Geo, Wong Woon, and those big fellows have got six big houses.

Q.—How many smaller ones?

A.—Seventy-five or seventy-six. Last year I got two boys and we counted eighty-two gambling-houses in this city. Duffield said if we didn't stop he would break our heads.

Q.—Who is Duffield?

A.—He is a policeman who watches houses of prostitution and gambling-houses. He gets lots of money.

Q.—How much?

A.—Five dollars a week from the gambling-houses, and four bits a week from each prostitute.

Q.—Do you know of white boys going to Chinese houses of prostitution?

A.—Yes; plenty of them.

Q.—How old boys have you seen there?

A.—Ten or fifteen years old. Women don't care how old they are, as long as they got money.

Q.—Have you seen many boys twelve and fifteen years old there?

A.—Plenty of them.

Q.—How many women have been arrested to be tried to-day?

A.—I have forgotten. The first day we got nine. I don't know how many they got this next time. Yesterday, when the trial was coming on, these big boss fellows with lots of money scared off the witnesses. I tried to make them not afraid; but it was of no use.

Q.—Do they frighten the Chinese by threatening to kill them if they testify in the American Courts?

A.—Yes, sir. Plenty of times the big company scares the little company. When there is any trouble, the companies go against each other sometimes. When one man kills another, one company tries to get him hung, and the other to get him free, if they can't settle it themselves. Sometimes they spend lots of money to get a man hung.

Q.—From what part of China do most of the Chinamen here come?

A.—Near Canton mostly; but there are plenty of Tartars in this country.

Q.—Do you know any Christian Chinamen?

A.—Yes.

Q.—How many?

A.—Ten or fifteen. Some believe little. Some just go to school to learn to read; that is all. Some believe everything.

Q.—Suppose a Chinawoman got away, what would they do?

A.—Sometimes her owners put up money to get her back again; sometimes they make the man who got her pay money to them for her. If a man take a woman away from a house of prostitution, they tell him they put his life out.

Q.—Do you know of any Chinamen being killed for taking away women from those houses?

A.—One boy got killed up in Ross Alley nearly four years ago. These big fellows hired men to kill him. Three men ran up and shot him, and ran a knife into him; and that is the reason other boys are afraid to help women.

Q.—How old were you when you came to California?

A.—About nine years old.
Q.—How old are you now?
A.—Nearly twenty-four.
Q.—How many gambling-houses were there two months ago?
A.—Over eighty.
Q.—How much a month do they pay the police?
A.—Five dollars a week each one. These four big fellows, besides that, collect thirteen dollars a month to pay a white man to get them out of trouble. The lottery-houses pay eight dollars a month.
Q.—How many lottery-houses are there?
A.—Two or three hundred. When I have tried to get into gambling-houses to see who were there, so I could arrest them, they wouldn't let me in. The bosses tell them, when they see me coming, to shut the door. I get a green boy from the mountains to go into a house of prostitution, so he can talk and see what kind of a house it is, so I can make him swear.
Q.—Whom are you assisting in this matter?
A.—The boys working in this city here make twenty or twenty-five dollars a month, and they spend this in the houses of prostitution and gamble it off. They come to me and say: "You get the gambling-houses and houses of prostitution shut up, and you will be a great man." Charley Duffield put one fellow in jail one hundred days for nothing, because he was helping me. Yesterday I had ten or twelve boys to swear in Court against the gamblers and the whore-house fellows. I told them not to be afraid, that nothing would happen to them. When they found out that they would get hurt if they swore, they all run away. They put up a notice on a wall to put out my life for one thousand and five hundred dollars, but when I went to get it they tore it down.
Q.—Did you ever see any other notices offering rewards for killing Chinamen?
A.—Plenty of them.
Q.—Where do they have them posted?
A.—On a five-story house on Jackson Street. These big fellows had a place where they kept their books and money, and a list of all the men interested in gambling-houses and houses of prostitution. I knew I could not get in there, and told Ying Low to go there and see if he saw any books on their table. The first time he saw plenty of books, and I went and got policemen to go there, but those big fellows all cleared out. I think they will have another meeting in two weeks or ten days, and I guess I can catch them then. Last month Wong Woon put up eight thousand dollars, that he got from gamblers, to fight the law. Whenever a gambler or a prostitute gets into trouble, they spend some of this money to get them out and fight the law. Yesterday I had fifteen witnesses to swear against these fellows, but when Wong Woon saw that he asked for a continuance, and this morning I have only got two. My company tells me to break up these houses, and the six companies have put up a notice saying that if any more notices of reward are put up, they will fight.

Dr. H. H. Toland sworn.
Mr. Haymond—Doctor, how long have you practiced medicine in this State?
A.—Twenty-three years.

Q.—And during that time have you had one of the leading positions, from a medical point of view, in this city?

A.—Yes, sir.

Q.—You are the founder of the "Toland Medical University"?

A.—Yes, sir.

Q.—A member of the San Francisco Board of Health?

A.—Yes, sir.

Q.—Of what institution were you a graduate?

A.—Transylvania University, Kentucky, in eighteen hundred and thirty-two—one of the first Western universities that was established at Lexington, Kentucky.

Q.—It has been stated that these Chinese houses of prostitution are open to small boys, and that a great many have been diseased. Do you know anything about that?

A.—I know that is so. I have seen boys eight and ten years old with diseases they told me they contracted on Jackson Street. It is astonishing how soon they commence indulging in that passion. Some of the worst cases of syphilis I have ever seen in my life occur in children not more than ten or twelve years old. They generally try to conceal their condition from their parents. They come to me and I help screen it from their parents, and cure them without compensation. Sometimes parents, unaware of what is the matter, bring their boys to me, and I do all I can to keep the truth from them.

Q.—Are these cases of frequent occurrence?

A.—Yes, sir. You will find children from twelve to fifteen that are often diseased. In consequence of neglect, they finally become the worst cases we have to treat.

Q.—What effect will that have upon the health of the community, in the end?

A.—It must have a bad effect, because a great many of these children get secondary syphilis, and it runs until it becomes almost incurable. Under the most favorable circumstances it takes a long time to eradicate it, but when it becomes constitutional, it is an exceedingly difficult thing to cure it. When they come to me for treatment, they sometimes have secondary syphilis; sometimes chancre; sometimes a tertiary form. Under most favorable circumstances it takes two or three years to eradicate syphilis.

Q.—Unless you have complete control of the patient for that time, is it not certain that the seeds of the disease remain in the system through life?

A.—It destroys life. I can show a dozen cases in the County Hospital, where, if they recover, it will be after a long course of treatment, and some of them will not recover at all. The whole system becomes poisoned and debilitated. They are so diseased, and the system is so exhausted, perhaps by a big sore, or something of that sort, that they cannot be cured.

Q.—When syphilis assumes a secondary and tertiary form, what effect will it have upon the children of such persons?

A.—The disease is hereditary, and will be transmitted to the children. I have positive evidence of that in a family that I have been treating, where the children are diseased. The father had the disease when he married a healthy woman, and of three children born, every one exhibited symptoms of syphilis.

Q.—From your observation, what would you say as to the effect it must have upon this community if these Chinese prostitutes are allowed to remain in the country?

A.—It will fill our hospitals with invalids, and I think it would be a very great relief to the younger portion of the community to get rid of them.

Q.—Judge Hager says, when he was in the United States Senate, and endeavored to take some steps to prevent immigration of this people, he was met by the proposition that their coming to this country tended to advance Christian civilization, and the humanitarians of the East would not aid him for that reason. What is your opinion?

A.—It does not tend to the advancement of Christian civilization, but it has the contrary effect. There is scarcely a single day that there are not a dozen young men come to my office with syphilis or gonorrhœa. A great many of them have not means to be treated properly, and the disease runs on until it becomes constitutional; and in nine cases out of ten it is the ruin of them. I have treated a great many boys, and I have treated the parents. Sometimes the parents would come, and after going through a course of treatment, would bring their children.

Mr. Pierson—To what extent do these diseases come from Chinese prostitutes?

A.—I suppose nine-tenths. When these persons come to me I ask them where they got the disease, and they generally tell me that they have been with Chinawomen. They think diseases contracted from Chinawomen are harder to cure than those contracted elsewhere, so they tell me as a matter of self-protection. I am satisfied, from my experience, that nearly all the boys in town, who have venereal disease, contracted it in Chinatown. They have no difficulty there, for the prices are so low that they can go whenever they please. The women do not care how old the boys are, whether five years old or more, as long as they have money.

Q.—Then the maintenance of this population in our midst, instead of advancing civilization, would seem to be a crime against it?

A.—That is my opinion.

Mr. Donovan—Have you ever read or heard of any country in the world where there were so many children diseased as there are in San Francisco?

A.—No, sir. I lived in a town of one hundred and fifty or two hundred students, and we had not many public houses, but the students were not near so diseased, in proportion to their number, as are the boys here in this city.

Mr. Haymond—Can you approximate the number of boys affected here during any given year?

A.—I cannot tell exactly, because my attention has not been particularly directed to it; but I treat half a dozen every day in the year of three hundred and sixty-five days.

Q.—Is not that a fearful condition of things?

A.—It is most frightful. Generally they are improperly treated, and the syphilis or gonorrhœa runs on from week to week until stricture results, and that is almost as bad as constitutional syphilis, because it requires a long time to cure it.

Q.—Do you know anything about the cleanliness of the Chinese quarter of this city?

A.—I have treated a good many Chinamen. I perform nearly all their surgical operations, and have found them cleanly in person.

Their clothes are generally clean. In some places they are very much crowded. I have never examined the quarters. I have only been in the stores, where I have been called on surgical business. The Chinese do not like to be cut, and it is only seldom you can get a chance to operate on them. They have no surgeons in China. The Chinese doctors do not understand the circulation of the blood, and they know nothing of surgery or surgical diseases. They are not allowed to dissect. They have made no advancement at all in the science of surgery.

W. M. Webster sworn.

Mr. Haymond—What is your business?

A.—Agent for the Associated Press.

Q.—How long have you resided in California?

A.—Since eighteen hundred and sixty-two.

Q.—Were you ever in China?

A.—In the summer of eighteen hundred and sixty-one.

Q.—What part of China?

A.—Shanghai.

Q.—What do you know of the social and moral condition of that people, the condition of their cities, etc.?

A.—Shanghai was the nastiest city I ever saw. The streets were very filthy, while public privies—which are nothing more than open sheds—are scattered along the public thoroughfares. Some of these places were running over—the refuse matter flowing over the streets in the vicinity, sometimes a foot deep on the sidewalks. The streets are very narrow, the widest being about ten, fifteen, and twenty feet in width, and full of all kinds of garbage. There is an indescribable combination of stenches arising from these sources, which is simply horrible.

Q.—Are there any Christian Chinamen there?

A.—Not that I am aware of.

Q.—Do you know whether the missionaries have made any advances in christianizing them?

A.—I do not know.

Q.—How do the Chinese quarters of this city compare with Shanghai?

A.—As far as the streets are concerned, they are cleaner here. How it is as regards the interior, I cannot say.

Q.—What is your opinion as to the moral condition of these people, gauged by the European standard?

A.—Very low, indeed, as regards the condition of the laboring classes. They seem to be much worse there than they are here. They seem to be more oppressed there than here. I can't say that I ever saw any evidences of slavery, but I have seen some very harsh treatment of laborers by foremen or overseers. They are worked very hard and forced to live on very little of the cheapest food.

Q.—What was the meaning of the term "coolie," in China, when you were there?

A.—I understood it to mean a laboring man.

Q.—From your observation, what do you think of the continuance of this Chinese immigration?

A.—It must be very bad. It must injure the morals of the people here and ruin business.

Q.—Does it tend to the advancement of Christian civilization?

A.—Not at all. I think the whites will learn more heathenism from the Chinese than they will christianity from us.

Q.—From what part of the East did you come.

A.—Maine.

Q.—Have you ever been connected with the press, except as agent for the Associated Press?

A.—Not regularly. I have done some newspaper work, however, from time to time.

Q.—Is it not the almost universal opinion here that this Chinese immigration is a great evil?

A.—That is the only expression of opinion that I have heard. A great many seem to favor a limited immigration, though all are opposed to the present system.

Q.—Is it your opinion that the presence of the Chinese here tends to elevate them or degrade the whites?

A.—To degrade the whites, I should say.

Q.—We have just examined Dr. Toland in regard to diseases contracted in Chinatown by white boys. What is his standing as a physician and surgeon?

A.—It is very good. I understand that he stands at the head of his profession, and is a man of great learning and thorough scientific attainments.

Dr. J. C. Shorb sworn.

Mr. Pierson—What is your profession?

A.—Physician and surgeon.

Q.—How long have you been such?

A.—Since eighteen hundred and fifty-nine.

Q.—From where did you graduate?

A.—The University of Pennsylvania—Philadelphia.

Q.—How long have you resided in California?

A.—I came to California, as a surgeon in the army, in the winter of eighteen hundred and sixty—December, I think—and I have been here ever since. I have resided in San Francisco since eighteen hundred and sixty-four.

Q.—Practicing your profession all the time?

A.—Yes, sir.

Q.—You are a member of the San Francisco Board of Health?

A.—Yes, sir. I have been a member now two months. On the first organization of the Board of Health, I was a member for three years—during eighteen hundred and seventy-one–two–three, I think.

Q.—Are you familiar with the Chinese quarter of this city?

A.—I am not, nor do I want to be.

Q.—Have your duties, as a member of the Board of Health, called you into that quarter?

A.—No, sir.

Q.—Do you know anything of its condition as regards cleanliness?

A.—Only such idea as I would get from driving through it. The duty of examining the quarter devolves upon the Health Inspector, and not on the members of the Board of Health.

Q.—Do you know what influence Chinese prostitution has upon the white population?

A.—Very bad—exceedingly so.

Q.—What is the effect on the youth of San Francisco?

A.—The presence of Chinese women here has made prostitution

excessively cheap, and it has given these boys an opportunity to gratify themselves at very slight cost. They get syphilis and gonorrhœa cheaper in that way than any way I know of. Now and then these boys have a "windfall," and go among white girls and distribute these diseases very generously. I have had boys from twelve years up to eighteen and nineteen—any numbers of them—afflicted with syphilis contracted from Chinese prostitutes.

Q.—From your own experience, can you give us any idea of the extent of this evil among boys?

A.—It would be very hard to give you a definite idea.

Q.—Is it very general?

A.—Yes; and I suppose my experience must be the experience of all the physicians in San Francisco in full practice.

Q.—Have you any opinion as to the influence the Chinese have upon civilization here?

A.—I have some idea about that, of course, but I have not studied the question to any great extent. It is well known all over the world that it is better for any country where the laborers are consumers; and to have this Chinese population of any benefit to this country, they should consume the products of this country.

Q.—Then you regard the Chinese as non-consumers?

A.—Of course I do.

Q.—What effect is the prevalence of these syphilitic diseases going to have upon future generations?

A.—No one can pretend to map out the ravages which syphilis will make. You do not know exactly when it dies out in the system. You don't know to what extent it may affect generations yet unborn.

Q.—Is it regarded by medical men as hereditary?

A.—The disease can be transmitted, and the peculiar condition of the system of the progeny will very easily enable you to trace this disease.

Q.—Is syphilis, in the tertiary form, ever cured?

A.—Yes; occasionally. Nature revolts at the presence of this poison in the system, and sometimes succeeds in getting rid of it. The vital principle is sometimes strong enough to effect a cure without medicine. But this tertiary form generally gets hold of weak or exhausted constitutions, and there are generally other troubles besides syphilis.

Q.—Do you not find, in the case of boys who have contracted syphilis, that they are practically incurable because of neglect?

A.—Boys who get that kind of a disease are not generally ashamed to come and tell you about it; at least that has been my experience.

Q.—You are satisfied, from the revelations made by patients, that the most of it is contracted from Chinese women?

A.—Yes; some of my worst cases in boys have come from Chinese prostitutes.

Q.—Do you think that this Chinese immigration tends to the advancement of Christian civilization?

A.—My ideas are exactly opposite. I do not see how any sensible man can reach a conclusion of that kind. No man with any knowledge of the facts can do so.

Q.—Do you know any Christian Chinamen?

A.—No; I do not know any, but I hear there are some in town.

Q.—What is the standing of Dr. Toland in his profession?

A.—Excellent.

Q.—He is known all over the State of California?

A.—Yes, sir.

Q.—Is there any generally received opinion among medical men that the habitual use of opium destroys the procreative powers?

A.—Unquestionably. It breaks down the nervous system completely, and has a very serious effect on other powers. It deranges digestion, and when this is deranged all the powers of the body must necessarily fail.

James H. Bovee sworn.

Mr. Haymond—How long have you resided in California?

A.—Since eighteen hundred and fifty.

Q.—In what part of the State?

A.—In San Francisco, except three years.

Q.—What is your business now?

A.—I am in no business at present, but for the last four years I have been jail-keeper in the Sheriff's office.

Q.—Do you know anything about the Chinese quarters?

A.—Yes, sir.

Q.—What is the condition of those quarters as regards cleanliness?

A.—I don't know that you can go to any part of the world and find as dirty a place as the Chinese quarters here.

Q.—What is the extent to which gambling and prostitution is carried on in the Chinese quarter?

A.—At present I do not think there is any gambling, but before this excitement it and prostitution were very prevalent.

Q.—Can the Presidents of the six companies live there and not know anything of this?

A.—It would be impossible for them not to know all about it.

Q.—What do you know of offers of rewards for assassinations of persons for giving testimony in American Courts?

A.—I don't know anything about that, but I have heard of such things.

Q.—Do they interfere with the administration of justice here?

A.—Yes, sir. Whenever a man is arrested the first thing he does is to try to bribe the officer to let him go. Then they will try to bribe anybody who has anything to do with the prosecution.

Q.—Suppose they are arrested and brought into Court; is it an easy matter to obtain evidence from Chinese?

A.—Yes; they can obtain it. The Chinese will swear to anything. I do not think that they have any regard for our oaths at all.

Q.—Are these prostitutes bought and sold and held in bondage?

A.—Yes; that has always been my idea.

Q.—How do they treat their sick and helpless?

A.—I have seen them thrown out on the street and on the sidewalk, and I have seen them put into little rooms without light, bedding, or food. There they were left to die.

Q.—What opportunities have these women to escape, if they should desire?

A.—I don't see that they have any at all, for where a woman escapes, a reward is offered and she is brought back. Where they can get her in no other way they use our Courts.

Q.—What proportion of the Chinese are law-breakers, and breakers of the ordinances of the city?

A.—I think nearly the whole Chinese population, from the biggest merchant down to the lowest thief. Several years ago I know that their head merchants were keepers of gambling-houses and houses of prostitution.

Q.—Have you ever seen a Christian Chinaman?

A.—I have seen those who have pretended to be such, but they will pretend to be anything, if it is of any advantage to them.

Q.—Do you know where the Globe Hotel is?

A.—I do.

Q.—How many people occupied that building before these raids were made?

A.—From eight hundred to one thousand people.

Q.—About how many white people would occupy a building of that kind?

A.—One hundred would fill it comfortably.

Q.—Do you know the building on Jackson Street leased to Chinamen by the Rev. Dr. Gibson?

A.—I do.

Q.—What is its condition?

A.—It is crowded with Chinamen.

Q.—How does it compare with the Globe Hotel for filth?

A.—Worse.

Q.—Have you been in the basements in that quarter?

A.—Yes; and in all these places, in all the rooms, you will find Chinese crowded together two and three tiers deep. In the Globe Hotel you can find them under the sidewalk, living in a horrible condition.

Q.—About what proportion of criminals in the County Jail are Chinese?

A.—One-fourth, and more than that sometimes.

Q.—What effect has the presence of this population on the morals of the community?

A.—Bad; especially upon the boys. I have noticed a great many boys—fifteen, sixteen, seventeen, and eighteen years of age—in the Chinese alleys, amongst Chinawomen. This is very readily accounted for, from the fact that Chinese women charge only two and four bits, and as a rule these boys have not much money. They, therefore, go where there is the least cost.

Ah Chung sworn.

Mr. Haymond—How long have you been in California?

A.—Five or six years.

Q.—How old are you?

A.—Eighteen.

Q.—What have you been doing in California?

A.—Cooking.

Q.—For white people?

A.—Yes.

Q.—Do you know how many Chinese prostitutes there are in San Francisco?

A.—I think about one thousand.

Q.—Who own them?

A.—Wong Woon, An Geo, Bi Chee, and Wong Fook Soi.

Q.—Where do they get them?

A.—They buy in China and bring here.

Q.—What do they give for them in China?

A.—About one hundred and fifty dollars.
Q.—What are they worth here?
A.—Some nine hundred and some eight hundred dollars.
Q.—Do they steal some of them in China?
A.—They buy them.
Q.—Do they buy and sell girls in China?
A.—Yes, sir.
Q.—Do you know how many gambling-houses there are in San Francisco?
A.—I think about two hundred.
Q.—What do the Chinamen do with anybody who testifies in Court against the women?
A.—An Geo, Wong Woon, and Ah Fook put up money to kill him.
Q.—Do you know whether any paper is ever put up offering money to kill Chinamen?
A.—Yes. I saw them.
Q.—Have they threatened to kill you if you testify?
A.—Yes. I am a little scared.
Q.—What are you afraid of?
A.—Afraid shoot me.
Q.—Do you know of anybody being killed?
A.—Yes.
Q.—What for?
A.—One boy he testify against women, and they kill him with a knife

Ah Gow sworn.
Mr. Haymond—Can you speak English?
A.—Yes, sir.
Q.—How long have you been in San Francisco?
A.—One year.
Q.—How long in California?
A.—Three years.
Q.—Where have you lived?
A.—At Half-moon Bay.
Q.—What did you work at?
A.—Making cigars.
Q.—For white people?
A.—No; for a Chinaman—Ah Wah.
Q.—To what company do you belong?
A.—Ning-yeung.
Q.—Do you know anything about threats made against Chinamen for testifying in the American Courts?
A.—An Geo, Bi Chee, and Wong Woon say they shoot me.
Q.—What for?
A.—They say I pick out prostitutes in Court.
Q.—Are you a witness now?
A.—Yes, sir.
Q.—Do they threaten to shoot you if you tell the truth?
A.—Yes, sir.
Q.—Do you know anything about notices being posted up offering rewards for killing men?
A.—Yes. I have seen them.
Q.—What were you put in jail for lately?

A.—George Duffield said I bothered the women and the gamblers by coming into Court against them.

Q.—Do you know how much money the Chinese pay these officers?

A.—The gamblers, five dollars a week; each woman, four bits; lotteries, eight dollars a month.

Q.—What do the people who own women do, when they become sick and helpless?

A.—I suppose they take care of them.

Q.—When they are sick and going to die, do they put them on the street?

A.—Sometimes.

Q.—Do these people who own women whip them?

A.—The boss women whip them all the time.

Q.—Do you live in the Chinese quarter?

A.—Yes, sir.

Q.—Are you afraid?

A.—Sometimes. I do not go out at night, but stay in the house and lock my door.

H. H. Ellis sworn.

Mr. Haymond—What is your occupation?

A.—I am Chief of Police of the City and County of San Francisco.

Q.—How long have you resided here?

A.—Since June, eighteen hundred and forty-nine.

Q.—What has been your occupation?

A.—I have been attached to the police department for upwards of twenty years.

Q.—Are you acquainted with the Chinese quarters of this city?

A.—Yes, sir.

Q.—What is their condition in relation to cleanliness?

A.—Very foul and filthy.

Q.—Do you know of any quarter of any American or European city that will compare with it for filth?

A.—No, sir.

Q.—It is in testimony that there are about thirty thousand Chinese living in this city, the most of them residing in seven or eight blocks. Do you know what proportion of that population is criminal?

A.—I should say that there are about one thousand five hundred or two thousand regular criminals.

Q.—Including those who violate the city ordinances in relation to fires and health, and those who live off the wages of the criminal classes, what is the proportion?

A.—I think almost the entire population.

Q.—Excluding from consideration the Chinese quarter, how are the laws and ordinances enforced in this city, as compared with other American cities?

A.—Favorably. The number of arrests are greater in proportion to each man employed. I have here a table of the arrests made in twenty cities of the United States. They range from eight to one hundred and seven per man, and this latter number is credited to San Francisco. Outside of the Chinese quarter, the laws are administered admirably, although we have a very small force of men. The force of officers in the twenty cities referred to ranges from one to each two hundred and fifty-eight inhabitants to one in one thousand four hundred and forty-five; Nashville having the most officers per capita, and San Francisco the least.

Q.—What are the difficulties in the way of enforcing laws in cases where the Chinese are concerned?

A.—The Chinese will swear to anything, according to orders. Their testimony is so unreliable that they cannot be believed.

Q.—What is the greatest difficulty in the way of suppressing prostitution and gambling?

A.—To suppress these vices would require a police force so great that the city could not stand the expense. It is difficult to administer justice, because we do not understand their language, and thus all combine to defeat the laws.

Q.—What is their custom of settling cases among themselves, and then refusing to furnish testimony?

A.—It is generally believed to be true that the Chinese have a Court of arbitration where they settle differences.

Q.—After this settlement is made, is it possible to obtain testimony from the Chinese?

A.—If in secret they determine to convict a Chinaman, or to acquit him, that judgment is carried out. In a great many cases I believe they have convicted innocent men through perjured evidence.

Q.—Do you know anything about offers of rewards being posted up in this city for the murder of Chinamen?

A.—Yes, sir. I have had such notices taken down and interpreted.

Q.—What influence does the presence of the Chinese have upon the morals of the white race?

A.—Very injurious.

Q.—In what respect?

A.—I regard the prostitution question as the worst feature of it, for great numbers of young men visit Chinawomen.

Q.—Are those women held as slaves?

A.—Yes, sir; they are held under a sort of contract, but they very seldom work it out.

Q.—Is it difficult for those women to escape from that life?

A.—Yes, sir. When they do escape they are brought back by force, or arrested for some alleged offense.

Q.—Do you know any Christian Chinamen?

A.—I know some Chinamen who profess to be Christians.

Q.—How many have you known in twenty years?

A.—Not more than half a dozen altogether, and I have not any faith in their sincerity.

Q.—Why not?

A.—Because I think it is done from interested motives entirely.

Q.—Then there has been no success at all connected with missionary labors in that field?

A.—Not so far as my observation goes here and elsewhere. In Australia, China, Peru, and other places, missionaries have not succeeded in christianizing Chinese to any extent.

Q.—Does their presence in this country tend to the advancement of Christian civilization?

A.—It has the contrary effect.

Q.—In what estimation is Chinese testimony held here by men acquainted with the administration of justice?

A.—They look upon their testimony with great suspicion. As a class their testimony is unreliable.

Q.—Is it not frequently the case that on preliminary examinations they swear to one state of facts, and on the trial directly the opposite?

A.—Yes, sir.

Q.—Do you know anything about money being collected for the purpose of paying men around here to see that they were not molested in their criminal pursuits?

A.—I have heard rumors of such things, but have never known anything definitely.

Q.—What is the condition of the Chinese quarter generally?

A.—Filthy beyond description.

NINTH DAY.

San Francisco, April 21st, 1876.

David C. Woods sworn.

Mr. Haymond—How long have you resided in this State?

A.—Twenty-five years, off and on.

Q.—What position do you hold?

A.—Superintendent of the Industrial School.

Q.—How long have you occupied that position?

A.—Two years and three months.

Q.—Do you know anything about the effect the presence of a large Chinese population has upon the boys that are growing up here?

A.—I think it has a very bad effect. I find that the larger proportion of boys who come to the school, large enough to cohabit with women, are afflicted with venereal diseases.

Q.—How many boys are usually in that school?

A.—One hundred and eighty, on an average.

Q.—What proportion do you think are affected with that disease?

A.—I think that, during the time I have been there, fifty have come with venereal diseases.

Q.—Do you attribute that to the presence of Chinese prostitutes in this city?

A.—They tell me so themselves. I question them, and they say they got it in Chinatown?

Q.—What are the ages of those boys?

A.—We have had them as young as thirteen, with gonorrhœa; they have all sorts of venereal diseases. There is no time that I have had less than two or four down with them.

Mr. Donovan—How many boys have entered that institution since you have been there?

A.—Two hundred and fifty or three hundred, I think.

Q.—And fifty of them have been afflicted with disease?

A.—At least that number; some come there with it very apparent. It develops in others after they have been there a few days. Some are so badly diseased that it is impossible to cure them.

Q.—Do you have physicians?

A.—Yes, sir; I also doctor some of them myself. I am an old sea captain, and understand those diseases pretty well, because they are very prevalent among sailors.

The following resolution was adopted by the committee:

Resolved, That H. H. Ellis, Chief of Police of the City and County of San Francisco, be and is hereby requested to detail a competent officer to collect statistics as to the number of Chinese employed in the various avocations in San Francisco.

HONG CHUNG sworn.
Mr. Donovan—How long have you been in this country?
A.—Twenty-four years.
Q.—Are you in business here?
A.—I am Inspector for the Sam-yup Company.
Q.—Have you declared your intention of becoming an American citizen?
A.—Yes, sir.
Q.—Have you got your first papers?
A.—Yes, sir; last December.
Q.—Are many other Chinamen going to become citizens?
A.—Yes, sir.
Q.—A great many?
A.—Yes, sir.
Q.—Will all become American citizens?
A.—Yes, sir.
Q.—And stay here?
A.—Yes, sir.
Q.—Will they become candidates for the office of Governor of the State as soon as they are citizens?
A.—May be; I don't know. They are going to become citizens. I like to be citizen. American man make no good laws for Chinaman. We make good laws for Chinaman citizens.
Q.—Would you like to be Governor of the State of California?
A.—Of course. I like the State of California a long time; I like a free country.
Q.—Would you like to be Governor?
A.—I cannot be Governor. I like the State of California, and like to be a citizen of the American man's people.
Q.—Would you like to hold office under the free American Government?
A.—No, I wouldn't do it.

Committee adjourned to meet in the State Capitol building, at Sacramento.

TENTH DAY.

SACRAMENTO, May 2d, 1876.

Committee met in Sacramento, in the State Capitol building, at two o'clock, pursuant to adjournment. Mr. Haymond in the chair.

CHARLES P. O'NEIL sworn.
Mr. Haymond—How long have you resided in California?
A.—Twenty-seven years.
Q.—How long have you resided in Sacramento City?
A.—Twenty years.

Q.—How long have you been on the police force here?
A.—Twenty years.
Q.—What has been your duty; have you been a special or a regular?
A.—For the last fourteen years I have been a special and a Deputy Sheriff.
Q.—In what part of the city?
A.—Principally on I Street, in the Chinese quarter.
Q.—What part of the city do the Chinese quarters take up?
A.—On I Street, from Sixth to Second.
Q.—What is the condition of the streets in that part of the city, in regard to cleanliness, as compared with other portions of the city?
A.—It is very good, for the Health Officer makes them keep the streets clean.
Q.—About how many Chinese do you suppose there are in the city?
A.—In and about the city I suppose there are about two thousand.
Q.—What employments do they follow—that is, the major portion?
A.—Those outside the city, gardening, working in the sugar mill, woolen mill, bucket factory, working around the flour mills, and working out as servants.
Q.—Are there any Chinese women here?
A.—Yes, sir; there are a couple of hundred, the most of them being prostitutes.
Q.—How many Chinese families are there in this city—men with their wives and children?
A.—There are not a great many. It is a very unusual thing for Chinamen to bring their families here from China, so much so that I never even heard of such a case. In conversation with me, they always speak as if opposed to such a thing.
Q.—Do you know how these women are held—whether they are owned by anybody, or whether anybody claims to own them?
A.—Only from hearsay. I have heard them (the Chinamen) frequently say that they bought them. On one occasion I was called into a Chinese house, and there saw four hundred and fifty dollars pass between a woman and a man. They wanted me to be a witness to the fact, and I witnessed it. Some time afterwards the woman told me that her boss had sold her for four hundred and fifty dollars. That was the contract I witnessed, but it being in Chinese I did not understand it at the time. The woman soon after committed suicide. She did not like this man to whom she had been sold, and committed suicide by drowning. From my experience as an officer, I know that these women are kept under close surveillance.
Q.—Is it possible for them to escape, or is there any reasonable probability that any of them could escape from that servitude?
A.—No; not without they are protected by the white people. I have known them to attempt to escape, and have known them to have been sent for and brought back. To do this they use different means, principally money. They use, also, the machinery of the American Courts to enforce these contracts, it being customary to have these women arrested for larceny or some crime, in order to get the more secure possession of them. In the prevention of this thing the principal difficulty lies in the fact that we don't understand their language. We do not know what they are getting at, and they will tell such well concocted stories that it is almost impossible to get at

the truth as we can with white persons. A Chinaman has a right to go before a magistrate and make out that a crime has been committed by a person, and a magistrate, having no means of ascertaining the truth, must issue his warrant.

Q.—As a people, what is the rule as to the reliability to be placed upon their oaths?

A.—It depends a great deal on circumstances. They will protect one another in a great measure. There are some of the Chinese merchants that are very good people, but then there are a great many others that they can use for almost any purpose that they want.

Q.—Do you know anything about any organizations existing among the Chinese for the protection of their members against the laws of this country, or for the enforcement of their own laws independent of the action of the authorities?

A.—The only thing I know about that is this: A case was tried in the County Court, a short time ago, where some parties were convicted of robbery. One of the members of the Chinese Wash-house Association violated some rule, and they forced him to pay sixty dollars. The parties were arrested and convicted, and I believe that the case is now before the Supreme Court.

Q.—It was in some proceeding of a Chinese tribunal that it was adjudged that he should pay sixty dollars?

A.—Yes, sir; and they enforced that judgment, and took the sixty dollars, with the aid of a pistol. Mr. Fratt was very active in his prosecution of the offenders, and in his protection of this Chinaman. The difficulties in the way of administration of justice are our ignorance of their language, and because they band together to defeat that administration. I have not known of cases where Chinese witnesses swore to one thing at the preliminary examination, and another at the trial; but I have known them to go away. I have hear them say they settled the matter all up, and when the case came on there were no witnesses.

Q.—Is it done in crimes of any magnitude, as murder and burglary?

A.—Yes, sir; almost anything can be settled.

Q.—How many Chinese houses of prostitution are there here?

A.—Twenty-five or thirty.

Q.—How many Chinese are there in Sacramento?

A.—About two thousand.

Q.—What is the white population?

A.—About twenty-two thousand.

Q.—Do you know anything about young men and boys frequenting these houses of prostitution?

A.—Young men and boys formerly frequented these houses of prostitution, but it has been done very little of late, because of the watchfulness of the officers on duty. I used to have a great deal of trouble every week whaling boys off from I Street. The Chinese, of course, encouraged their visits, and I did all I could to stop them. These houses are now only partly open. The last Grand Jury rather closed up gambling and houses of prostitution, as a general thing.

Q.—Do you think that it would be possible for the Chief of Police of this city, or the police authorities, to suppress those houses entirely?

A.—Yes, sir; by arresting the people as fast as they would open them. It would be hard, perhaps impossible, to obtain any convictions, but that proceeding would, I think, stop it.

Q.—Do you know how these women are treated by the persons who own them?

A.—It looks to me like they were very closely confined in the houses. I have known the masters and mistresses to whip the women, but I have never heard of it a second time where I have gone and cautioned them. When they become sick and helpless, they turn them out to die. I have known two cases where they have put them in empty houses and left them there to die. In one case I took the woman and had her conveyed to the hospital, where she died. I found her in a high fever, alone, in an unfurnished room. She was sitting in a corner, moaning. I found the party who hired the room and the party who put her there. I went for him, but he "got up and dusted." I haven't seen him since. The Chinese have some superstition in regard to persons dying in their houses, and that will probably account for the manner of treatment. They believe that to let one die in the house brings bad luck.

Q.—Do you know anything about any Chinese gambling-houses?

A.—Yes, sir; there are Chinese gambling-houses around there.

Q.—How many?

A.—There are none just now, for they have been closed up; but there used to be all the way from four to sixteen or seventeen. About three persons were engaged in each house, or forty or fifty engaged directly in the gambling business.

Q.—What proportion of the Chinese on I Street do you suppose belong to the criminal classes; that is, engaged in prostitution, living off the fruits of prostitution, gambling, living off the fruits of gambling, petty larcenies, etc.?

A.—On I Street there are from one hundred and fifty to two hundred of what we call "highbinders," living off the houses of prostitution, and they are mixed up with the gamblers. You might call them hoodlums. They band together and make raids on the gambling-houses and on the women, and make them give them money. They live in that way; always ready for a fight at any moment among themselves, and against anybody that may oppose them. They go together in gangs, and will number about two hundred. With the women, this criminal class will number at least four hundred, or one-fifth of the entire Chinese population of the city. The petty thieves, shop-lifters, etc., range with these highbinders, and go along picking articles from doorways, etc. On J Street one will probably go inside to buy something, when a confederate or two will walk off with a pair of pants or boots, or anything that can be carried off.

Q.—From your experience, as an officer, what effect do you think that population has upon the morals of this city?

A.—I don't think it has much effect upon the morals of this city.

Q.—Why?

A.—There are not enough of them.

Q.—Do you know anything about any of the men being held in servitude, or under labor contracts?

A.—No, sir.

Q.—Do you know anything about any boys being diseased because of the Chinese women?

A.—Not for the last two or three years. During this time the officers and myself have been vigilant, and generally have driven these boys off the street when they came there. The Chinawomen have the reputation of being diseased as a general thing, but of this I have no personal knowledge.

Q.—Do you know of any cases of leprosy in this city?

A.—There is one knocking around town somewhere—a man. I haven't seen him lately; he was around Fifth Street. There was another here but he died, and this old fellow came here, I think, from Stockton. There are some Chinese in our hospital, but I do not know how many.

Q.—Have they any respect for our oath?

A.—None, sir. From my judgment, after twenty years' experience as an officer, I can say that they will swear whichever way their interests run; or will swear for any pecuniary gain—that is, the most of them. Of course there are some who are honest and straightforward, but they are exceptions. As a population, the Chinese are largely criminal, when we consider perjury in the list. They are ready to do anything for their own interest and immediate advancement.

Q.—Through the exertions of yourself and some other officers you prevented boys from going to these quarters?

A.—Yes, sir.

Q.—Were these women always ready and willing to solicit these boys to enter their houses?

A.—Yes, sir; whenever they would come along.

Q.—Stop at the window and knock for little boys passing?

A.—Stand at the door or window, and say, "Come in; come in." I never saw small boys there; never any boys less than thirteen or fourteen years old.

Q.—Don't you think boys of that age too small for that offense?

A.—Not in California. They might be back East. I have found such boys in these houses and driven them out. I have also known cases where young girls, dressed up as boys, went to these places—out of curiosity, perhaps.

Q.—Do you know any Christian Chinamen?

A.—I knew one.

Q.—How long since?

A.—Several years ago, in San Francisco.

Q.—Have you ever known of any Christians here?

A.—No, sir; nor do I believe that there ever was one made in California.

Q.—Do you know of any Chinese mission here?

A.—Oh, yes.

Q.—Who runs that mission—white people?

A.—Yes, sir; a great many young ladies go there to instruct the Chinese. They instruct men only—men and boys.

Q.—Do these young ladies ever attempt to teach the women anything?

A.—No, sir. Go to the churches every Sunday evening and you can see them teaching the Chinamen.

Q.—What are they teaching them?

A.—The Bible and all those good things.

Q.—What effect does that teaching have on them?

A.—It makes confirmed scoundrels of them.

Q.—Do you know anything about any opium dens?

A.—Most of their houses are so. They have places to smoke opium in almost every house. There are three or four places were white women went to smoke, but I have not seen any of them since last fall.

Q.—How are the Chinese, as a race, given to the vice of opium smoking?

A.—About as much as American people to taking their regular "tod."

Q.—You say that this christianity they are taught makes confirmed scoundrels of them?

A.—There are very few Chinamen I have seen—of course there are some exceptions—that become "Christians," and learn to talk good English, who do not become rascals. They go to these schools solely to learn English. I have heard Chinamen frequently say that they went to these places simply to "catchee English." I have asked them why they went, and that is the reason they have always given me. They laugh at the idea of being converted to christianity. On one Sunday there was a Chinese missionary down on I Street, singing hymns, and directly opposite the Chinese were having their religious festival, commonly called "driving the devil out." There was an old Chinaman there, Billy Holung, who has been around here for twenty years, and turning to him I asked what the Christian performance was. He said it was a Christian church. I asked him what he was talking about, and he said: "He is talking about Jesus Christ; he is damn fool—he never see Jesus Christ." There is a mission here, too. I do not know how many members it has. There are Chinamen who claim to be converted, who preach every Sunday on Third and I Streets. There are about fifteen or twenty of them, I think. A Chinaman leads it. I have not seen a white man there more than once since they went there. I do not believe in Chinese religious sincerity, so far as christianity is concerned.

Q.—Do the Chinese come here to stay?

A.—No, sir.

Q.—How long do they remain?

A.—They stay until they gather so much money, and then they leave for China. There are some here who have made two, three, and four trips to their own country.

Q.—What is considered a fortune among the Chinese?

A.—Between two hundred dollars and three hundred dollars is considered a pretty good stake by the working classes.

Q.—Are they satisfied to go back when they get that?

A.—Yes.

Q.—What do the Chinese do around here?

A.—They lease grounds and raise garden produce, principally for San Francisco. They work in the beet sugar factory, in the woolen mills, and in the flour mills. They also work as servants and farm hands.

Q.—Do you know of any who are making shirts or doing sewing?

A.—I don't think there are over two or three places here where they do that kind of work. Nearly all of it is done in San Francisco.

Q.—What are they doing at the sugar factory?

A.—They are raising beet and making sugar. The company employs them so it can compete with Eastern white labor.

Q.—Do you know anything about one portion of the Chinese supporting another?

A.—That is done in this way: Servants working out are obliged to support those out of employment. Six or seven of them live in a room together, and to support those doing nothing those working in families are compelled to take grub from the houses.

Q.—Do they steal it?
A.—Yes, sir.

Ah Dan sworn.
Mr. Haymond—How long have you been in California?
A.—Almost ten years.
Q.—From what part of China did you come?
A.—Back of Canton.
Q.—How old are you now?
A.—I believe I am twenty-eight.
Q.—What have you been doing since you came to California?
A.—Cooking in kitchens and working in restaurants.
Q.—Have you been living with Americans most of the time?
A.—Yes, sir.
Q.—Have you ever been interpreter in the Police Court?
A.—Yes, sir.
Q.—Have you any fears about testifying here and telling all you know? Are you afraid?
A.—I ain't much afraid. I came up here to swear, and I must tell all I know.
Q.—Have ever any threats been made against you for testifying in the Police Court, or for interpreting truly?
A.—Yes, sir; I am afraid because Chinamen got too much to gas about. Because one got convicted he think it all a put up job by me. In Sacramento City two interpreters killed.
Q.—Do you know how Chinamen who come to California come here?
A.—Yes. Some come themselves, paying their own fare out of money they have earned working out; when they have no money they borrow it, agreeing to pay a good rate of interest. Sometimes, where a man is honest, no security is required; but where he is not good the lender takes a mortgage on whatever property he may have.
Q.—How do the women come here?
A.—Sometimes they come here, when little young girls, and sometimes they come here for husbands.
Q.—Do you know whether any of them are stolen and brought here?
A.—Some are.
Q.—Do you know whether any are bought in China and brought here?
A.—I guess there are some. I don't know that they are owned here by Chinamen; but some men tell me they own women.
Q.—Do they buy and sell these women here?
A.—Yes; I believe that.
Q.—How much does a woman sell for here?
A.—Sometimes four hundred or five hundred dollars; sometimes more, sometimes less.
Q.—You never sold any?
A.—No, sir.
Q.—What do they do with these women when they are sick and are going to die?
A.—When these women get sick and unable to work and make more money, if they have friends, they are cared for; if they have no friends, nobody looks after them. Sometimes a woman gets and lives with one man; but if they can, the owners bring her back. If they can't get her back any other way, they sometimes kidnap her.

Q.—Do you know the six companies?

A.—Yes, sir; I guess so. They are to take care of Chinamen belonging to their own company. They have nothing to do with the women. They deal only with men. They charge Chinamen so much, so as to buy building, just like Capitol, maybe, which the company owns. When Chinaman gets into trouble, he gets taken care of; when he wants to go from one city to another, the company furnishes money, and he pays it back again. Suppose he don't pay it right away, he pays it after a while. If he don't pay, they never kill him. I have never heard anything of the kind. If a young man, able to work, wants to go to China, he must first pay his debts; but if he is old and poor, and can't pay up, they let him go home. Each Chinaman pays the company ten dollars. This money is used to buy a house and pay expenses, same as white people buy a State Capitol. In case a Chinaman is injured by another Chinaman, his company tries to enforce the American law for the punishment of the offender.

Q.—You say there were two interpreters killed in Sacramento?

A.—Yes, sir; one was Ah Quong, and one Ah Gow.

Q.—How long ago?

A.—I wasn't in California the first one; Ah Quong, two years ago.

Q.—What was he killed for?

A.—Because he interpreted in Court. Chinamen thought he ought to have American man get Chinaman clear. They thought he had power to do it; but he couldn't do it, and they killed him.

Q.—If you are interpreting in Court, and you don't get a man clear, will they kill you?

A.—No, sir; I am not afraid when I do what is right.

Q.—Have they threatened to kill you if you did not get Chinamen clear?

A.—No; not yet. Sometimes they get talking on the street about gambling-houses on I Street, and Chinamen blame me for stopping them.

Q.—What do they threaten to do—threaten to kill you?

A.—Talking about killing me.

Q.—Do you know District Attorney Jones?

A.—Yes, sir.

Q.—Did you tell him last week that some of them threatened to kill you?

A.—Yes, sir; some of them. A man came to me a few days ago and told me they were going to kill a Police Court interpreter, advising me to leave the city, because he said somebody would come and kill me; some men had put up rewards, and some men whom I did not know were coming from San Francisco to kill me. I was before the Grand Jury and explained the game of "tan," and for this they put up the reward, and I am to be killed by three men from San Francisco I don't know. The reward offered for my life is five or six hundred dollars. I have heard of rewards of this kind being put up here and elsewhere. I have not seen any here, but have in San Francisco. They are in Chinese, and posted up, saying that these men will make agreement, if some man kill another, to pay the murderer so much money. These agreements for murder are red papers written in Chinese, and say they will give so much money on condition you kill so-and-so, naming the person. If the murderer is arrested, they will get good counsel to defend him. If he is sent to prison, they will pay him so much money to recompense him, and if he is hung they will send so much money to his relatives in China.

Q.—Did you go to officer Jackson and ask him not to subpœna you, if he could help it, in the Hung Hi case?

A.—Yes. I said to him, "I don't know about the case. If you put me on the stand, and it don't go as they want it, they will blame me."

Q.—Didn't you tell him you were afraid they would kill you?

A.—I did tell him so.

Q.—You were afraid?

A.—Yes, sir. I told Charley O'Neil some put up money to kill me. He told me not to fear—to keep a look out for myself. In case I testify here to all I know, I'm afraid they will kill me.

Charles T. Jones sworn.

Mr. Haymond—How long have you been District Attorney of this county?

A.—A little over two years.

Q.—Do you have any difficulty in administering justice, where Chinese are parties?

A.—During my term of office I have had considerable to do with Chinese criminals, and always have great difficulty in convicting them of any crime. I remember well the case of Ah Quong, spoken of a few moments ago by Ah Dan. At the time I was defending three parties charged with kidnaping, and I had Ah Quong as interpreter, knowing him to be honest and capable. The circumstances of the case were these: A Chinaman wanted to marry a woman then in a house of prostitution. She desired to marry him, and he went with two of his friends to the house. She went with them. They drove out of town to get married, when the Chinamen who owned her heard of it, and started some officers after her. She was arrested and surrendered to these Chinamen, with instructions to bring her into Court next day. I had this man to interpret for me, being well satisfied that she would swear that she was not being kidnaped. The next day the owners brought into Court a woman whom the defendants informed me was not the one at all, but another. The attorneys for the other side insisted that it was, believing the statements of their Chinamen to that effect. The case was postponed for two or three days, when it was shown that the woman offered was not the one taken away. This interpreter told me they would kill him as sure as these defendants were not convicted. We went out of the Court-room, and he told me he was afraid to go on I Street. I told him he hadn't better go then, but I did not think they would trouble him. Half an hour afterwards he was brought back, shot in the back, and a hatchet having been used on him, mutilating him terribly. This was in broad daylight, about eleven o'clock in the morning, on Third and I Streets, one of the most public places in the City of Sacramento. There were hundreds of Chinese around there at the time, but it was difficult, in the prosecution of the case, to get any Chinese testimony at all. It happened that there were a few white men passing at the time, and we were enabled to identify two men, and they were convicted and sent to the State Prison for life, after three trials. They attempted to prove an alibi, and after swearing a large lot of Chinamen they said they had twenty more. The Chinese use the Courts to gain possession of women. Sometimes it happens that where a man is married to a woman, they get out a warrant for his arrest, and before he can get bail they have stolen the woman, and carried her off to some distant place. I have had Chinamen come to me to find out how many witnesses I had in cases. If they found out, they would get sufficient testimony to override me. Before I was District Attorney I have had Chinese come to me to defend them, and ask me how many witnesses I wanted, and what was necessary to prove in order to acquit.

Q.—Do you often find that upon preliminary examinations and before the Grand Jury there is enough testimony to warrant a conviction, but on the trial these same witnesses swear to an exactly opposite state of facts?

A.—Very frequently.

Q.—To what do you attribute that?

A.—I attribute that to the fact that they had tried the case in Chinese Courts, where it had been finally settled. I have records in my office of a Chinese tribunal of that kind, where they tried offenders according to their own rules, meted out what punishment they deemed proper, etc. These records were captured in a room on I Street, between Fourth and Fifth. There was a Chinaman here who opened a wash-house on Second Street, underneath the Orleans Hotel. It appears that he was a member of the Chinese Wash-house Association, and that they had a rule that no wash-house should be opened within ten doors of one already opened. This new house was opened within the prescribed limits, and the association held a meeting. One of the charges was that he was in partnership with a white man—a foreigner, their rules forbidding any such arrangement, and they fined him, I think, thirty dollars. The Chinaman went to Mr. Fratt, who told him he would protect him. Then they held another meeting, and, as was proved on the trial of these cases, they determined that he should pay one hundred and ten dollars, or they would kill him. They sent out three of their number, and they met him on Third, between I and J. One had a knife, another a pistol, and the other one made a demand, telling him that if he did not pay one hundred and ten dollars they would kill him immediately. He had sixty dollars in his pocket, and he gave them that. He went and told Mr. Fratt, and these three men were arrested for robbery. The society held another meeting, and the whole meeting was arrested as conspirators, these records being captured. I had them translated by an interpreter from San Francisco, and used them on the trial of the robbery cases. The records recite that the members enter into a solemn compact not to enter into partnership with a foreigner; that this man did so, and the company offers so many round dollars to the man who will kill him. They promise to furnish a man to assist the murderer, and they promise, if he is arrested, they will employ able counsel to defend him. If convicted, he should receive, I think, three dollars for every day he would be confined, and in case he died, certain money would be sent to his relatives. These records appeared in evidence and were admitted; also, a poster that was taken from a house, offering a reward for the killing of this man. This poster was placed on a house in a public street. Being written in Chinese, of course they alone knew its contents, and informed us of them. I have frequently had Chinese come to me with offers of pecuniary reward if I would let off some Chinese criminal. They generally come alone, but never broach the subject in the presence of white men. This man, Ah Bean, who keeps a store on the corner of Fifth and I Streets, has done that. When he returned from China the first thing he did, on seeing me, was to say: "Charley, you District Attorney now and I am very glad. We will make a heap of money. There is heap Chinese here. Some pay out too much to lawyers. Now, whenever a Chinese case happens you fix it up; Chinamen pay you so much money; you take half, I take half." They don't seem to understand that that involves moral turpitude. Being as careful as they are to have no white witnesses around when they make their offers, of course I could not convict them of bribery. This Ah Bean is a specimen Chinamen, and would attract your attention immediately. He pretends to be higher than the rest of the Chinese here and holds himself as much better than the balance.

Q.—Can you rely upon the oaths of Chinamen?

A.—No, sir; not at all, whenever their interests are in the least concerned. They will swear whichever way they may deem most advantageous, irrespective of truth, justice, or honesty.

Q.—Have you ever known a Christian Chinaman?

A.—I have known Chinamen who pretend to be Christians, and I have heard them preach and pray. I think this Chinese christianity is all a mere pretense. I would not trust a Christian Chinaman any quicker than I would any other, but I would be a little more suspicious in that case, because they become sharper.

Q.—Why do they go to the Christian Sunday-schools?

A.—They go to learn English. I have had Chinamen, who pretended to be very devout Christians, tell me that the only reason they went to Sunday-school and church was to learn English without any expense to themselves.

Q.—Suppose a Chinaman should assist the officers in bringing Chinese criminals to justice—would that be a dangerous thing for him?

A.—I think it would. I am satisfied that they have their own tribunals, where they try all these cases.

Q.—What chance have these women, who are held in prostitution, to escape?

A.—They have a very small chance.

Q.—In case of escape, do they ever resort to the Courts, in order to regain possession of the women?

A.—Yes, sir.

Q.—Do you think the presence of Chinese in California tends to the advancement of Christian civilization?

A.—I do not.

Q.—About what proportion of the Chinese here belong to the criminal classes?

A.—A large portion do, while I believe that every Chinaman will steal when he gets a chance. I believe the Chinese merchants here, in a manner, control the petty thieves, receive their stolen goods, and get them out of trouble when arrested.

Q.—Do you think it possible to entirely break up these houses of prostitution and gambling in this city?

A.—It would be very difficult. The Chinese resort to perjury in all cases, and many white men find it impossible to identify Chinamen.

The Committee adjourned until ten o'clock to-morrow.

ELEVENTH DAY.

SACRAMENTO, May 3d, 1876.

JAMES DUFFY sworn.

Mr. Haymond—How long have you resided in the City of Sacramento?

A.—Since eighteen hundred and fifty-two.

Q.—Do you know anything about the Chinese quarter?

A.—Yes, sir.

Q.—Do you know anything about the condition of their houses, as to cleanliness?

A.—They are horribly dirty. I have never been in a Chinese house yet that wasn't more like a water-closet than a house.

Q.—You are an expressman?

A.—Yes, sir.

Q.—How are the streets kept?

A.—I Street is very dirty. They throw a great many slops into the street and into the back yards, and between them all there is a terrible mess.

Q.—Do they live as white people do?

A.—No, sir. You and your wife could not live where thirty of them live.

Q.—Do you know anything of boys visiting houses of prostitution?

A.—I have seen small boys visit their houses of prostitution. In one instance I saw a woman entice a boy of about eleven years of age into her house. I got a policeman, George Harvey, and had both parties arrested. The woman, I think, deposited ten dollars for her appearance, but forfeited it next morning.

Mr. Donovan—Do you know of white people being discharged to give place to Chinamen?

A.—I have heard white ladies say so. They said they would prefer white help, if they would work for the same price as Chinamen.

Q.—Do you know of any boys being diseased by having visited the Chinese quarter?

A.—No more than I have heard.

Q.—What is the common report?

A.—That no one goes there except he gets diseased.

Q.—What is the common report as to truth-telling among the Chinese?

A.—A Chinaman will tell a lie for ten cents, and swear to it.

Q.—What is their character for honesty—are they generally considered honest, or thieves?

A.—There might be one in the city perhaps that would not steal, but you would have to look pretty hard to find him. I don't think there is a Chinaman in this city that would not steal. They are all thieves, liars, and perjurers.

Mr. Haymond—Why can they afford to do work cheaper than white men?

A.—They can work cheaper than the white man, because they have no families to support, and therefore live much cheaper. Their living does not cost them over fifteen cents per day. Take a laboring man here who has a wife and two children dependent upon him, and his expenses at the very least are two dollars and fifty cents a day, and he must live very economically to make that amount do. Where a white laboring man has no family, his necessary expenses will be from one dollar and seventy-five cents to two dollars a day. He can board for twenty dollars a month, and his washing, clothing, etc., will make up the balance. Most of the Chinese here wear clothes of Chinese manufacture, consume goods imported from China, and all their dealings are against the American interests. Where they do not board themselves, they can be accommodated—boarded and lodged—at houses in Chinatown for one dollar and fifty cents a week, and less.

Q.—When Chinese become hopelessly sick, what do they do with them?

A.—I know of cases where women, hopelessly sick, have been turned out to die of disease or starvation, or both. I have been with undertakers after the bodies of such persons. One we found alone in a wash-house, dead. There was no furniture in the room, and nothing for the sick woman to subsist upon. When a Chinaman dies, you can hardly get another Chinaman to touch the body, or even the coffin containing it; and it is often a difficult job to get any help from them at their funerals.

JAMES COFFEY sworn.

Mr. Haymond—How long have you lived in California?

A.—Twenty-one years.

Q.—What have you been engaged in during that time?

A.—Driving stage most of the time. For the last two years I have been on the police force in Sacramento.

Q.—In what part of the State were you driving stage?

A.—All over.

Q.—In the mining section?

A.—Yes, sir.

Q.—Where they employed Chinese?

A.—A few.

Q.—What was the condition of the Chinese quarters in the various mining towns?

A.—Very poor.

Q.—How do they live?

A.—Most generally in tents, in those days.

Q.—In communities by themselves?

A.—Yes, sir.

Q.—Since you have been on the police force here, have you had occasion to visit the Chinese quarters?

A.—Very often.

Q.—In what condition are their houses, and how do they live?

A.—They are in very poor condition, and the Chinamen live more like hogs than men. A great many are living in basements below the streets, except a few women who live on the first floors.

Q.—Do you know anything about young boys visiting Chinese houses of prostitution?

A.—I have seen several.

Q.—Of what ages?

A.—Twelve, fourteen, and sixteen years old.

Q.—Do you know whether any of them have been diseased?

A.—I do not.

Q.—Do you know whether these women are owned or not?

A.—They are bought and sold just like we buy and sell cattle. The merchants here, who claim to be connected with the six companies, also claim ownership of these Chinese women.

Q.—Do you know what they do with these women when they become sick and helpless?

A.—Some are taken care of, and some are placed in rooms by themselves to die. Then hardly anybody goes to see them. They are turned out to die. I have known two cases of that kind in Chinatown during the last year—one man and one woman.

Q.—Have these women any chance to escape from this servitude?

A.—It is very hard for them to escape. There is somebody on the alert at all hours of the day and night. When they do escape, the laws of this country are used to reclaim them, in many instances. Sometimes they are arrested for trumped up crimes, and sometimes taken back by force.

Q.—What is your experience as to the reliability of Chinese testimony in Court?

A.—It is not to be relied upon at all.

Q.—Do the police have much difficulty in ferreting out crime where the Chinese are interested?

A.—Yes, sir. We do not understand their language, and it is impossible to get interpreters whom we can trust.

Q.—Have you ever seen any Christian Chinamen?

A.—I have never seen a really Christian Chinaman, nor do I believe that there is a single Chinaman who believes in the Christian religion. I don't think there is one in existence. I have seen Chinamen at Sunday-schools singing, and they say they go to learn the American style of religion. I have had a good deal of business with Christian Chinamen, and from my experience I have learned to watch them more closely than I do the unregenerated. I have found them meaner and more unprincipled than the ordinary Chinese?

Q.—Has this Chinese population a good effect upon the city, or a bad one?

A.—Bad, I think. I cannot see any good that can come from it.

Matt. Karcher sworn.

Mr. Haymond—How long have you lived in the City of Sacramento?

A.—Twenty-five years.

Q.—What has been your occupation during that time?

A.—I kept a bakery for about fourteen years, and was connected with the police force for eleven years. During four years I was Chief of Police here.

Q.—Do you know that part of the city known as the Chinese quarter?

A.—I do.

Q.—How do they live, and what is their condition as to cleanliness?

A.—They live in small rooms, filthy, as a general thing—so much so that several times, when going in them, I have had to come out and vomit. They are as filthy as can be.

Q.—Is there any difficulty in enforcing the laws of the State, where the Chinese are parties?

A.—There is a great deal—caused, first, by our not being acquainted with their language, and in the second place, the Chinese, as a general thing, will swear to anything. I have never yet come across one that would not perjure himself where his interests were concerned. I did think at one time that I had found one that I could believe under oath, but I have changed my mind. I would not now believe one under oath, unless he were corroborated by other circumstances. I would want the corroboration to be proof in itself.

Q.—Is that the general estimation in which Courts and juries hold their testimony?

A.—Yes, sir.

Q.—Do you know who own or claim to own the Chinawomen who are prostitutes here?

A.—Merchants here, who pretend to be respectable—Chinese merchants, I mean.

Q.—Are they buying and selling these women?

A.—That is my opinion, from my experience.

Q.—How are they treated?

A.—Where one is young and good-looking, and makes plenty of money, she is well treated. Those who are unable to make much are treated very badly.

Q.—How young are the youngest that you know of as being held?

A.—I have seen them as young as fifteen years.

Q.—What chance have they to escape from this life, if they desire?

A.—They have very little chance.

Q.—Why is that?

A.—Because the Chinese will swear to almost anything, and if one is taken away by another, she is simply run off to another locality to be sold into slavery again. Sometimes the farce of marrying is gone through with in order to get the woman, who may be beyond their reach. As soon as the newly-made husband gets possession of his bride he turns her over to her former owners.

Q.—Do you know of cases where they have had Chinamen arrested and convicted of crime simply because they have interfered with them?

A.—Yes, sir. The arresting officer and the District Attorney have to be very careful lest they be made the instruments of sending innocent men to State Prison. Sometimes, where several men are arrested, one will be offered whom we may convict if we will let the others go. Several men were arrested here some time ago for robbing Harper's shoe store. These fellows put up a man who admitted that he was guilty, but I did not believe he had anything to do with it. These Chinese leaders offered to furnish me with all the evidence I wanted, if I would have a *nolle pros.* entered in the other cases.

Q.—Do you know anything about their putting up offers of rewards upon walls and street corners, written in Chinese, for the murder or assassination of given Chinamen?

A.—Yes. Of course I could not read Chinese, but I secured some of these posters, and had an interpreter from San Francisco come up here and interpret them. They were rewards for the murder of some Chinamen who did something contrary to their laws. They have their own tribunals where they try Chinamen, and their own laws to govern them. In this way the administration of justice is often defeated entirely, or, at least, to a very great extent. I know this because I was present at a meeting of one of their tribunals about seven years ago. There was some thirty or forty Chinamen there, one appearing to act as Judge. Finally, the fellow on trial was convicted and had to pay so much money, as a fine for the commission of the offense with which he was charged. Generally, their punishments are in the nature of fines; but sometimes they sentence the defendant to death. In cases in the Police Court we have often found it difficult to make interpreters act. They would tell us that they would be killed if they spoke the truth; that their tribunals would sentence them to death, and pay assassins to dispatch them. About two years and a half or three years ago, Ah Quong was killed. During the trial, at which he was interpreter, there were a great many Chinamen. I stationed officers at the doors, and then caused each one to be searched as he came out of the room, the interpreter having told me that he feared they would murder him. Upon these Chinamen I found all sorts of weapons—hatchets, pistols, bowie-knives, Chinese swords, and many others. There were forty-five weapons in all, I think, concealed about their persons in all kinds of ways. The interpreter testified in that case, and half an hour after leaving the Court-room he was brought back, shot and cut with hatchets. He was terribly mutilated, and lived only a few moments after being brought to the station-house. The murderers were arrested, but attempted to prove an alibi, and had a host of Chinese witnesses present for that purpose. Although there were some hundreds of Chinese present at the time of the murder, the prosecution was forced to rely upon the evidence of a few white men who chanced to see the deed committed. We were opposed at every turn by the Chinamen and the Chinese companies. As a general thing it is utterly impossible to enforce the laws with any certainty against those people, while they will themselves use our laws to persecute innocent men who have gained their enmity. They seem to have no ideas concerning the moral obligation of an oath, and care not for our form of swearing.

Q.—Have you ever seen any Christian Chinamen?

A.—Never. Some make a pretense of being Christians.

Q.—For what purpose?

A.—Principally to further their own ends in some way or other—get into the confidence of families, where they are working—get into the confidence of the master or mistress and stay there for probably a year or two, and afterwards, if they have a chance, they rob them. Several instances have occurred in this town.

Q.—Don't you find this to be the case frequently: Robberies are committed in families; you suggest it is a Chinese domestic, and they protest against it, and afterwards you make proof of it?

A.—Yes, sir; that has occurred frequently. In one particular instance, a certain lady in this town felt very indignant that I even mentioned such a thing as that her Chinaman should commit a robbery. I had simply asked how long she had had the Chinaman.

Q.—Was she engaged in instilling christianity into the Chinese?

A.—She was engaged in that good work.

Q.—And this was a Christian Chinaman?

A.—Yes, sir.

Q.—And you managed to convict him of the robbery, even to the satisfaction of that indignant lady?

A.—Yes, sir.

Q.—They are cunning and expert thieves?

A.—Yes, sir.

Q.—What is the character, as to truth and veracity, of these christianized Chinamen?

A.—I wouldn't take their word for anything.

Q.—Would they perjure themselves as readily as do the unchristianized?

A.—I believe so.

Q.—What effect does this Christian teaching have upon the Chinese?

A.—It makes them keener and more conscienceless—worse in every way. They learn the English language, and the smarter they get the worse they get, and the more expert in thieving. I know Chinamen who have been here for a long time, and I cannot see that they have been improved by their contact with the whites. On the contrary, they have learned all of our rascality and none of our virtues. I don't think it is natural for a Chinaman to learn anything good. I have known one Chinaman a good many years. He was considered by a good many people, and is now, what they call a "way up" Chinaman—one of the better class. His name is Ah Bean.

Q.—Is he a Christian?

A.—He pretends to be. He is rather smart—has learned telegraphy, etc.

Q.—He is the fellow who tries to bribe public officers, is he?

A.—Yes, sir.

Q.—He is a way up fellow and a good Christian?

A.—Yes, sir. At one time I thought he was a pretty good Chinamen, but now I don't think there is a worse Chinaman on I Street or on the Pacific Coast, because he has learned so much. The more they learn the worse they become.

Q.—What has been the effect in this city of the employment of Chinese? Has it displaced white labor to any great extent in the lighter avocations?

A.—Yes, sir; to a great extent.

Q.—Do you think that they drive servant girls from their places, deprive them of an opportunity of making an honest living?

A.—Yes, sir.

Q.—And has that fact added to the ranks of prostitution?

A.—Yes, sir.

Q.—Do you know of any such cases?

A.—Yes, sir. I recall two very distinctly, where white girls have been driven to prostitution by being thus driven from their employments.

Q.—They first come into contact with these Chinamen in the honest walks of life, and are them displaced by them. Next they meet them in the lower walks, and still the advantage is against them.

A.—Yes, sir. That condition of affairs exists to an alarming extent.

Q.—Then, instead of the presence of Chinese tending to the advancement of Christian civilization, it has a directly opposite effect?

A.—Yes, sir.

Q.—It is claimed by the Chinese missionaries in this State, that from sixty to one hundred have become christianized. Taking that to be true, how many white people have been ruined by their presence here during the last twenty-five years?

A.—The percentage against them is very great. Many more whites have been ruined in this city alone than have been converted in the whole State. I do not think that Chinese become converted to christianity at all. I don't think it is possible.

Q.—In San Francisco at an early day, and in Sacramento, there were few boys fourteen, fifteen, and sixteen years of age in the country?

A.—Yes, sir.

Q.—And the places occupied by boys in other countries were filled by the Chinese?

A.—Yes, sir.

Q.—So that the result was, that when boys came along in the natural growth of the country there was no work for them to do?

A.—That is correct.

Q.—We have an element in San Francisco, and a small element here, known as hoodlums. Might not the growth of that element be justly attributed to the presence of this people in our midst?

A.—I think nine-tenths of it may. In other countries boys find employment in this light work, but here it is done by the Chinese. Boys of tender age have been found in Chinese houses of prostitution frequently.

Q.—Would those boys be liable to visit the houses of white prostitutes?

A.—They would not be so liable.

Q.—Why is that?

A.—The prices are higher, and boys of that age will not take the liberties with white women that they do in Chinatown. In addition to that, it can be said on behalf of the white women that they would not allow boys of ten, eleven, or fourteen years of age to enter their houses. No such cases have ever been reported to the police, while the instances where Chinese women have enticed these youths are very frequent. Some three years ago two boys, one thirteen and the other fifteen, were taken from a Chinese house of prostitution and brought to the station-house. One belonged here and the other to San Francisco. I met the San Francisco boy about a month afterwards, and found him suffering from a loathsome disease, which he said he contracted in that house.

Q.—Do you know what they do with their sick when they become helpless and unable to make more money?

A.—Put them in some out-house, or on the sidewalk, to die?

Q.—Without food or bedding?

A.—Generally. I have found men and women, both, in that condition. I have found them by accident, while hunting for other things—stolen goods, criminals, etc.

Q.—You found women without food or drink, and without covering?

A.—Yes, sir.

Q.—And death would have come from disease or starvation, or both?

A.—Yes, sir.

Q.—Is that the common way of disposing of these women when they become useless?

A.—Yes, sir, if not the only way.

Q.—They are less cared for than are useless domestic animals by the white race?

A.—A great deal less.

Q.—What is the general effect of the presence of this race upon the morals of this country?

A.—Bad.

Q.—Is this population a criminal one?

A.—Principally.

Q.—Do you know of any good that comes from their presence?

A.—I have never heard of any, nor can I think of any.

Q.—Leaving San Francisco out of consideration, have you ever known so many people, in any city, crowded together in the same space that they are crowded here?

A.—No, sir.

Q.—Have you ever known as vicious a population concentrated in any other city?

A.—No, sir.

Q.—Do you know of any cases of leprosy here?

A.—I know of one case of leprosy here. The leper is a loathsome looking object, and no one will dare to touch him. They will not receive him at the hospital, and there is no place at the station-house for him. He could go into any store in this city and take whatever he pleased.

Q.—Would it be possible to close up houses of gambling and prostitution entirely in the Chinese quarters?

A.—I think that it would be an utter impossibility. To do it would require a police force large enough to have a man stationed on I Street every fifty or one hundred feet. More policemen would be required for the Chinese quarter than for all the rest of the city. Taking into consideration the present state of taxation, the extra expense would be more than we could stand.

Q.—The Chinese are about one-tenth the population of the city?

A.—Yes, sir.

Q.—Do they pay one-hundredth part of the tax?

A.—No, sir; I don't think they pay one-thousandth part.

Q.—Do they own any real estate?

A.—I do not know of any case. I have heard that one Chinaman owned a piece of land, but I do not know anything about it.

Q.—Would the houses in which they live be habitable for any other class of people?

A.—No, sir. A few recently erected might be cleansed, but most of them would have to be torn down and rebuilt.

Q.—Tell us how they regard our laws and ordinances relating to health and fire; how they live; whether they buy things here or from Chinese merchants; whom they have displaced, and what would be the effect of sending large numbers of them East?

A.—They totally disregard the fire and health ordinances. They build fires in their rooms on the floor, under the sidewalks and on the sidewalks. The danger of the destruction of the city by fire is very great, especially when a north wind is blowing. The Chinese live together, fifteen or twenty in a small room, and do their cooking there and sleep there. This enables them to live upon probably ten cents a day, or seventy cents a week, while a white laborer would be under an expense, at the very least, of twelve dollars a week. The Chinese use Chinese clothing, live upon Chinese rice, and deal with Chinese merchants. The Chinese washerman has taken the place of the white washerwoman. He has usurped the place of the white girl in families. He has driven white laborers from the factories, the fields, and the ordinary work of laborers. He has invaded a large portion of our manufacturing institutions, displacing white labor, male and female. He has been enabled to do this from the fact that he works for less than is necessary to support the most economical of white laborers. It has been stated in Eastern papers that the Chinese on this coast are abused, and that they are not protected by the laws. That is not so. It is because the laws have been well enforced in California that the people have stood this thing so long as they have. If we should send a population of this kind to any large city in the United States, and the workingmen should understand the character of the Chinese as we understand it, they would rise up and prevent their settling among them.

George Hing sworn.

Mr. Haymond—How long have you been in California?

A.—Twenty-three years. I went home about two years and a half, and came back about nine years ago.

Q.—What do you do now?

A.—I keep store, and work for the railroad company.

Q.—How many Christian Chinamen are there in California?

A.—I don't know. There are probably somewhere near one hundred.

Q.—Are they Christians, or do they pretend to be Christians?

A.—Some keep it a long time.

Q.—From what part of China did you come?

A.—About two days from Canton.

Q.—Do you know how these Chinawomen get here?

A.—No.

Q.—Do you know whether they are bought and sold here?

A.—No.

Q.—How many Chinamen are there in California?

A.—I think about one hundred and thirty thousand or one hundred and forty thousand. That is too much. China merchants don't like too much to come.

Q.—Does the Chinese Government like to have these people come here?

A.—I don't know.

Q.—Do the six companies know who own these Chinawomen here?

A.—No, sir.

Q.—Do you know anybody that owns one?

A.—No, sir. I am traveling on the road most of the time.

Q.—How long have you been working for the railroad company?

A.—About eight years.

Q.—If the six companies were to tell the Chinamen who own women that they must send them away, would they do it?

A.—I think not. We have no right to say anything of that kind. I attend to my business, and don't interfere with anybody else.

Ah You sworn.

Mr. Haymond—How long have you lived in California?

A.—Sixteen years.

Q.—From what part of China did you come?

A.—Canton.

Q.—How long have you lived in Sacramento?

A.—Thirteen years.

Q.—What have you been doing in Sacramento?

A.—Keeping a butcher shop.

Q.—Do you know whether Chinawomen are bought and sold here
A.—No.
Q.—What do these Chinamen do here?
A.—I don't know.
Q.—Do many Chinamen bring their wives here from China?
A.—Yes.
Q.—How many in California?
A.—I can't tell.
Q.—How many in Sacramento?
A.—I can't tell how many—about two, three, or four here, I guess.
Q.—How do they get these other women? Do they buy them or steal them?
A.—I cannot tell.
Q.—When those women get sick and are going to die, do they put them in houses by themselves, without food or water?
A.—In case a woman got no husband, and don't know enough to go to the hospital, they put her out that way.
Q.—Why don't the Chinese companies take care of them when they are sick?
A.—The company can't attend to much business of that kind.
Q.—How many gambling-houses were there in Sacramento before this excitement?
A.—I don't know. I am a business man and don't know anything about that.
Q.—Did you ever gamble yourself?
A.—Since I came back from China I never gambled.
Q.—Where do you live?
A.—On I Street, between Second and Third.
Q.—Are there any women that live close to your store?
A.—Yes; some family women.
Q.—Do any other kind of women live there?
A.—I can't tell.
Q.—Are there any bad women around there?
A.—I don't know.
Q.—Do you know the meaning of the word "coolie" in China?
A.—No.
Q.—Do you know any Chinese Christians?
A.—Some believe and some do not.
Q.—How many believe?
A.—I don't know.
Q.—Do you know any?
A.—I don't know any at all.
Q.—Do you know Ah Bean?
A.—Yes, sir.
Q.—Is he a Christian?
A.—He did not used to believe, but he does now.

Billy Holung sworn.
Mr. Haymond—How long have you been in California?
A.—Since eighteen hundred and forty-eight.
Q.—What have you been doing?
A.—The first time, mining.
Q.—How long have you lived in Sacramento?
A.—Since eighteen hundred and sixty-two.
Q.—What have you been doing in Sacramento?

A.—Worked in a saloon first time for an American man on Front Street—Pony Exchange.

Q.—How do these Chinawomen come here—the women that are prostitutes?

A.—I don't know.

Q.—Who own them?

A.—I don't know.

Q.—Did you ever see rewards offered for killing men?

A.—Never heard of that.

Q.—Do you know anything about Ah Quong being killed?

A.—Yes, sir.

Q.—What was he killed for?

A.—I don't know.

Q.—Who killed him?

A.—I don't know.

Mr. Lewis—Did you ever buy a woman yourself?

A.—No. I don't do that kind of business.

Q.—Six years ago, when you were in the Pony Exchange, did you not buy a woman and give six hundred dollars for her?

A.—Yes, sir; I bought me a wife.

Q.—What became of her?

A.—I own her.

Q.—What is she doing?

A.—Dressmaking.

Q.—Where, in San Francisco, is she living?

A.—On Jackson Street, up stairs.

Q.—How many other women are with her?

A.—She is alone.

Mr. Donovan—What do you do for a living?

A.—Keep a store.

Q.—How often do you see your wife?

A.—Sometimes.

Q.—Does she pay you what money she makes?

A.—Yes, sir. The money she gets for dressmaking. I pay for her support.

Q.—Are you married to her?

A.—Yes, sir.

Q.—Why don't you keep her in Sacramento?

A.—She quarrels with me.

Q.—Did you ever whip her?

A.—No, sir.

Q.—How much money does she give you?

A.—I pay sixty dollars every month.

Lem Schaum sworn.

Mr. Haymond—How long have you resided in California?

A.—About fourteen years, sir.

Q.—From what part of China did you come?

A.—One hundred and fifty miles from Canton.

Q.—Where were you educated in English?

A.—Down at Oakland.

Q.—By whom?

A.—By Mr. Rowle, the Rev. Dr. Moore, and Dr. Gamble.

Q.—How old were you then?

A.—I came here when I was about fifteen.

Q.—Did you have any relatives in California?
A.—Yes, sir; my father was here.
Q.—How long have you been in Sacramento?
A.—Pretty nearly four months.
Q.—Where did you live before that?
A.—I lived at the bay.
Q.—Where did you live in San Francisco?
A.—Mostly with my father. When I wanted to study I went to Oakland.
Q.—Are you a Christian Chinaman?
A.—Yes, sir.
Q.—How long since you first believed in the Christian religion?
A.—Since about eighteen hundred and seventy.
Q.—Have you tried to make Christians out of your countrymen here?
A.—I tried that; but it is very hard work to do it.
Q.—Do some of them pretend to be Christians when they are not?
A.—Only those grown-up fellows; the young boys do not. Boys working around see the American customs, and we can instruct them in no time; but the old ones think Confucius' is the only good religion, and with them it is very hard work.
Q.—Are there a good many Buddhists among them?
A.—Yes, sir.
Q.—None of them ever become Christians, do they?
A.—They will not. They don't know anything about Christianity, and you can't make them understand it. They never will take your word for it.
Q.—You don't know of any Chinamen who believe in the doctrines of Buddha that have been converted to the Christian religion?
A.—Yes; one or two, down at the bay.
Q.—How many Christian Chinamen do you think there are in California altogether?
A.—About four years ago we formed a Chinese Young Men's Christian Association at the Rev. Dr. Loomis' place. There were twenty-eight of us when we formed that society, but the number has grown up to about five hundred.
Q.—Do you think that many are Christians?
A.—I think about half are real Christians.
Q.—Do you know how these bad women are brought here?
A.—They are stolen and bought in China, and brought here the same as we buy and sell stock.
Q.—Their condition is a very horrible one, then?
A.—Yes, sir.
Q.—Do you know how they are treated?
A.—Yes, sir. The parties who own them generally treat them pretty roughly. If they don't go ahead and make money the owners will give them a good thrashing.
Q.—Suppose you were to convert one of these women, would she have any chance to get away from them?
A.—Yes, sir; they do down at the bay. The Rev. Dr. Gibson has a Chinese woman's home; so has the Rev. Dr. Loomis. When a Chinese woman gets away and goes to either of these places she is taken care of and protected until she can do something for her living, or find a respectable Chinaman to marry with.

Q.—Don't they try to steal those women back?

A.—They can't do it. They would if they could, but they can't do it.

Q.—How many are there, do you know?

A.—I made inquiry about them about four months ago; twenty or thirty were at Gibson's, and fifteen or twenty at Loomis'.

Q.—They protect them there?

A.—Yes, sir.

Q.—Is it not very common, when those women try to get away, for the people who own them to have them arrested for larceny, and things of that kind?

A.—Yes, sir.

Q.—They are held by fear of punishment if they try to escape?

A.—Exactly.

Q.—There are cases where Chinamen have cut them all to pieces with knives for running away, are there not?

A.—I never have seen any, but this is what I have heard.

Q.—They torture them?

A.—Yes, sir.

Q.—Do they buy and sell these women here?

A.—Yes, sir.

Q.—And hold them in slavery?

A.—Exactly.

Q.—Do you know anything about turning these women out to die when they become sick from disease, and unable to make money?

A.—I have not heard of anything of that kind; but when they are sick, and expect they are going to die, they are taken care of.

Q.—The police officers here have testified that they have found these sick people where they have been left in outbuildings, without food or water?

A.—I presume they do that. I have not seen any case of that kind, and I am not positive.

Q.—You have not associated with these people?

A.—I have not associated with them at all. I am sick of them; I got enough of them.

Q.—You have seen the Chinese quarters? Do you think that it is good for the Chinese, or for the Americans, to have those people living as they do?

A.—I think it is very bad for both Chinese and Americans.

Q.—As a general rule, taking the one hundred and fifty thousand of them in California, they don't learn much good after they come here, do they? Don't they learn the vices of the country?

A.—That is your own fault. No Chinaman can take a walk up and down the street unless you find an Irishman or a Dutchman strike them down. They struck one down and I told them I would have them arrested and put in the County Jail for six months. A great many Chinamen desire to learn to read and write English, and then also our methods of business, or any kind of work; perhaps the arts or sciences.

Q.—They live very cheaply, don't they?

A.—They must live cheaply, sir. They have got to live cheaply, because they only get about fifteen dollars a month, or three or four dollars a week.

Q.—A great many live in the same house?

A.—Yes; a great many live together, because they have not got money enough to have rooms as you have.

Q.—Do you known the house Dr. Gibson rents to them in San Francisco?

A.—He didn't rent that at all. They come in there free.

Q.—The house on Jackson Street, near the theater?

A.—That is our mission.

Q.—He rents it to Chinamen, don't he?

A.—No, sir. He has got nothing to do with it; he has no money to invest in that business.

Q.—Who does rent it?

A.—I think some American rents to Chinamen, and the Chinamen rents to the Chinese, but don't know.

Q.—Suppose it was proven to you that Gibson rented that building to Chinamen, what would you think of Dr. Gibson?

A.—I would think that he would be a very bad man.

Q.—It has been in testimony that he does rent that building to Chinese, and that he makes a profit out of it. What do you think of that?

A.—I think he would be a very bad man if he does that.

Q.—That is a very bad place, is it not?

A.—It is a very dirty place—enough, almost, to kill a man. It is so strong there that I can't go around Jackson Street now.

Q.—It is in a very filthy condition?

A.—Exactly.

Q.—What did you do before you went into the mission?

A.—I was in the mines. My father owned some mines; but my profession was geologist and mineralogist.

Q.—Did you ever study that profession much?

A.—Yes, sir.

Q.—Where did you study it?

A.—At home in China. I guess I know as much as any of them at home—more, too.

Q.—Do you know whether the Chinese Government is in favor of its people coming here or not?

A.—It is not in favor of it, but the government can't help itself. The policy of the Chinese Government has been exclusive. It desires to keep its people at home. This immigration is mostly from the Province of Canton.

Q.—Suppose the mass of that immigration was stopped, do you think it would have any influence on our commercial relations with other parts of China?

A.—No. I think this immigration must stop. I say it is not only ruining Americans, but it ruins the Chinese. Their wages, we notice, come down every day. A short time ago Chinamen got thirty-six dollars a month working on the railroad. What do they get now? Twenty-six dollars per month—one dollar a day. This immigration must be stopped in some way.

Q.—Do you think, if proper representations were made to the Chinese Government by intelligent Chinamen, as to the state of affairs here, they would willingly aid in stopping it—stopping this immigration of the lower classes here?

A.—The government, I am afraid, would not be able to do it. It has eighteen provinces, and a revolution in every province almost.

Q.—It is claimed that if we were to attempt to stop it ourselves the Chinese Government would be offended?

A.—No, they would not be offended; but they would be very glad to do that, the same as I am. The Chinese Government would be only too glad to prevent their people coming to this country.

Q.—What is the general opinion of Christian Chinamen with whom you associate in this State as to the policy or impolicy of having this Chinese immigration continue without any limits?

A.—We think that this immigration must be stopped. It must be stopped in some way, and then we can look after those Christians educated in this country. We want to stretch forth our hand as far as we can so as instruct them about a better world than this. That is our object, and a good many of them are going back to preach at home. Looking at this thing from a Christian standpoint, I think that christianity is not advanced by this immigration, and I would give anything in the world to have it stopped.

Q.—In the Eastern States, when we proposed to check this immigration, or to limit it to the better class of Chinese, we were met with this proposition: that Chinese immigration to this country would have the result of christianizing China. I understand you to say that the immigration, such as is coming here now, don't tend to the advancement of christianity?

A.—It does not.

Q.—So it would be better, then, from your standpoint as a Chinaman, to stop it, for by stopping it you would make more Christians?

A.—Yes, sir.

Q.—Do you know anything about the organization of the six companies, and what their purposes are?

A.—Yes, sir. The six companies see so many of our nation coming to this country poor that they try to provide for them; but lately they telegraphed to the Chinese Hospital at Hong-kong not to let any more come here. We don't know how we stand here now. It is not friendly. There is going to be a row. Those who arrived at San Francisco lately had not, of course, heard anything of this, but I think it will check immigration. I have heard Chinese merchants talk about this matter, and they say this immigration must be stopped if they want to live. They don't know how in the world they can stand it.

Q.—What is the opinion of the Chinese merchants in Hong-kong and Shanghai, and other Chinese ports? Are they in favor of stopping it?

A.—Those fellows at home have nothing to do with emigration from Hong-kong to this country.

Q.—There is no fear that if we were to stop immigration it would interfere with our trade with the Chinese people?

A.—None whatever. The Chinese merchants want it stopped, and the whole thing can be done in a friendly way.

Q.—Do you know anything about notices of rewards being posted up in Chinese quarters in San Francisco or here, for the punishment of certain men—a notice of this kind: Five hundred dollars or six hundred dollars will be given for the assassination or murder of some Chinaman?

A.—I do. That is a Chinese custom. When members of a company do anything against the rules of that company they are punished. Suppose one member of a company comes to me and says: "Go and steal a woman from a Chinaman," and I do so for him. Because I favor him, his enemies prove I stole the woman, and put up a reward of five hundred or one thousand dollars to have me killed. That is the way they do.

Q.—Do they post those rewards up publicly?

A.—I think not; I think they do that in secret.

Q.—Has it been your experience that those secret judgments are carried into execution?

A.—They pop it to you every time.

Q.—Almost every time a judgment is entered that a man shall die, and they offer so much money to have him killed, the man is killed?

A.—Exactly.

Q.—They take every advantage?

A.—Yes, sir.

Q.—That is regarded as a death sentence?

A.—Yes, sir. The man knows he has to die, but gets out of the way if he can.

Q.—That makes it difficult for any Chinamen, if they are disposed, to protect women?

A.—Yes, sir.

Q.—If a Chinaman takes a woman to the mission, that sort of a reward will be offered?

A.—Yes, sir; most likely.

Q.—Do you know of their custom of settling cases that get into the Courts? For instance, a Chinaman is arrested for kidnaping one of these women. Do you know anything about their settling that among themselves and keeping the testimony away from the Courts?

A.—I believe they do that.

Q.—They have some sort of a tribunal in which they settle this thing for themselves?

A.—Yes, sir.

Q.—Have they a tribunal which punishes for offenses against their customs?

A.—Yes, sir. For instance, suppose I should march myself out and kill a Chinaman. I am brought before the company and made to pay a fine. They take the money and send it back to the family of the killed party to support his mother.

Q.—If you kill a member of the See-yup Company, the See-yup Company will determine, through this tribunal, that you shall pay so much money?

A.—Yes, sir.

Q.—Suppose you pay that money?

A.—Then I will be all right.

Q.—They would not try to punish you by law?

A.—No, sir.

Q.—Suppose you refuse to pay the money?

A.—I must go through the American Courts.

Q.—And they will convict you?

A.—Exactly.

Q.—If you do pay the money they will protect you against the American laws?

A.—They let the whole matter drop.

Q.—And keep witnesses out of the way?

A.—Yes, sir.

Q.—It is impossible, then, to administer justice, under our laws, to this Chinese population?

A.—Exactly; it is impossible.

Q.—Do you know anything about Chinamen coming here under contract to work so long after they get here?

A.—Yes, sir; when men have no money to get to California they borrow it and make a contract to work until they have refunded that money. There are very few cases where the lenders have lost anything, for the working classes of the Chinese, as a rule, keep all such contracts faithfully. When Chinamen desire to go back to China the Pacific Mail Steamship Company will not sell them tickets unless they have a check or ticket from the six companies, or from the missionaries. This is done to protect the creditors of the Chinamen living in this country.

Q.—Do you know to what extent christianity is being spread in China?

A.—Very strong now.

Q.—You are glad to see that, of course?

A.—Oh, yes! glad to hear of it.

Q.—Do you know what denominations are making the most converts?

A.—The Presbyterians in Canton; but I thing Methodists in Shanghai and Wong-bow. The Catholics are getting along more slowly.

Q.—To what denomination do you belong?

A.—To the First Congregational Church.

Q.—Do you know how many Christian Chinamen there are in this city?

A.—I guess about twenty-four.

Q.—And how many in San Francisco?

A.—Three hundred and sixty or three hundred and seventy. There are a little over one hundred running around the country. I think the genuine Christians in California will number about two hundred.

Q.—Do you preach to them?

A.—Yes; but I do not preach for a salary.

Q.—Have you any other business?

A.—My business is geologist.

Q.—What do you do for a living here?

A.—I have an uncle who keeps a store, and he is going home. He wanted me to collect his debts, and wrote to me to come up and stay with him for a while.

Q.—Is he a Christian?

A.—No, sir.

Q.—How do the Chinese generally regard Christian Chinamen?

A.—With a great deal of prejudice. This is because they know we are better than they are.

Q.—If the Chinese merchants here were to unite together, could they not give criminals up to justice if they desired?

A.—I do not know.

Q.—Can the six companies send lewd and improper characters back to China or stop their immigration?

A.—Yes, sir; in a measure by advice, but they have no power to command it to be done.

SAM LEE sworn.

Mr. Haymond—How long have you lived in Sacramento?

A.—I came back from the mountains a few days ago?

Q.—What part of the mountains?
A.—Bakersfield.
Q.—Have you ever seen rewards posted up—offering rewards for the murder of Chinamen?
A.—Yes; in San Francisco.
Q.—What do those papers say?
A.—Just put up to say they pay one thousand dollars or five hundred dollars to kill.
Q.—Any names signed?
A.—No, sir.
Q.—How do you know who will pay?
A.—They go and find out before they do it.
Q.—Do you know any Christian Chinamen?
A.—No, sir. I went to school once to learn something. I wanted to learn to speak English, and the American law.
Q.—What you understand by religion, then, is learning English?
A.—Learning American man's law and what the American man knows.

TWELFTH DAY.

SACRAMENTO, May 4th, 1876.

O. C. JACKSON sworn.
Mr. Haymond—How long have you been in California?
A.—Since eighteen hundred and sixty-three.
Q.—How long have you resided in Sacramento?
A.—Since eighteen hundred and sixty-three.
Q.—What is your present occupation?
A.—Regular police officer in the City of Sacramento.
Q.—How long have you been connected with the force?
A.—I have been an officer since eighteen hundred and sixty-nine, but not on the regular force all the time.
Q.—Are you familiar with the Chinese quarters of this city?
A.—Yes, sir.
Q.—What is their condition as regards cleanliness?
A.—It would be simply ridiculous to compare it with the white part of the city. It is filthy in the extreme.
Q.—How do they live? Do many live in the same house?
A.—They are packed in, three tiers deep. I have visited Chinatown hundreds of times in search of Chinese thieves, and have seen them stowed away head and feet together, in cellars and under sidewalks, and all their surroundings of the most filthy character.
Q.—Do you know how these Chinese prostitutes are held—whether in slavery or not?
A.—I think they are all held in slavery. They are all bought and sold the same as horses and cows, bringing prices according to age and beauty.
Q.—Do you know how they are treated?
A.—As slaves, and punished as the owners may choose.
Q.—What sort of punishments are inflicted?
A.—I do not know, only from hearsay.
Q.—What chance have these women to escape if they should so desire?

A.—Very little chance. Where they do get away they are generally caught and brought back to the owners again.

Q.—Do they resort to the processes of our Courts in order to recover women who have escaped?

A.—Yes, sir; in a great many cases to my knowledge. They will swear out a warrant for her arrest for grand larceny or some felony. Sometimes it is sworn out against the man who has her, and sometimes against both. As soon as they get possession of the woman, they trifle with the cases until they fall through. It is almost impossible for a woman to escape.

Q.—Do you know what is done with these women when they become sick, helpless, and incurably diseased?

A.—Where they see that they will be of no further use to make money, they turn them out on the sidewalk to die. I have seen men and women also turned out to die in this manner. I have found dead men while searching for stolen property, and have had the Coroner attend to them. The Chinese are very superstitious in regard to sickness and death, and will have nothing to do with their unfortunate fellow countrymen. A great many die in out-of-the-way places, abandoned by the Chinese, without food or drink.

Q.—Do you know whether Chinese prostitutes have been in the habit of soliciting young boys of tender age?

A.—I do not remember any cases of late occurrence. Since the present Chief of Police went into office there has been little of that business, as he has kept the places shut up. Previous to that, these women were in the habit of soliciting openly. I have seen in these houses boys of ten, thirteen, fourteen, and fifteen years of age.

Q.—Have you ever heard of boys of that age visiting white houses of prostitution?

A.—No, sir. I never knew of any such case.

Q.—Do you believe the white women would allow it?

A.—No, sir.

Q.—This is frequent in the Chinese quarter?

A.—It has been.

Q.—How is their testimony received in Court?

A.—I would not believe a Chinamen under oath, for they will swear whichever way interest or prejudice directs. They are in the habit of compromising felonies and offenses. They have their own secret tribunals, where they try men for offenses. I was present at one of their meetings a short time ago, and they questioned me very closely regarding certain Chinamen whom they accused of furnishing evidence. This week, in the County Court, we had a trial of a Chinamen whom I arrested for stealing from the Congregational Church school-room. He was caught in the room by the Chinaman who keeps it in order, and held until I got there and took him into custody. There were three Chinamen there when he was arrested and searched, besides Mrs. Shane, the teacher. Two of these Chinamen begged the white witnesses on several occasions not to go to Court and testify, else they would be killed by order of their countrymen. In the Police Court they were not needed and were not called. Two or three nights before the trial came on in the County Court, this Chinaman, Fon Fon, came to my residence very much excited, and wanted me to go down town with him. I asked him what for, and he said the Ky-che-lung was holding a meeting, and he wanted me to go before it. He said they were meeting to make him pay one dollar a day for every day this man had been in jail, or else hire a lawyer to get him out, saying that if the man was convicted and he did not pay this money, he would be killed. He also said that he had not dared to go down I Street since the man's arrest. I went to the meeting of the Ky-che-lung and was questioned very closely. To see what they were up to I evaded their questions, and finally told them this man had nothing to do with the matter. This was what they were after, and one told me he did not believe me. On the trial the two other Chinese had disappeared, and an attachment had to be sent for Fon Fon. On the stand he perjured himself, declaring he knew nothing of things that occurred there the day of arrest. He was very much scared and doubtless acted under orders. The Chinese told me that the whole matter had been settled. The great number of offenses committed by Chinese among themselves are settled long before they come to issue in our Courts. They use threats and intimidation among themselves, but never towards the whites.

Q.—Do you know anything about the murder of Ah Quong?

A.—Yes, sir. That was as Mr. Jones stated.

Q.—Do you know anything about the posting up of offers of rewards for assassinations?

A.—I have had them, but of course could not read them. I have had them translated. They offer so much for the murder of a particular individual, and agree to protect the murderer.

Q.—Do you know any Christian Chinamen?

A.—No, sir.

Q.—Do you know whether the employment of Chinamen in this city, in the place of white girls, has led to the prostitution of the whites in any degree?

A.—I cannot say. My opinion is that the presence of the Chinese tends to degrade the working classes, but I can't say that I know of any instances where white girls have been driven to prostitution because of the Chinese.

Q.—How much a day can Chinese laborers of the lower classes support themselves upon?

A.—They can live on ten cents a day. White men cannot board themselves for less than fifty cents a day. The Chinese evade all the tax they can. A poll-tax receipt is passed around from one to the other, and they swear themselves clear of paying whenever they can.

Q.—Do they import much of their food and clothing from China?

A.—Yes, sir. They spend very little money with Americans. They come here, stay until they get some money together, and then go home again. While they are here, they are sending money home all the time.

Q.—From what you have seen, do you think the presence of the Chinese here tends to the advancement of Christian civilization?

A.—It has the reverse effect. It is also degrading to white labor; instead of learning good, they are learning vice. They are becoming educated only in thievery, and perjury, and everything bad.

Q.—In the administration of justice, do the officers meet with any assistance at the hands of the more respectable portion of the Chinese?

A.—They stand in the way of the administration of the law, from the head men down to the lowest thieves. They are a nation of thieves, the lowest being under the direction and management of the more intelligent, who know the laws, hire lawyers, procure testimony, and act as receivers of goods stolen. When you are on I Street, searching for information, you can't find a man but what will answer to all your questions, "No sabe." Sometimes they put up jobs on their fellow countrymen, and convict them of crime, whether guilty or not. They have no respect for our laws, and consider them only of use in so far as they can use them to work their own personal ends. They settle everything in their own councils, and as the thing goes there, so it goes elsewhere.

Q.—What is the great difficulty in the administration of the law?

A.—Our ignorance of their language; and unless white witnesses are very familiar with Chinese faces, they have great trouble in identifying them. Officers have no difficulty on that score, but others do.

Charles P. O'Neil recalled.

Mr. Haymond—Do you know anything about the murder of the first interpreter?

A.—Yes, sir. He belonged to the Ning-yeung Company, which broke off from the See-yup Company. He was considered as a pretty bad sort of man, for he was going after some Chinamen pretty lively. He was in the habit of assisting to make convictions, trumping up false charges, etc.

Q.—How do you know they were false?

A.—They were proved so to be afterwards.

Q.—How was he removed?

A.—They sent to China for a man to come here and kill him. Letters were sent to this Chinaman at Folsom, where he was living, and also telegraphic dispatches, warning him that he was to be murdered. He immediately came to Sacramento City and went into a gambling-house. He was sitting down, leaning over the table, and this man that was to kill him was standing opposite. This fellow walk behind the interpreter and shot him. As he fell, he shot him a second time, and then rushed to the street. This was about six o'clock in the evening. He walked about forty steps up the street. He then crossed the street and walked about one hundred and fifty feet further. Then he threw his pistol in a doorway, went probably seventy-five feet further, and jumped down into a yard and disappeared. He went to China and was there pretty nearly a year, when he came back and died in San Francisco, just about the time we discovered his whereabouts. Before he did this killing he had gone to China. He was then sent for by the companies and came back. He was in the State only three or four days when he killed his man.

Mr. Donovan—What reason had they for wanting this man murdered?

A.—There was a white man murdered in Amador County by some Chinese in his employ. He was a Mr. Griswold, a wealthy ditch owner. The Chinese fled to Marysville. Ah Gow, the interpreter, was living there then, and he went to white men and said "The murderers of Mr. Griswold are in a wash-house across the street. Arrest them, and we will make the reward." The men were arrested, taken to Amador County and hung. That is why Ah Gow was killed.

Q.—Do you know what company brought this man out?

A.—No, sir; I only learned that from the Chinese a year after the murderer left. The head of one of the companies in San Francisco was arrested for conspiracy, and brought to Sacramento. On the preliminary examination he was discharged. He was a very old man, and was the one who presided at the meeting at which the reward was offered for the murder.

Q.—Was he a Ning-yeung man?

A.—No. Ah Gow was a Ning-yeung man.

Q.—When was this?

A.—Twelve years or more ago. Professional fighters are in the constant employ of the companies. These fighters committed several murders here some time ago, but we could not catch them. Several were arrested, but nothing could be proven. The Chinese told me that they had settled the thing in their own tribunals, and that ended it.

Committee adjourned to meet in San Francisco, Monday, May twenty-sixth, eighteen hundred and seventy-six, at eleven o'clock A. M.

THIRTEENTH DAY.

SAN FRANCISCO, May 26th, 1876.

F. L. GORDON sworn.

Mr. Donovan—Do you know of any persons being killed among the Chinese by hired assassins?

A.—I know of three.

Q.—What is your business?

A.—For some years I have been publishing a Chinese newspaper in this city. I am not doing that just now.

Q.—How long were you engaged in that business?

A.—Three years this month.

Q.—Do you ever transact any other business for these people?

A.—Yes, sir; I have done mercantile business with them, printing, collections, etc. I have collected poll-tax, and done general business with them. I have been frequently called from the city on business for Chinese. The last time was at Vallejo, in regard to a shooting scrape at the quicksilver mines three or four miles from that place. The Chinese sent for me to go there and look after things. When I got there I found that the trouble had resulted from an attempt made to shoot Ah John. Two men were arrested, and they sent to San Francisco and hired eleven others to go up and swear that they did not attempt to shoot anybody. Ah John then sent down and got fourteen or fifteen to swear that they saw the shooting. Two men were brought there to swear, whom I knew were in San Francisco when the difficulty occurred.

Q.—Do you know of any cases where they have hired men to kill others?

A.—Yes, sir. The first case I know of is that of Ah Suey, a member of the Wong-tung-sing Society. He did something contrary to their rules in regard to the collection of money. I was in Ah Suey's house the very day he was killed. He knew there was a reward offered for his death, and he had not gone out for some days. He told me he was going to collect some money, and would go to China in a sailing vessel. I told him I heard there was a reward offered for his death, and he had better look out. During the day he went into Washington Alley thirty or forty feet, when he was shot in the back, and instantly killed.

Q.—Who offered the reward?

A.—I heard that the society offered it. I think the amount was eight hundred dollars.

Q.—Have you seen rewards of that kind posted up?

A.—Yes, sir; they are written on red paper.

Q.—Mention some other cases.

A.—A Chinaman on Jackson Street was sent for by Chinamen, to whom he had loaned money, and was told that if he would go to a certain room on Jackson Street they would pay him. Two men waited for him there, and they killed him.

Q.—Was there any evidence of a reward having been offered for his death?

A.—I heard it spoken of in this way, before it happened: that there would be money paid for his death. I was in a house two days before the killing, and there heard the matter spoken of. I am perfectly satisfied that his death was the result of a reward.

Q.—Do you know of any other case?

A.—There was a priest in Spofford Alley, who was told that if he gave any testimony against other Chinamen, he would be killed. He was badly cut soon after, but I think he recovered. Mr. Locke and myself waited two or three hours for the man to come to do the cutting, in order to arrest him. We knew the fellow who had threatened to do it. After we left, the attack was made.

Q.—What was the date of these two murders?

A.—I think one was a year ago in February, and the other was a month or two later. I know of a case where a woman was cut because she would not consent to be blackmailed. A Chinaman, Ah Chuck, went into a house of prostitution and Chin Cook, a prostitute, borrowed his pocket-knife, and, after using it, laid it on the table. In a few minutes he said he was going, and wanted his knife. It had disappeared from the table, and he said she would have to return the knife or pay him for it. He said it cost him one dollar and twenty-five cents, and he would come the next night for the money. Mr. Locke was sent for, and he told her to pay no attention to it; that the Chinaman was trying to blackmail her. She gave Locke two dollars and fifty cents, and told him to buy as good a knife as he could for the money. He did so, and she offered the man the knife. He refused to take it, saying his knife was a broken one and he didn't want a new one. She pawned some of her clothing for twelve dollars, but he would not take that. He then said his knife was worth eighty dollars, and told her he would slash her if she did not pay it. He afterwards cut her with a knife. She screamed and tried to get under the bed, when he cut her again. Mr. Locke and myself found him on Clay Street and arrested him. The next day he was bailed out, when he went up there and cut her again with a hatchet. Another woman, Chin Woey, was cut in the head and arm and face for refusing to pay thirty dollars blackmail to two Chinamen, one of whom kept a gambling-house and the other a wash-house. Locke and myself arrested the gambler, and he was bailed out. The next day he and two others laid in wait for me with iron bars. My revolver, however, frightened them, and they retreated.

Q.—Was there a reward offered for your death?

A.—Yes, sir. There was a reward of six hundred dollars offered for me, and one of two hundred and fifty dollars offered for a Chinaman in my employ. In March, of this year, I was told not to go to a certain house on Clay Street, or I would be killed. One day I went there, and was asked into a room where several Chinamen were—two with iron bars, one of whom had threatened to kill me. The door was locked after me, and these men advanced. I sprang to the door, drew a pistol, and kept off the Chinamen while I unlocked the door from behind and ran into the street and escaped. Saw a notice offering a reward for my death posted up in Chinatown. Cut it down, and have the translation. It says that any man who wants to get rich suddenly can do so by killing me, for six hundred dollars will be paid for my death. It was authorized by the "Wash-house Society." I had threatened to sue them and recover three thousand four hundred dollars on a contract for printing, and they thought they could escape payment by murdering me. My Chinese servant knew of this arrangement, and was my friend, so they offered two hundred and fifty dollars for his death.

Q.—What are "hatchet men"?

A.—Fighting men; a class of men in Chinatown that can be hired to defend any house or store that is threatened, and will cut and kill indiscriminately. About a year and a half ago a store at number nine hundred and seven, or number nine hundred and nine Dupont Street, was threatened. A riot took place, and hired "hatchet men" broke into the store, shooting, cutting, and destroying. Some months ago a riot occurred at number eight hundred and ten Dupont Street, regarding the employment of Chinese in shoe factories, and the retention of wages. Store-keepers hired "hatchet men," and they fought the strikers. Nine were wounded, and fifteen or twenty arrests made. None were convicted. Know a large number of professional fighters here.

Q.—What do you know of the character of the Chinese for honesty, as a general rule?

A.—As far as I have seen, I think that Chinamen who act honestly do it from policy, and not principle. A good many Chinamen with whom I have been thrown in contact have been straightforward, but I believe that was only policy.

Q.—Do you know of any regular system of blackmail among the Chinese?

A.—Yes, sir; about three months ago three Chinamen went around to do their regular collecting. They belong to a society having its headquarters on Ross Alley. They went around among Chinese prostitutes, and told them that a new Chief of Police had come in, and, unless he received a handsome present, would shut up the houses. They collected from one and a half to five dollars from each one, and it was divided among the members of that society.

Q.—How many Chinese prostitutes are there in this city?

A.—About one thousand eight hundred. They are divided into two classes, one for white men and the other for Chinamen. With the white-men prostitutes the Chinamen will have nothing to do, saying that if a Chinawoman degrades herself by prostituting with white men she is too low for a Chinaman.

Q.—Do you know anything about money being paid to protect gambling-houses?

A.—Yes, sir. Some two years ago one of these Chinamen went

around among the gambling-houses, and told them that by paying a license of from eight to thirty dollars a month they could escape arrest; but if by mistake they should be arrested their fine would be paid from this money. If they did not pay this license they would be arrested, and their business broken up. Nearly all the gambling-houses paid it, and these men went around for months collecting it. A special officer went around to see that the collections were made.

Q.—Do you know whether Chinese prostitutes are free or slaves?

A.—They are owned sometimes by men and sometimes by women. I know many cases of their being bought and sold. There are many leading Chinamen here who have shares in Chinese houses of prostitution. Among them are Ah Fook, who has charge of the joss-house at the head of St. Louis Alley; Yee Yum, on Jackson Street; Him Lung Mok, who has a store on Dupont Street, nearly opposite Commercial.

Q.—Do you know whether Chinamen sell their wives?

A.—Yes, sir. I had a Chinamen working for me two and a half years ago who got sick and out of money. He put his wife into a house of prostitution, and let her out for so much a month. After she had been there three or four weeks he sold her to the proprietors of the house. His name was Yung Sung.

Q.—Is there any way for these women to buy themselves free?

A.—Those in houses for white men have no chance; but those for Chinamen receive many presents of money, etc., which are for their own use.

LEE KAN sworn.

Mr. Pierson—How long have you been in California?

A.—Since eighteen hundred and fifty-two.

Q.—What business have you been in?

A.—Interpreter for the Bank of California for nine years.

Q.—From what part of China did you come?

A.—From Canton.

Q.—Do you know how many Chinamen there are in San Francisco?

A.—About thirty thousand.

Q.—What class of Chinamen do we have here, as a general thing?

A.—There are some merchants, but the most of them are laborers; we call them farmers in China.

Q.—What do you mean by a coolie in China?

A.—Those who are sold to slavery to some parties, to work for so many years.

Q.—Do you know anything about the six companies in San Francisco?

A.—Yes, sir.

Q.—Do you know the heads of those companies?

A.—Yes, sir.

Q.—Do all the Chinamen that come to San Francisco come consigned to those companies?

A.—They come by themselves. When they come here an inspector for each company boards the vessel, and looks after them.

Q.—Do you know of any Chinamen that come here under contract, to work until they earn their passage money?

A.—Not with the six companies. They may borrow from their friends and relatives, and then, when they earn money here, pay them back.

Mr. Donovan—Do you know anything about buying and selling women for purposes of prostitution?

A.—I know very little about that, for I am not in that line of business.

Q.—Do you know any men engaged in that business?

A.—I do not know whether I do or not. I have merely heard it talked about.

Q.—Do you believe it to be true that women are bought and sold for purposes of prostitution?

A.—Yes, sir.

Q.—Do you know any Chinese Christians?

A.—Yes, sir.

Q.—Are you one?

A.—No, sir.

Q.—Are these men real Christians, or are they only pretending to be?

A.—I cannot tell.

Q.—As a rule, are they not such persons as would become Christians, or anything else, for a good position and a good salary?

A.—I cannot tell.

Q.—Would all of them become Christians for good salaries, and good positions?

A.—I guess so.

Q.—Do you hear any of them say that Sunday-school is a good place to learn English?

A.—Yes, sir.

Q.—Did it strike you that they were more anxious to learn English than to get religious teachings?

A.—Yes, sir.

Q.—Do the Chinese respect this mission here?

A.—I think so.

Q.—Have the Chinese companies tried to stop the Chinese from coming here?

A.—Over a month ago they had a meeting of merchants and company men, and they sent a dispatch to China. A good many Chinamen had paid their passage money before they got the news. I think, from this time, there won't be so much immigration, because the merchants have sent another dispatch to their agents or correspondents, not to send any freight on vessels carrying more than one hundred passengers.

Q.—About how many Christian Chinamen are there here?

A.—Not more than two hundred.

Q.—Do those men discard the Chinese habit and costume?

A.—No, sir.

Q.—Do they wear their queues?

A.—Yes, sir.

Q.—Are they more respected than they were before they became Christians?

A.—No, sir.

Q.—Are they more honest?

A.—No, sir. They only change their religion. They are no better than they were before, when they were heathens.

Q.—Are the Chinamen coming here able to get employment as fast as they come?

A.—No, sir.

Q.—Have the wages of Chinamen been reduced very much during the last ten years?
A.—Yes, sir.

JAMES R. ROGERS, the officer detailed by the Chief of Police, at the request of the committee, to collect statistics regarding Chinese in San Francisco, pursuant to the resolution of the committee heretofore adopted, submitted the following report:

GENTLEMEN: In compliance with the instructions received from your honorable committee, I have endeavored, in the limited time in which I was engaged in the matter (six days), to obtain and collect for your information details relative to the different industrial pursuits which are either monopolized by the Chinese or are fast becoming so. From the fact that this class of our community have reduced the prices to what would be almost starvation to our white men and women, thereby showing the cause, in a great measure, of the lack of employment in our city, and the prolific cause of our young men growing up in idleness, and our women, in very many instances, driven to the last resort, of which our city will furnish abundant proof, these are matters of the most serious consideration. It would require, as will be apparent to your committee, considerably more time to collect for your information reliable and thoroughly accurate data regarding the inroads made upon the different avocations whereby our citizens are gaining their livelihood; but, as before stated, the extremely limited time allowed me must be my excuse for giving the general summary which I have the honor to offer for your consideration.

CIGAR MAKING.

There are about three thousand three hundred Chinese employed in the business of cigar making, earning from forty to ninety cents, and perhaps in some instances one dollar per day. There are in the vicinty of two hundred and sixty places where cigars are manufactured, the larger proportion of which are carried on by Chinese, and a very small number where Chinese and white labor are employed conjointly. The number of cigars manufactured in the First Congressional District of California during the last twelve months, nine-tenths of which have been made in the City and County of San Francisco and by Chinese labor, amounts to one hundred and twenty million five hundred and ninety-eight thousand. This includes about six million cigaritos. Deduct six million made by white labor, and the balance, one hundred and fourteen million five hundred and ninety-eight thousand, remains. Many of the cigaritos are manufactured from the butts of cigars picked up from the street, in front of cellars and bar-rooms, as can be seen gathered by Chinamen every morning on our public streets. These are again manufactured into material for smoking, and sold at the different Chinese depots at the rate of five cents per package, made up in the form of cigaritos.

OF LAUNDRIES.

There are about three hundred scattered throughout the city, averaging five men each. Some of these establishments employ double sets of hands and run day and night. It may safely be said there are fifteen hundred men employed, exclusively Chinese, in Chinese wash-houses in this city, while as many more are employed at the larger establishments of the same nature which are carried on by white management. Not less than three thousand men are employed in this business alone.

PEDDLING.

About three hundred are engaged in peddling fruit, vegetables, and fish, while many others are engaged in going from house to house selling laces, tape, needles, pins, matches, cigars, and human hair, which our ladies use to adorn their heads; in fact, almost all the material sold in our small retail dry goods stores can be procured from Chinamen at your door, and at prices which those who are doing a legitimate business cannot possibly compete with.

CLOTHING.

There are about thirty manufactories of men's clothing carried on by Chinese, the men doing the main portion of the work, while the women do the light finishing.

SLIPPER MANUFACTORIES.

Of these there are eleven, where large quantities of this article are made, the main work being done by men at the shop, and the finishing by Chinese women at their homes during the day; in fact, nearly all of this article is from Chinese labor.

SHOES AND GAITERS.

A very large number of men are employed and an immense amount of material manufactured into merchandise of this nature, of which my limited time does not allow me to give you the full details, but there is no doubt but what eight-tenths of the ladies' and children's gaiters and shoes made in this city are of Chinese manufacture.

MANUFACTURE OF LADIES' AND CHILDREN'S UNDERWEAR.

Shirts, night-dresses, chemises—in fact, every article of such nature—are being made up in large quantities by Chinamen and Chinese women; this to the dismay of our sewing girls, who vainly attempt to compete with Chinese labor. In very many of our retail stores where such merchandise as ladies' underwear is displayed for sale, the articles are the production and handiwork of a Chinaman, to the exclusion of the white girl, who, up to the present time, has made an honorable living by her needle.

LODGING-HOUSES.

There are about thirty known as such, where Chinese herd in large numbers, while there are very many more places of a similar nature. Very few of the domestics employed in families but what sleep in the Chinese quarter, sleeping in rooms containing from six men to twenty and forty, and even one hundred have been known to occupy a single apartment. Closed at all points, the atmosphere, upon entering one of these places in the morning, is beyond description. As a sanitary measure, this is a matter that should and has engaged the attention of the authorities; and the law known as the "pure-air law" was passed by our Legislature as a purely sanitary measure, and for the protection of our citizens and the prevention of an epidemic. This law is being enforced by the police department.

DOMESTICS.

There are about five thousand Chinese employed as cooks, nurses, dish-washers, bed-makers, and waiters. These are employed by families, lodging-houses, etc.

HOUSES OF ILL-FAME

Have been principally confined to the small streets and alleys in the Chinese quarter of this city, and comprise in number between one hundred and fifty and two hundred. These are occupied by a class of inmates brought to this country for the purpose of serving a term of years as prostitutes. During the day these women, as far as practicable, are employed at the various branches of industry—as working on shirts, slippers, men's clothing, women's underwear, etc. As this class of operatives do not receive pay for this extra work, it must naturally work a fearful injury to the honest white girl who depends upon her needle for her support. I need not describe in detail these places, or their disastrous tendencies upon our community, as the public press, from time to time, have fully advised you in all matters connected with this branch of our Chinese quarter.

THE MANUFACTURE OF SHIRTS

Of every description has been largely engaged in and is being carried on extensively by Chinese, giving employment to both men and this class of women.

OPIUM SMOKING.

This habit had formerly been practiced by the Chinese almost exclusively, every Chinese house being provided with the drug, together with all the implements for using the article. Regular depots are also established, where opium is smoked at regular and stated prices, where parties smoke until insensible, then sleep off the deadly effects. While this was practiced among the Chinese alone, no particular attention was given the subject, but very recently not less than eight places have been started, furnished with opium-pipes, beds for sleeping off the fumes, etc. These latter places were conducted by Chinamen, and patronized by both white men and women, who visited these dens at all hours of the day and night, the habit and its deadly results becoming so extensive as to call for action on the part of the authorities, and an ordinance was passed which had the effect of breaking up those places, but the practice, deeply rooted, still continues. The department of police, in enforcing the law with regard to this matter, have found white women and Chinamen side by side under the effects of this drug—a humiliating sight to any one who has anything left of manhood.

THE PRACTICE OF GAMBLING

Has been carried on very extensively in all its various branches. The many places where this vice has been carried on are now being kept closed by order of the Chief of Police—as far as practicable.

THE DIFFERENT ASSOCIATIONS,

Such as brokers, butchers, carpenters, employment offices, jewelers, watchmakers, pawn-shops, tinsmiths, barbers, joss-houses, and, in fact, very many other matters connected with this class of our community, had I the time I should be glad to give you the details; but, as before stated, the excuse must be given for this short report which I offer you.

Respectfully submitted,

JAMES R. ROGERS.

FOURTEENTH DAY.

SAN FRANCISCO, May 27th, 1876.

GILES H. GRAY sworn.

Mr. Pierson—What official position do you hold?

A.—Surveyor of Customs for the Port of San Francisco.

Q.—How long have you occupied the position?

A.—About three years.

Q.—Have you any data in your possession by which we can arrive at the number of Chinamen who have come to this country?

A.—The Custom-house records will show that. I have here a passenger list similar to that carried by every steamer in the China trade, and certified to by the United States Consul.

[Witness exhibited a passenger list similar to those carried by every steamer coming here from China, and which must be certified to by the United State Consul before vessels can clear. The list contains the names of the passengers, the sex, occupation, nativity, village or town, and whether they are free or hired emigrants.]

The certificate of the Consul reads as follows:

CONSULATE OF THE UNITED STATES OF AMERICA, AT HONG-KONG.

I, the undersigned, Consul of the United States for the Island of Hong-kong and the dependencies thereof, do hereby certify that the within-named persons, being inhabitants and subjects of China, to the number of eight hundred and seventy-six (876) are, each and all of them, free and voluntary emigrants, going hence to San Francisco, in the United States of America, on board the steamship Colorado, of New York, and that I am personally satisfied, by evidence produced, of the truth of the facts herein mentioned.

Done in conformity with the provisions of the Act of Congress entitled an Act to prohibit the coolie trade, approved February nineteenth, eighteen hundred and sixty-two; and an Act supplemental to the Acts in relation to immigration, approved March third, eighteen hundred and seventy-five.

Given under my hand and the seal of this Consulate, this fifteenth day of April, A. D. eighteen hundred and seventy-six.

[CONSULATE SEAL.] D. H. BAILEY, United States Consul.

The majority of the emigrants, as shown by these lists, are laborers, and it also shows that they are free. We do not permit a single Chinese individual to land here until this list is filed in the Custom-house. There is a law of Congress which prohibits the coolie trade. This is section two thousand one hundred and fifty-eight of the United States revised statutes. Section two thousand one hundred and sixty-two provides for the certificate, and there are severe penalties provided for bringing passengers to this port without that certificate. The Act of March third, eighteen hundred and seventy-five (page four hundred and seventy-seven of the session laws of eighteen hundred and seventy-four–five) provides for the prevention of the embarkation of lewd and immoral persons, criminals, etc. The Collector of the Port is instructed to prevent their landing, if they should gain a passage, and to return them to China in the ship which brought them. On the twenty-second of July last, the Collector and myself undertook to carry out this law, and we have thus far always detained the immigrants on board Chinese passenger vessels sufficiently long to give parties an opportunity to make complaint in regard to any of them as belonging to the prohibited classes. We detain them on board twenty-four hours, but there has yet never been a single complaint, for there is no one here with sufficient knowledge of the facts to proceed. The law is practically worthless, so far as this portion of it is concerned. When women come here, a letter is sent by the American Consul at Hong-kong, inclosing photographs of the women, and saying that he is satisfied that they do not come within the prohibited classes. [Witness exhibits a large number of photographs of Chinese women received in this manner.] Before women are permitted to go on board ships, they must have photographs taken at their own expense, and must swear to a certain state of facts. They must tell whence they came, where they are going, what their occupation is, whether married or single, why they go to a foreign country, etc., and produce witnesses who must also swear to a similar state of affairs. If the Consul is satisfied that they are respectable women, tickets are sold them, and they come here. When they present his certificate here, we cannot go behind that from mere suspicion. Since last July, there have arrived here not more than two hundred and fifty women, but previous to that every steamer brought two hundred and fifty and upwards. Very few prostitutes come now, the majority of the women immigrants being family women. There is a difference between the two classes, which an intelligent observer can generally perceive, and from my observation I think that, since last July, most of the women coming here are respectable. I have no doubt but that the importation of women for lewd and immoral purposes has stopped. The adoption of the "certificate" system has had that effect. If the same rules and regulations were applied to the men, I think it would practically stop their coming also. You might have a law passed providing for the payment of a heavy fee—say fifteen dollars, twenty-five dollars, or even fifty dollars—to the Consul before embarkation, and then none but the merchants could come to California. After the laborers pay for their passage, they have nothing left, and can raise no more money. Such a law would be within our power to enforce, and would not be open to the charge of unconstitutionality. All the Chinese immigrants who come here land at the Port of San Francisco.

On motion, a committee of one, Senator Rogers, was appointed to make arrangements for obtaining photographs of various parts of the Chinese quarter, for use of the Commission in the book now being printed.

The Commission then adjourned to meet in Sacramento, at the office of Hon. Creed Haymond, on Wednesday next, at twelve o'clock M.

FIFTEENTH DAY.

SACRAMENTO, June 3d, 1876.

JAMES GALLOWAY, being sworn, made the following statement:

My name is James Galloway; I am a lawyer by profession; age, fifty-eight years; came to California in eighteen hundred and forty-nine; have spent about twenty years in the gold mines of the Sierra Nevada Mountains; most of the time in the County of Sierra, in and about Downieville, Forest City, Sierra City; also, a portion in Nevada

County. I was for a number of years a practical miner, and for nearly all of the time in the mines, owner and operator. I am acquainted with the Chinese working in the mines, having employed Chinamen to work for me both in river and bank, or gravel, and occasionally in the tunnel diggings. I am also familiar with their habits and customs, and character, as residents of the mining regions, and their modes of working in the mines. Their habits are not essentially different from those I have seen in the valleys. They generally, indeed I may say universally, live in the meanest kind of hovels, sometimes constructed of the old lumber of an abandoned flume, other times in a canvas tent, but in the summer or mining season in brush tents, put up with posts and poles, and brush thrown over them. They are dirty in their habits, filthy around their camps; generally living on rice, but occasionally indulge in fresh pork, and also in a nice fat dog. I have the word of Chinamen who worked for me that they eat dog meat. Have known them to buy these animals. Have known them to eat chickens that they knew died of disease. They wear the Chinese dress, except some of them have our style of soft hats and boots, but many of them still wear the broad Chinese hat made from cane splits and manufactured in China. Nearly all their ware is evidently Chinese manufacture and made in China. They have their own merchants in the mining camps, from whom they buy all their rice and tea, and salt stuffs that are brought from China. They have their own garden plats, on which they raise their own vegetables; and it is curious to see how soon they will produce a crop of fresh peas, beans, and lettuce. They plant the peas and beans in hot sand, and when the sprouts are about one inch long they carefully take them up, wash them and thus have not green, but fresh peas and white beans sprouted. They eat green gourds and green pumpkins and green squashes.

Many of them in the mining camps smoke opium. Indeed, I think, more in proportion to their number smoke opium in the mines than in the valley towns, such as Chico, Marysville, and Sacramento, where I have lived. They import to nearly all the mining towns or camps lewd women, who ply their occupation in the mining camps, and ask and receive the patronage of the whites as well as of the Chinese. As a class their character in the mines is that of thieves. They have often been caught robbing sluice-boxes, houses, and stealing chickens, and frequently convicted, and often punished summarily by the discoverer. Those who have worked for me I always made a practice of watching. They have no morals that I could ever discover, except in carrying out contracts. In Sierra County they have often been charged with murder, but they are cunning and hard to convict. From eighteen hundred and fifty-five to eighteen hundred and sixty-nine, there must have been several thousand in the Counties of Sierra and Nevada. They nearly all raise the dead bodies of their companions and send them off, with the avowed intention of sending them to China.

Their operations in the mines have often been very profitable. These mines are nearly all worked by companies. Companies bring up scores of them and hire them out, or buy or locate claims, and set them to work on them. The company comes down in the evening and takes possession of the gold. These companies supply the rice and other provisions, tools, etc., for these fellows who work in the mines. When a person hires one or more of these Chinamen, it is usual, if not universal, to settle with the head man of the company; and if you turn off one he will bring you another. They appear to control all their movements, and take their earnings as though they were their property. Companies often locate mines on their own account, but generally get some person to locate the ground, and then buy from them, and thus they think they get a better title. They work much poor ground, but have also worked many hundreds of rich claims, and have taken out a large amount of gold. For several seasons I resided on the banks of the Yuba, and used to see their clean-up, and know that for years several companies made as high as from four dollars to twelve dollars per hand to the day. They soon become good miners. They are generally sober, patient, and slow, but constant workers. The Chinese, for several years, worked more men along the banks and in the beds of the different forks of the Yuba River than the whites, and made more money than the whites. This money (so far as my opportunities enabled me to judge, and my opportunities were of the best) nearly all left the mines in possession or ownership of Chinamen. They have no property, or but little in mining camps, or in the mines, that is worthy of the Assessors' or Tax-gatherers' notice. They get the gold, and go scot free as a general rule. Nearly all the ground they have worked could now be profitably worked by white labor—some of it would pay richly. They were not safe neighbors where they had large camps, and the whites were few. They are ingenious and imitative, and can work wet diggings as well, if not better than white men. In our mining towns they now occupy most of the domestic positions that women and girls did before their immigration to the mines. Many poor persons—widows, in some cases, with children—have been displaced by these Chinese laborers, especially is this the case in the laundry business and cooking. I am not much prejudiced against them, but did write some articles, in eighteen hundred and sixty-one and eighteen hundred and sixty-two, against the policy of our Government allowing this pauper labor amongst us. I wrote for my own paper, the *Sierra Citizen*, taking ground that they were carrying away our treasure, and would never become citizens—would not improve our country by building, or in any way add to the material wealth of the State. This is still my opinion. They do carry away our gold, and without any power of our getting any revenue from them. From my observation, I would say their presence in the mines is as injurious to our citizens living in them as in the cities, with this addition, that they carry away more wealth, and give less return, than in the latter places. Their morals are as bad. Their opportunities of committing outrages upon persons, and violating rights of property, are greater, while their punishment is less certain—being more difficult.

ANDREW AITKEN sworn.

Mr. Haymond—How long have you resided in California?

A.—Since the tenth day of August, eighteen hundred and fifty.

Q.—Have you lived in Sacramento ever since?

A.—No, sir. I have lived in Sacramento since the fall of eighteen hundred and fifty-three?

Q.—What is your occupation?

A.—I am in the marble business.

Q.—What knowledge have you as to the efforts that have been

made on this coast by the Christian people to convert and bring to christianity the Chinese people?

A.—My knowledge, as far as I have assisted and observed the labors of others, is that it is beneficial.

Q.—What is beneficial—what has been done?

A.—Teaching them to read the English language, studying scripture, and quite a number have been converted to christianity. There have been nine of them made members of the Presbyterian Church; of that number, one has died.

Q.—For what length of time have you observed these matters?

A.—I have been giving my personal attention for about three years—two years and a half or three years. I have been superintendent of the Chinese school in the Presbyterian Church. That school is on the corner of Sixth and L streets, and is under the management of the Presbyterian Session.

Q.—How long is it since it was established?

A.—About two years and a half or three years.

Q.—How many Chinamen are attending it?

A.—On an average, about sixty last year; sometimes more and sometimes less; mostly adults.

Q.—Eight or nine Chinamen have been converted?

A.—Nine joined our church, one died, and eight are now members. The first-named joined three years ago, and the balance within a year and a half. Generally, the same persons attend school regularly. There is a class that we call the "Bible class," composed of some six or seven, that are always there.

Q.—During the time that you have known of these missionary efforts have the members of the church been zealous, and has everything been done that can be done to bring about a conversion of the Chinese?

A.—Yes, sir. In the evening school they are taught to read, and in learning they are very quick and accurate.

Q.—Do you teach them concerning any of the principles of the government?

A.—No.

Q.—Do they seem to know anything of them?

A.—We have never attempted to do anything in that direction; we merely teach them to read.

Q.—Do you know of anything that could have been done by your church or its members, within the bounds of reason, towards educating and christianizing the Chinese, that has not been done?

A.—I think a little more might have been done had we started years ago; but since we started we have done everything that could be reasonably expected. I think our school is the largest school in the city.

Q.—Do you know anything about the condition of the Chinese in the City of San Francisco?

A.—Only by hearsay.

Q.—What effect do you think this Chinese immigration would have upon California should it be continued to the extent that it is now carried—three thousand five hundred or four thousand a month?

A.—I do not think it would be beneficial, especially the importation of so many lewd women; that is the greatest fault I see in the immigration of Chinese. I am not in favor of seeing a great influx of Chinese any more than any one else, but those that are here it is our duty to try and elevate and educate.

Q.—If one hundred and fifty thousand of these Chinese should settle in California it would be necessary that they should be raised from their present condition?

A.—Yes, sir.

Q.—What effect do you think their presence in this city has upon the morals of the community—do you think that it is good or bad, taking it as a whole?

A.—I think as a whole that it has not been good—that is, taking the worst class. The majority are rather inclined to corrupt the morals of others.

Q.—Do you know in what regard they hold women?

A.—No. I never had any conversation with them in regard to that.

Q.—Taking the Chinese members of the Presbyterian Church, what has been their conduct since—do you see any decided change in them?

A.—Yes, sir.

Q.—A very material one?

A.—Yes, sir. They seem to have a great reverence for anything that is religious. They are very attentive to lessons and learn to have a regard for praying. They seem to have more respect for prayer than even our own people.

Q.—How is it regarding their business relations—are they honest?

A.—I see no reason to doubt that.

Q.—Do you see any difference between them and the Chinese here?

A.—Yes, a marked difference. They do not associate with them, but keep by themselves. Those who are Christians associate with themselves or with white people.

Q.—Do you know what their opinion is about the effect of this large immigration into the country?

A.—I do not.

Q.—Do you find in this city, among the intelligent people, any desire to resort to force or violence against the Chinese here?

A.—No, sir.

Q.—And the general impression is the impression you have?

A.—Yes, sir.

Q.—You express the general feeling, when you say that they are here and must be protected, and that it would be a disgrace to our country to have any attacks made upon them?

A.—Yes, sir. That would show them that we are no better than they are.

Q.—Are there other mission schools in this city?

A.—The Methodist Church has one, and the Congregational folks have one.

Q.—Do you know how many students are attending them?

A.—No, sir.

Q.—Do you know how many church members there are?

A.—I think one or two belong to the Congregational, and one or two to the Methodists.

Q.—How is your school and mission sustained?

A.—The night-school is sustained by the Board of Presbyterian Missionaries. Mr. Loomis sends me money every month to pay the rent and the teacher.

Q.—Can you fix about the annual expense?

A.—One hundred and thirty dollars for rent; three hundred dollars for teacher; porter, three hundred dollars; total, seven hundred and thirty dollars, besides light and fuel. About one thousand dollars a year is the cost of keeping up that school.

Q.—In that, of course, you do not include the labors of yourself?

A.—There is no one paid except the teacher. All the other labor is voluntarily given. The gas is furnished by the church.

Q.—Are there any Chinese women attending that school?

A.—No, sir. There is one little half-Chinese girl that comes to our regular Sabbath-school.

Q.—Is she living with a white family?

A.—Yes, sir; but you could not tell but what she was pure white.

Q.—You do not find any prejudice among the members of your church to their education and advancement, do you?

A.—There is nothing said, but since this Chinese question came up some have absented themselves from school. Young men come in, and listen to the singing, and I sometimes ask them if they will teach, but they refuse, saying they don't like Chinamen, or make some such remark as that.

Q.—Do you know anything about the missionary labors in China?

A.—Only what I have read. I will say this, however, when the Chinese boys were admitted to the church, through the session, they underwent as clear an examination as any of our white people; in fact, they were more prompt with their answers in regard to the scriptures and the plan of salvation by a Redeemer.

Q.—Do they adopt the style of dress of white people?

A.—No. I do not think that has anything to do with it. Every nation has its customs in regard to dress, etc.

Q.—What is the employment of these persons that belong to your church?

A.—Some are engaged in washing, and some are servants.

Q.—Do you know how they are received by the Chinese who are not Christians?

A.—They are persecuted a good deal. I will state that a boy living with Judge Curtis, and who died a year ago, was as good a Christian as ever lived in the world. He was the first Chinese member of our church.

Q.—Do you meet with opposition from the mass of the Chinese?

A.—Yes, sir. During last year, last winter, they tried to kick up a fuss at the night-school, on Fourth Street, and I had to get a force of policemen to protect the school. They came there, and made noises, and tried to prevent boys from coming in. Since I got the police, there has been no disturbance.

Q.—These converts are not very well treated by the Chinese?

A.—No. They are persecuted.

Q.—Your converts do not associate with the mass of the Chinamen?

A.—They do not make them their associates as they did formerly. They have to associate with them more or less, the same as we Christians associate with our kind.

Q.—From the manner in which they are received they would not naturally associate with them?

A.—No.

Q.—Do they express any intention of returning to China?

A.—Some of them do. We had a colporteur here who returned to China with the determination to preach in his own country. Since he went away there is another young man who is filling his place and preaching in the Chinese language about five minutes every Sunday night to those who cannot speak English. Quon Loy was the teacher, and he had great influence among the Chinese. He was among them continually, was an industrious man and a good Christian.

Q.—Is not one of the difficulties in the way of the conversion of Chinese their migratory habits—that is, moving about from place to place?

A.—That would prevent more from uniting. One intended to join our church last spring, but he wished to go to San Francisco and unite with some of his acquaintances. I think it is a greater task for Chinamen to become Christians than it is for our own people, because they undergo more persecution and opposition amongst their own people; so it is a sacrifice they have to make. I have found these Chinese converts are very attentive to their duties, are present at communion service, and have as much regard for the solemnity of the occasion as any of us.

Q.—Have they any idea of the principles under which this country is governed?

A.—I do not know.

Q.—Don't you think it would be a good thing to educate them in that, in your mission schools?

A.—Yes, it would be. They seem to be very much taken up with reading, and, when they once learn, they read the papers. This Quon Loy writes as pretty a hand as you or I, and writes as pretty a letter as you would want to read. This boy, that lived with Judge Curtis, wrote a beautiful hand.

Q.—Senator Sargent has introduced a bill into the United States Senate, providing that hereafter not more than ten Chinamen shall be brought to this State on any one ship. What is your idea as to the passage of such a bill?

A.—I think it would be beneficial to restrict the immigration in that way. I believe in that fully.

Q.—What is the opinion of yourself and other members of your church as to whether the problem of converting the Chinese to christianity is to be worked out here, or whether it could be better worked out by the converts you make here returning to their own country?

A.—I think that if we could convert all those that are here, or even a portion of them, the balance would soon follow. A great many of those who are converted here will return to China, and preach the gospel to their own people. The missionaries we send to China will not have as much effect as the Chinese converts we send there. I do not believe any of us will see the fruits of the seed we are now sowing. It takes years for anything of that kind to show itself. A great obstacle in the way of their conversion is the fact that a great many churches take no steps towards educating them at all. I know this, that new ones coming to school don't know the first letter, and in three or four nights they know the alphabet. Their memory is remarkably clear, and their imitative powers are strong. Sometimes they stand up to repeat the ten commandments without missing a single word. They can repeat the Lord's prayer and the creed. We have the creed once every three or four nights.

Rev. H. H. Rice sworn.

Mr. Haymond—How long have you resided in California?

A.—Since February third, eighteen hundred and seventy-five.

Q.—What is your profession?

A.—A minister of the gospel. I am pastor of the Westminster Presbyterian Church, in this city.

Q.—State generally what efforts have been made by your church towards the conversion of the Chinese in our midst?

A.—There are two classes of efforts being made in relation to Chinese advancement, one secular and the other religious, although they are blended to some extent. We have a night-school on Fourth Street, taught by a member of our church, where the Chinese are taught to read, and are given the elements of an ordinary school education. We do not teach them anything about the principles of our government. I believe that ought to be taught by the government. The government ought to sustain Chinese schools, and, as far as possible, modify the ignorance of the Chinese race. The persons attending our school are mostly adults. We think it is our duty, because, the Board of Education has not thus far opened the public schools to the Chinese, to educate them, for we are convinced that Chinese immigration, if left to itself, will simply be a flood of heathenism poured on American soil. It is therefore the duty of the government to rise up and control it, and teach the Chinese American customs, and give them an education, in order to civilize them. Our mission night-school simply aims to give them a purely secular English education. They must be educated or excluded, and I do not believe it is possible to exclude them. The result of the meeting of the Chinese and the American civilizations is that the Chinese will come to this country, no matter what measures are taken to prevent it. Their education is, therefore, a public necessity, and a move in the nature of self-protection. The burden of educating them ought not, however, to be thrown upon the State of California, but should be sustained by the Federal Government.

Q.—It is exclusion on the one hand, or education on the other?

A.—I will say that it is exclusion or education, and you cannot exclude them.

Q.—You assume that it is a public necessity that they be educated?

A.—It seems so to me.

Q.—Do the Chinese come to this country to live?

A.—No.

Q.—They are here for some temporary purpose?

A.—Yes, sir.

Q.—They do not come as other immigrants do?

A.—Not as a rule, although there are some who come to live. My observation is very recent, and I can say very little regarding the civilizing effect of the contact with American manners and customs. I think, however, that such contact is good for them, and the best contact is generally found in these mission schools. Outside, they are not treated always as well as they should be, but the American people have the power to control and educate, if they will exert their strength.

Q.—The church recognizes the universal brotherhood of man?

A.—Yes, sir.

Q.—No State could recognize it, and exist; no family could recognize it, and live?

A.—It seems to me that the United States does recognize the principle of the brotherhood of the whole human race.

Q.—The State don't do that. Suppose you were to recognize in your family the universal brotherhood of man?

A.—We recognize that, in the family; it is not necessary for the whole world to be invited to the supper table. Some of us have pretty large families, and cannot all sit down at the same table. In regard to this matter of education, I will say, absolutely, that the State has a duty to educate the Chinese children as much as any other children. In regard to the religious education, I can corroborate the statements made by Mr. Aitken. The members of our church have told me they have, at times, received persecution from their countrymen. A Chinaman sacrifices much to become a Christian. Even in a worldly point of view they lose much, for they lose friendship to a great extent. I believe in the sincerity of our Chinese converts, and should they do anything wrong, they would be disciplined just the same as any of our white members. There seems to be a general misunderstanding as to what is a Christian Chinaman. Only those are considered so who have been baptized, and are members. A great many attend the school, but they are not Christians. The Chinese, at first, consider education and religion as synonymous, and when questioned will say they are Christians, when all they do is to attend school. They think that to be an American is to be a Christian. They call themselves Christians when they go to school. The church does not raise the question of how many converts are going to be made, how many are to become Christians, or what are to be the results. That does not affect us in the least; but it is a simple duty that we feel we owe, to teach them the Christian religion. The members of the church do not at all represent the sum total of the good influence exerted by our labors, nor would we consider christianity in this country a failure because the majority of the people have not united with any church. I do not think the home missionary work is being neglected because church people labor for the heathen of other nations, for I have found the most zealous workers in regard to foreign missions are also the most zealous workers at home. It is only a missionary religion that can live—all others decay. The religions of Brahma, Confucius, and Zoroaster are stagnating and dying, because they are not missionary religions. Buddhism and christianity are missionary religions, and are the strongest on earth.

Q.—What is your opinion as to the influence of the church in the East and in California?

A.—I think its influence in California is not so great as in the East. The early immigration to California was not religious, and the church had to come in for the leavings.

Q.—Suppose you were to put one million Chinamen on this coast, and add to that number those already outside of the pale, what effect do you think it would have upon the present generation?

A.—As Abraham Lincoln said, "I will wait for the river before I talk about the bridge."

Q.—Would we be as able to receive it as the older States?

A.—No, sir; I believe that Chinese immigration, if left to itself, is a detriment to this country, and the only loop-hole is in the fact that

it is a necessity—and whatever is, is right. The outcome is going to be good for this country, and for the old country. There must, however, be a conflict of races, and the final result is going to be beneficial. The effect of the presence of a certain class of Chinese here is more deleterious than the effect of the presence of the same class among our own people. Correspondingly bad classes among the white races would be less injurious to the community than bad classes among the Chinese. The moral effect is worse, but it is useless to try to exclude them, and it becomes our duty to elevate their civilization.

Q.—What do you think of Senator Sargent's proposition, restricting immigration to ten on a ship?

A.—I think it is rather idealistic. It would be difficult to limit it to ten; but assuming it could be done, I should have no objection to it.

Q.—Do you think that the church here has done as much as can be reasonably expected in this matter of the conversion of Chinamen—has the work been faithfully and efficiently done?

A.—Yes, sir; as far as I have seen the work, and I have seen it in San Francisco, here, and in San José. I think it has been done faithfully and efficiently by those who are working. I will not say that the church is doing all it could, but it is doing vastly more than the government could expect, and the government should be obliged to the church for carrying some of her burdens.

Q.—In your efforts to convert Chinese, do you meet with much sympathy from the outside population?

A.—No, sir. The church meets with very little sympathy in California.

Rev. J. H. C. Bonte sworn.

Mr. Haymond—How long have you resided in California?

A.—About six years.

Q.—In what part of the State?

A.—In Sacramento City.

Q.—What has been your profession during that time?

A.—I am Presbyter of the Protestant Episcopal Church, and Rector of Grace Church, in this city.

Q.—Have you had occasion to examine the effect which Chinese immigration is having upon the people of this State?

A.—Yes, sir. I have talked with the medical faculty in regard to the subject, and I have considered the question from a religious standpoint. The general moral effect has been very bad upon the young of this country. My judgment is based upon facts I have gained mostly from medical men in this city.

Q.—Men of standing in their profession?

A.—The ablest and best. The general effect, according to all the testimony I have gathered of their presence, has been deplorably bad in that direction. The conversion of the Chinese to christianity is a consummation hoped for and believed in by every Christian. I have no doubt whatever of the power of the gospel to regenerate the whole Chinese Empire. But Christian men differ as to the method by which this result is to be accomplished—the precise manner of reaching the Chinese. In the opinion of many good observers who have made this subject a study, this great result is to be accomplished through Chinese instrumentality, and in their own country; while others believe that China is to be reached through the conversion of the Chinese in America. The former believe that the character of a nation is not to be changed by mere preaching, but by a steady process of religious training and culture, under teachers of their own race. The missionary work of the past proves the fact that a heathen nation can be generally or permanently transformed only while in a settled condition, and while living in their natural surroundings. Christianity cannot be imposed upon China, but must be put into the Chinese; and this work will be slow until they undertake it themselves. The Chinese in California are not in a favorable condition to hear the gospel. They are here simply for the purpose of making money, and as they find the great body of our own people engaged in the same enterprise their love of money-getting becomes intensified by contact with our own people. They are, therefore, in a state of intense enthusiasm for gain, and sacrifice, like many of our own countrymen, everything for this one object. The Christian church in California finds one of its greatest obstacles in this passion among our own people, and if it operates disastrously in the work of converting our own people, it must be even more so in the Chinese work. Again, the Chinese now in this country are continually on the move, and it is almost impossible to keep up a continuous influence upon any one of them. We have control of them only for a few weeks or months, when they go to localities where nothing is or can be done for them. I cannot see, believing as I do in the necessity of thorough Christian training, an opportunity of doing them much good while in this country. Even those who may remain a year or two in the same place live under conditions which neutralize our efforts. The Christian teacher gains their attention only for a few hours, while their old ways and ideas have their continuous attention. They learn lessons, hear sermons, and learn Christian songs, then return to their inaccessible dens, where they again come under the sway of their old system. In my mind it is very doubtful whether a well-trained Christian could maintain his Christian character under similar conditions. Again, the Chinese are very keen observers, and let nothing pass unnoticed. We teach them christianity, but they see our hoodlumism and crime, and wonder that our people reject a religion which we seek to give them. They easily discern the fact that the Christian people are in a small minority. The missionaries in all lands have found their greatest obstacle in their own irreligious countrymen, and here the same obstacle operates with increased force. Under these circumstances we have no right to expect special results in the conversion of the Chinese who live among us. Besides, the Christian church in California is engaged in a severe struggle for its own existence. The nomadic habits of the people, their eager desire to make large fortunes, their lack of religious training, weakens the church very materially. The mass of the people of California came here at an early day, and they lived for many years without church privileges, and do not feel the necessity of churches as the people of older countries do. They do not stop long enough in their struggles to think that their early Christian training at home made them what they are, gave them their sense of right and wrong, imparted to them their great energy and hopefulness, and therefore they undervalue the church. For these and other reasons the Christian church in California is very weak. The church of the Pacific slope is not organized for the stupendous undertaking of converting the Chinese. The clergy are fearfully overworked, and besides, they have no special training for this peculiar work. The laity do not live long enough in a place to get into harness and learn the art of working among the Chinese. Besides, both men and women in California work harder than the people of any other country; are more intensely occupied, and have less leisure. The Christian church of the Pacific slope is therefore unprepared for this great emergency. The church has done its best, but that is comparatively little. It is foolish for Christian people in the East to expect much in the work of converting the Chinese, from the church of this country. In my judgment, the Chinese exercise as much influence among the people of this coast in favor of paganism as the church among the Chinese in favor of christianity. The Christian church will continue its work as long as the Chinese remain among us, but it will accomplish comparatively little, unless the church of the East throws its whole force into the work. The grand contest, which is to end with the conversion of China, must be carried on in China. The work in California, I fear, only retards our final success in China. What they see of christianity here, from their standpoint, must impress them very unfavorably. As a Christian minister, I take no part in this opposition to the Chinese. The Christian church believes, of necessity, in the brotherhood of man, and works for the salvation of all men indiscriminately, because they are men for whom Christ died. But this is a doctrine which the State cannot, at present, administer or establish. The State is organized for the protection and development of local institutions, ideas, and interests, and cannot permit the presence of systems that threaten its existence. The church is organized to establish the kingdom of Christ throughout the world, and means to do it. The Chinese question is therefore mainly a question for statesmen, and must be determined from their standpoint.

Q.—Do you think that the missionary work in California has been well and faithfully done, and that it has borne as good fruits as possible, under the circumstances?

A.—Undoubtedly.

Q.—Do you know anything about the difference between the Japanese and the Chinese?

A.—I have had more intimate associations with the Japanese than with the Chinese, and there is certainly a very wide difference between the two nations.

Q.—Do the Chinese have any appreciation of a republican form of government?

A.—I have never found one that had the faintest conception of what it was.

Q.—How are the Japanese?

A.—They seem to have an instinctive knowledge of our institutions. I have read essays by even young Japanese girls, and they seem to have an instinctive insight into things as they are. As far as I have seen the Japanese, they have come to the conclusion that the secret of all our greatness is in the Christian religion. I talked with one of the most distinguished Japanese gentlemen that ever came to this country, and he told me that while they might carry over a great many of our fine arts and fine things, still they could not retain them unless they took our christianity to sustain them. In dress and appearance, Japanese coming here try to imitate Americans. They stop at hotels, etc., and live like Americans. I am utterly amazed at the difference between the Japanese and the Chinese. I am convinced that through Japan we are to work the conversion of China.

Q.—What do you think of Senator Sargent's proposition to restrict immigration to ten on a ship?

A.—It would be certainly a very desirable thing, if it can be done. If further immigration were stopped, I think that the churches, by a concerted action, could reach these Chinese here, and, perhaps, make our efforts in China of more avail. The nomadic habits of those here are a great drawback. There is scarcely a Chinaman here that has not been in from ten to twenty places on the coast, and it is very difficult to christianize such roamers.

STATISTICS

SHOWING THE AREA AND POPULATION OF THE CHINESE EMPIRE; OUR TRADE WITH CHINA; CHINESE POPULATION IN CALIFORNIA; ETC.

The following is taken from the *San Francisco Journal of Commerce*, a paper of high repute. The figures have been verified by the committee:

The area of the Chinese Empire is much greater than that of the United States, and about equal to that of the great Empire of Brazil. Next to that of Russia it is the largest in the world, and contains incomparably the greatest population—a population comprising at least one-third of the whole human race.

The following are the latest estimates of area and population:

	Area sq. miles.	Population.
China	1,534,953	405,213,152
Manchuria	362,313	3,000,000
Mongolia	1,288,035	2,000,000
Thibet	643,734	6,000,000
Corea	90,300	8,000,000
Lienkhien	2,310	1,000,000 (Lienkhien and Liaotong together)
Liaotong	2,982	
Totals	3,924,627	425,213,152

The area, population, and chief cities are as follows:

Province.	Provincial Capital.	Area Eng. sq. miles.	Population.
Chih-li	Pekin	58,949	28,114,023
Shan-tung	Tse-nan-foo	65,104	28,958,764
Shan-se	Tae-yuen-foo	55,268	27,260,228
Honan	Kae-fung-foo	65,104	23,037,171
Keang-soo	Nanking	92,661 (Keang-soo and Gan-hwuy together)	37,843,501
Gan-hwuy	Gan-king-foo		34,168,059
Kiang-si	Nan-chang-foo	72,176	30,426,999
Foo-keen	Fuh-choo-foo	53,480	38,888,432
Che-keang	Hang-choo-foo	39,150	26,256,784
Hoo-pih	Woo-chang-foo	381,724 (Hoo-pih and Hu-nan together)	37,370,098
Hu-nan	Chang-cha-foo		18,652,507
Shen-se	Se-gan-foo	154,008 (Shen-se and Kan-suh together)	10,207,256
Kan-suh	Lan-choo-foo		15,193,135
Sze-chuen	Ching-too-foo	166,800	21,435,678
Kwang, or Canton	Kwang-choo-foo	79,456	19,147,030
Kwang-si	Kwe-lin-foo	78,250	7,313,895
Yun-nan	Yun-nan-foo	107,869	5,561,320
Kwei-choo	Kwei-yang-foo	64,554	5,288,219
Totals		1,524,953	405,213,152

This immense population could send out one-quarter of one per cent. as colonists to our shores, and then equal in numbers all the white population of the Pacific Coast. Were they sufficiently civilized, well armed, learned, and intelligent, they could spread their rule over the world, and be as dreaded in the nineteenth and twentieth centuries as were the hordes of Atilla, Gengis-Khan, and Tamerlane (all from Chinese territory), from the fifth to the fifteenth.

The internal trade of China is immense, the foreign is comparative small—the exports being only about one hundred and twenty-five million dollars annually, while the imports, exclusive of coin and bullion do not exceed twenty-five million dollars. The Chinese money of account consists of taels, consisting each of ten mace, or one hundred candareens, or one thousand cash. Three taels are equivalent to one pound sterling or four dollars eighty-six cents and sixty-five one-hundredths—one is therefore equal to one dollar sixty-two cents and two hundred and sixteen one-thousandths, while a cash is equal to one and thirty-one fiftieth mills nearly, six of them being about equal to a cent. These cash, made of copper, are the only coin current, gold, silver, and foreign coin being valued according to its weight and fineness. The principal weights are the tael or leang, one and one-third ounces avoirdupois; the catty, one and three-quarter pounds, and the picul, one hundred and thirty-three and one-third pounds.

Our imports from China, as well as our exports thither, are, on the whole, constantly increasing, though there was a heavy decline in quantities and values of some articles in eighteen hundred and seventy-five, as compared with the previous year, and though the quantity and value of tea and sugar imported has declined during many years.

The following tables give details for the past two years:

IMPORTS.

Articles.	1874.		1875.	
	Free.	Dutiable.	Free.	Dutiable.
Cigars		$962		
Coffee	$151,585		$162,823	
Hemp, raw		244,989		
Jute, etc.		1,570		
Opium		236,632		$757,640
Oil		139,746		
Rice		812,261		1,141,462
Silk, raw	626,424		209,336	
Silk manufactures				106,370
Silkworm eggs	8,386			
Spices		59,832		
Sugar		481,273		183,656
Tea	1,096,400		518,926	
Tin, in bars, etc.	27,458			
Miscellaneous	115,679	612,385	149,280	1,459,304
Totals	$2,025,932	$2,689,650 2,025,932	$1,040,365	$3,648,432 1,040,365
Grand total		$4,715,582		$4,688,797

EXPORTS—DOMESTIC.

1874.	Wheat Flour.		Ginseng.		Fish of all kinds.	Coin and bullion.	Potatoes.		Quicksilver.		All other commodities.	Totals.
	Barrels.	Value.	Pounds.	Value.			Bushels.	Value.	Pounds.	Value.		
January	11,099	$65,816	7,753	$9,099	$1,478	$180,639	20	$12			$14,393	$271,437
February	12,891	76,028	85,583	91,705	2,336	319,992	51	20			21,691	511,802
March	3,078	19,813	12,915	13,500	583	219,272	6	7			12,395	265,570
April	5,989	26,125	29,514	26,847	3,027	923,200			7,650	$9,563	28,511	1,017,273
May	11,946	64,386	13,141	14,335	20,411	1,671,845					44,064	2,815,040
June	14,341	78,490	9,000	9,000	23,111	593,201	3,251	2,926			20,510	727,238
July	12,909	70,980	27,475	26,990	31,259	353,767	4,421	3,345			27,930	514,271
August	11,745	60,644	46,092	48,517	39,163	449,268	7,078	3,712	15,300	22,185	32,769	656,258
September	16,117	75,977	17,655	20,800	2,243	429,266	2,489	1,448			27,937	557,671
October	15,726	72,947	53,817	58,522	29,999	525,738					28,332	715,538
November	4,418	20,426	16,448	20,662	3,873	214,555	679	584	11,475	17,250	11,113	288,463
December	12,931	61,310	53,879	74,960	8,413	280,891			26,775	41,119	17,601	484,294
Totals	133,190	$692,942	373,272	$414,937	$165,896	$6,161,633	17,895	$12,084	61,200	$90,117	$287,246	$7,824,855
1875.												
January	12,145	$64,390	61,303	$104,985	$1,347	$695,662			7,650	$11,858	$27,888	$906,130
February	15,850	72,160	55,642	79,523	6,757	667,736			22,950	32,278	20,175	879,629
March	1,009	5,039			514	117,450			9,180	12,525	7,291	142,819
April	11,941	59,994	66,979	87,809	16,250	530,936			123,200	89,301	28,815	813,105
May	11,927	59,440	28,602	30,800	45,300	414,547			85,593	56,827	28,116	635,030
June	9,951	46,813	12,756	15,635	34,329	531,150			42,075	27,327	35,967	691,221
July	7,848	39,410	18,389	19,717	43,559	229,519	901	$883	206,528	139,759	26,860	499,707
August	3,105	18,566	33,142	43,233	37,240	344,786	5,966	4,107	130,760	90,537	36,492	574,961
September	9,195	52,576	35,279	39,594	38,655	345,897	5,906	4,791	160,809	107,566	23,325	612,404
October	10,515	57,372	39,796	40,764	215,004	597,158	1,717	1,459	142,273	106,572	21,575	1,039,904
November	8,367	47,796	43,245	43,005	15,645	618,448	2,581	2,065	322,228	212,689	31,881	972,029
December	7,539	47,715	64,747	71,544	3,427	581,618	18	10	79,434	54,283	17,184	775,781
Totals	109,292	$571,271	459,880	$577,109	$458,027	$5,674,907	17,089	$13,315	1,332,959	$942,522	$605,569	$8,542,720

The imports of the principal articles compare as follows for the two years:

Articles.	Pounds.	Value.
Tea, 1875	1,881,651	$518,926
Tea, 1874	2,828,570	1,096,480
Decline 1875	946,919	$577,554
Sugar, 1875	5,528,529	$183,656
Sugar, 1874	15,462,603	481,273
Decline 1875	9,934,074	$297,617
Rice, 1875	46,883,850	$1,141,462
Rice, 1874	31,645,536	812,261
Increase 1875	14,738,314	$329,201
*Coffee, 1875	751,192	$162,823
*Coffee, 1874	775,069	151,585
Decrease 1875	23,877	†$11,238
Silk, 1875	----------	$315,706
Silk, 1874	----------	626,424
Decrease 1875	----------	$310,718

*Singapore and Manila. †Increase.

There has thus been a decrease in the quantity and value of almost every article of prominence except rice and coffee, but the increase in articles of food and clothing consumed by the Chinese, and of which they import the greater part, has almost made up for this.

The exports of principal articles of domestic merchandise for the past two years compare as follows:

Articles.		Amount.	Value.
Flour, 1875	Barrels	109,302	$571,271
Flour, 1874		133,190	692,942
Decline 1875		23,888	$121,671
Ginseng, 1875	Pounds	459,880	$577,109
Ginseng, 1874		373,272	414,937
Increase 1875		86,608	$162,172
Fish, 1875		----------	$458,027
Fish, 1874		----------	165,896
Increase 1875		----------	$292,131
Quicksilver, 1875	Flasks	8,712	$942,522
Quicksilver, 1874		400	90,117
Increase 1875		8,312	$852,405

A slight decrease is here shown in flour, but an increase in everything else, and a remarkable one in quicksilver. This year the increase promises to be still larger, as during the first quarter the exports of flour to China have equaled fifty-six thousand eight hundred and ninety-six barrels, valued at two hundred and thirty-six thousand six hundred and fifteen dollars and six cents, and those of quicksilver five thousand four hundred and thirty-four flasks, valued at two hundred and fifty-seven thousand nine hundred and two dollars and fifteen cents. If the exports of both these articles to China continue in the same ratio for the remainder of the year, we shall have sent to that country in eighteen hundred and seventy-six as much as we sent in eighteen hundred and seventy-four and eighteen hundred and seventy-five together.

The number of Chinese in the city and State has been variously estimated at from thirty thousand in the former and one hundred thousand in the latter, to ninety thousand in the former and two hundred and ten thousand in the latter, respectively. To-day, for the first time, the *Journal of Commerce* gives accurate details of the arrivals and departures since eighteen hundred and fifty-two, obtained from official sources:

Statement of Chinese passengers arrived and departed at the Port of San Francisco, California.

Year.	Arrived.	Departed.
1852	20,026	1,768
1853	4,270	4,421
1854	16,084	2,339
1855	3,329	3,473
1856	4,807	3,028
1857	5,924	1,932
1858	5,427	2,542
1859	3,175	2,450
1860	7,341	2,090
1861	8,430	3,580
1862	8,175	2,792
1863	6,432	2,942
1864	2,682	3,910
1865	3,095	2,295
1866	2,242	3,111
1867	4,290	4,475
1868	11,081	4,210
1869	14,990	4,895
1870	10,870	4,230
1871	5,540	3,260
1872	9,770	4,890
1873	17,075	6,805
1874	16,085	7,710
1875	18,021	6,305
First quarter 1876*	5,065	625
Total	214,226	90,089
		214,226
Excess of arrivals		124,137

* The Hon. T. B. Shannon, Collector of the Port of San Francisco, gives the number of arrivals and departures of Chinese at that port in the second quarter of eighteen hundred and seventy-six, up to June sixteenth, as follows:

Arrivals ---- 7,096
Departures ---- 1,120

The excess of arrivals during the second quarter of the year eighteen hundred and seventy-six, added to the *Journal* estimates, would fix the Chinese population at one hundred and sixteen thousand.

The excess of arrivals over departures previous to eighteen hundred and fifty cannot be determined, but as the whole population in eighteen hundred and fifty numbered ninety-two thousand five hundred and ninety-seven, it is fair to estimate the Chinese portion at ten thousand. This would give the excess of arrivals over departures since eighteen hundred and forty-eight at one hundred and thirty-four thousand one hundred and thirty-seven, from which must be deducted the deaths, the births being so few and far between as not to form any element with calculation.

The deaths among the Chinese population is about two per cent. per annum. At this rate the deaths since eighteen hundred and forty-eight would reach twenty-four thousand nearly, which, taken from the surplusage of arrivals over departures, leaves one hundred and ten thousand as the Chinese population of the coast, of which twenty-five thousand to thirty thousand are in this city.

That the benefits expected to flow from the cheap labor of this vast multitude have not been derived can be easily seen. During their residence in the State they have earned one hundred and eighty million dollars, of which only a very trifling percentage has been spent here. Given instead of these one hundred and ten thousand Chinese one hundred and ten thousand white workmen, with their families, reaching three hundred thousand, and earning and spending sixty million to seventy million dollars a year, and see what a change for the better would occur. See the large number of merchants that would do a profitable business, the army of jobbers and manufacturers and retailers that would be supported, the tens of thousands of houses that would be wanted, and the general prosperity that would flow from such an altered state of things.

ASSESSED VALUATION OF PROPERTY BELONGING TO CHINESE.

The committee addressed circular letters to each County Assessor in the State, and from returns received, the assessed value of all property, real and personal, assessed to Chinese in this State, does not exceed one million five hundred thousand dollars. The rate of State tax is sixty-four cents on each one hundred dollars in value, and if the whole tax was paid, the revenue derived by the State from the property tax laid upon property held by Chinese would not exceed nine thousand six hundred dollars.

The assessed value of all the property in the State is, in round numbers, six hundred millions.

The total population of the State is about seven hundred and fifty thousand, and the Chinese population is more than one-sixth of the whole.

The Chinese population, amounting to at least one-sixth of the whole population, pays less than one four-hundredth part of the revenue required to support the State Government.

NATIVITY OF CONVICTS

In the California State Prison, June fourteenth, A. D. eighteen hundred and seventy-six.

United States.	
Alaska	1
Alabama	5
Arkansas	2
California	155
Connecticut	10
Delaware	2
Florida	12
Georgia	4
Illinois	6
Indiana	7
Iowa	1
Kentucky	12
Louisiana	12
Maine	6
Maryland	11
Michigan	7
Massachusetts	16
Missouri	39
Mississippi	2
New Hampshire	2
New York	163
New Jersey	7
North Carolina	2
Ohio	22
Oregon	3
Pennsylvania	46
Rhode Island	5
South Carolina	7
Tennessee	7
Texas	2
Vermont	4
Virginia	10
West Virginia	4
Wisconsin	6
Total	600

Foreign.	
Austria	1
Australia	3
*China	198
Canada	23
Chile	6
Central America	1
Denmark	1
England	49
France	15
Germany	54
Ireland	98
Italy	12
Mexico	39
Portugal	6
Peru	1
Russia	1
Sweden and Norway	10
Switzerland	1
Scotland	11
Spain	6
Wales	3
West Indies	5
Newfoundland	1
Total	545

Summary.	
United States	600
Foreign	545
Total	1,145

CHARLES AULL, Turnkey.

* The State appropriates ten thousand dollars per month for the support of the State Prison, the earnings of the prisoners falling that much short of maintaining the prison. It will be seen that the net cost to the State for each prisoner is about thirty cents per day; and this without taking into consideration the cost of prison buildings.

The net cost to the State of keeping one hundred and ninety-eight Chinese prisoners in the State Prison is not less than twenty-one thousand six hundred dollars per annum, a sum twelve thousand dollars in excess of the whole amount of the property tax collected from the Chinese population of the State.

www.ingramcontent.com/pod-product-compliance
Lightning Source LLC
LaVergne TN
LVHW011230110826
845150LV00006B/1597